IN THE NAME OF

ALLAH

THE ALL-COMPASSIONATE, ALL-MERCIFUL

YOUR MONEY MATTERS
THE ISLAMIC APPROACH TO BUSINESS, MONEY, AND WORK

- Title: *Your Money Matters*: *The Islamic Approach to Business, Money, and Work*
- Author: Mohammad Rahman, Ph.D.
- English Edition 1 (2014)
- Layout Design: IIPH, Egypt Branch
- Cover Design: Samo Press Group, Beirut

YOUR MONEY MATTERS
THE ISLAMIC APPROACH TO BUSINESS, MONEY, AND WORK

دليلك لإدارة أموالك وفق الشريعة

Mohammad Rahman, Ph.D.

الدار العالمية للكتاب الإسلامي

INTERNATIONAL ISLAMIC PUBLISHING HOUSE

Copyright © 2014 International Islamic Publishing House
King Fahd National Library Cataloging-in-Publication Data

Rahman, Mohammad
Your Money Matters: The Islamic Approach to Business, Money, and Work. / Mohammad Rahman. — Riyadh, 2014

288 pp ; 21 cm

1- Islamic finance   2- Personal finance - Islamic
I- Mohammad Rahman   II- Title

332.121 dc

Legal Deposit no. **1435/3495**
ISBN Hardcover: 978-603-501-253-9

International Islamic Publishing House (IIPH)
P.O. Box 55195 Riyadh 11534, Saudi Arabia
Tel: 966 1 4650818 / 4647213 — Fax: 966 1 4633489
E-mail: editorial@iiph.com — iiphsa@gmail.com
www.iiph.com | www.iiph.com.sa

CONTENTS

PART THREE

PRONUNCIATION AND TRANSLITERATION CHART

Arabic script	Pronunciation	Trans-literated form
أ	short 'a', as in *cat*	a
آ — ى	longer 'a', as in *cab* (not as in *cake*)	â
ب	/b/ as in *bell*, *rubber* and *tab*	b
ت	/t/ as in *tap*, *mustard* and *sit*	t
ة	takes the sound of the preceding diacritical mark sometimes ending in h (when in pausal form): ah, ih or ooh; or atu(n), ati(n) or ata(n) when uninterrupted	h or t (when followed by another Arabic word)
ث	/th/ as in *thing*, *maths* and *wealth*	th
ج	/j/ as in *jam*, *ajar* and *age*	j
ح	a 'harsher' sound than the English initial /h/, and may occur medially and in word-final position as well	ḥ
خ	as in *Bach* (in German); may occur initially and medially as well	kh
د	/d/ as in *do*, *muddy* and *red*	d

Arabic script	Pronunciation	Trans-literated form
ذ	as in *this*, *father* and *smooth*	dh
ر	/r/ as in *raw*, *arid* and *war*; may also be a rolled 'r', as pronounced in Spanish	r
ز	/z/ as in *zoo*, *easy* and *gaze*	z
س	/s/ as in *so*, *messy* and *grass*	s
ش	as in *ship*, *ashes* and *rush*	sh
ص	no close equivalent in English, but may be approximated by pronouncing it as /sw/ or /s/ farther back in the mouth	ṣ
ض	no close equivalent in English, but may be approximated by pronouncing it as /d/ farther back in the mouth	ḍ
ط	no close equivalent in English, but may be approximated by pronouncing it as /t/ farther back in the mouth	ṭ
ظ	no close equivalent in English, but may be approximated by pronouncing 'the' farther back in the mouth	<u>dh</u>
ع	no close equivalent in English: a guttural sound in the back of the throat	'
غ	no close equivalent in English, but may be closely approximated by pronouncing it like the French /r/ in 'rouge'	gh
ف	/f/ as in *fill*, *effort* and *muff*	f

Arabic script	Pronunciation	Trans-literated form
ق	no close equivalent in English, but may be approximated by pronouncing it as /k/ farther back in the mouth	q
ك	/k/ as in *king*, *buckle* and *tack*	k
ل	/l/ as in *lap*, *halo*; in the word Allah, it becomes velarized as in *ball*	l
م	/m/ as in *men*, *simple* and *ram*	m
ن	/n/ as in *net*, *ant* and *can*	n
هـ – ه – ﻪ	/h/ as in *hat*; unlike /h/ in English, in Arabic /h/ is pronounced in medial and word-final positions as well	h
و	as in *wet* and *away*	w
و	long 'u', as in *boot* and *too*	oo
ي	as in *yard* and *mayo*	y
ي	long 'e', as in *eat*, *beef* and *see*	ee
ء	glottal stop: may be closely approximated by pronouncing it like 't' in the Cockney English pronunciation of *butter*: *bu'er*, or the stop sound in *uh-oh!*	(omitted in initial position)

Diphthongs

Arabic script	Pronunciation	Trans-literated form
أُو، ◌ُو	long 'o', as in *owe*, *boat* and *go*	au, aw
أَي، ◌َي	long 'a', as in *aid*, *rain* and *say*	ay, ai, ei

Diacritical marks (tashkeel)

Name of mark	Pronunciation	Trans-literated form
◌َ fatḥah	very short 'a' or schwa (unstressed vowel)	a
◌ِ kasrah	shorter version of ee or schwa (unstressed vowel)	i
◌ُ ḍammah	shorter version of oo	u
◌ّ shaddah	a doubled consonant is stressed in the word, and the length of the sound is also doubled	double letter
◌ْ sukoon	no vowel sound between consonants or at the end of a word	absence of vowel

ARABIC HONORIFIC SYMBOLS

(ﷻ)	*Subḥânahu wa Ta'âlâ*	The Exalted
(ﷺ)	*ṣalla Allâhu 'alayhi wa sallam*	Blessings and peace be upon him
(﷿)	*'alayhi as-salâm*	May peace be upon him
(﵁)	*raḍiya Allâhu 'anhu*	May Allah be pleased with him
(﵂)	*raḍiya Allâhu 'anhâ*	May Allah be pleased with her
(﵃)	*raḍiya Allâhu 'anhumâ*	May Allah be pleased with both of them
(﵄)	*raḍiya Allâhu 'anhum*	May Allah be pleased with all of them
(﵅)	*raḍiya Allâhu 'anhunna*	May Allah be pleased with all of them (females only)

HADITH GRADE TERMS

Sound: *ṣaḥeeḥ*

Reliable: *ḥasan*

Weak: *ḍa'eef*

Odd: *ghareeb*

Authentic: includes sound, reliable, or any grade in between

Acceptable: *sakat 'anhu;* the grader of the hadith did not comment on it, meaning that he found nothing unacceptable in it

ABOUT THE WORD 'LORD'

The word lord in English has several related meanings. The original meaning is 'master' or 'ruler', and in this sense it is often used to refer to human beings: 'the lord of the mansion' or 'Lord So-and-So' (in the United Kingdom, for example). The word *Lord* with a capital L is used in the lexicon of Islam to refer to the One and Only God — Allah. In Islam, there is no ambiguity about the meaning of this word. While it is true that one may occasionally use the word *lord* (whether capitalized or not) to refer to a human being, in Islamic discourse the reference of this term is always clear from the context. Whereas for Christians, Hindus and other polytheists, the word *Lord* with a capital L may refer to Allah, to Jesus or to some imagined deity, for Muslims, there can be no plurality of meaning. Allah alone is the Lord, and the Lord is Allah — not Jesus, not Rama, not any other being.

The Editor

WHEN JIHAD
REFERS TO FIGHTING

Although jihad is often translated into English as 'holy war', it must be noted that war has never been described as 'holy' in any of Islam's primary texts or even early Islamic literature. Linguistically speaking, jihad is an Islamic term that applies to a broad spectrum of activities, ranging from daily striving to meet the day's challenges, to the striving against one's desires and self, to the struggle to provide for one's family. Its basic definition is 'the act of striving or struggling in the way of Allah'. Therefore, jihad is not limited to war; it includes struggling with one's soul, speech, body and wealth so that the message of Allah reaches all humans willing to receive it.

Islamic scholars have referred to different types of jihad, such as jihad against the self (to understand Islam, act upon it, call others to it and be patient with the difficulties of making this call), jihad against the Devil (repelling Satanic whispers, doubts and lusts), jihad against the tongue (controlling it, using it to enjoin what is good, forbid what is wrong, spread the correct teachings of Islam and answer false ideologies), jihad against aggression with the purpose of protecting Islam and the lives, honour and property of Muslims) and other types of jihad like jihad against the hypocrites, jihad against oppressors and jihad against mischief makers.

Jihad — in the context of fighting — has specific rules and conditions that need to be met before jihad is initiated. The first rule is that people are not to be fought because of what they believe, or to coerce them to accept Islam. The second rule is to 'fight only those who fight you' and never initiate unprovoked aggression *(Qur'an 2: 190)*. That means that Muslims are only allowed to fight back, rather than initiating fighting; but 'fighting back' includes fighting against actual aggression as well as proactively addressing real threats of aggression. In both cases, Muslims are instructed to be prepared and ready to defend their nation before they actually engage in military conflict. There are additional conditions, but the above-mentioned conditions are vital for putting jihad in its broader meaning in the proper context.

Another condition of the sort of jihad which involves fighting is that it should take place only under an Islamic authority that 'raises the banner' for such jihad. It is not following the Sunnah at all for any individual or self-appointed group of Muslims to wage war on behalf of a nation. Instead, Muslims should be united under the single authority of an imam or khaleefah (caliph), except in the case where an individual needs to defend his own family and property, or to help his neighbour to do so. This is proved by the example of the early Muslims as well as texts in the Qur'an and the Sunnah:

❨When there comes to them [the hypocrites] a matter related to [public] safety or fear, they spread it about; if only they had referred it to the Messenger and to such of them as are in authority, those among them who are able to think through the matter would have understood it.❩   *(Qur'an 4: 83)*

«Hudhayfah ibn Yaman asked the Prophet (ﷺ): What if (the Muslims) have no single leader (they are divided into disputing groups)? The Prophet (ﷺ) answered: If they have no single leader or unified group, then leave all these disputing groups, even if you have to bite on a tree until your death.» [part of a longer hadith recorded by Bukhari]

There are other conditions for jihad. In general, the rules laid out for war in Islam should be upheld unless there is some legitimate need or strategy when fighting occurs that would necessitate going against those rules. A Muslim should not kill himself or herself *(Qur'an 4: 29)* nor kill another Muslim, except by accident *(Qur'an 4: 92)*. Women, children, the elderly and other non-combatants should not be harmed. Land should not be destroyed, nor trees cut down. Corpses should not be mutilated. Islam should not be imposed upon non-believers. Rather, if combatant non-Muslims choose on their own to embrace Islam, even if only as a deceitful trick, it should be accepted by the Muslim leadership, and fighting should stop. Peace should be sought before lives are lost. Treaties and agreements should be upheld. Prisoners should be well-treated. Above all, justice must be done.

❨Fight in the path [according to the rules set by Allah] of Allah only those who fight you, but do not commit aggression [transgress limits]. Allah does not love aggressors. ...And fight them until persecution is no more, and religion is [freely embraced] for [the individual's faith in] Allah. But if they desist, then let there be no aggression except against transgressors.❩   *(Qur'an 2: 190, 193)*

❨Allah does not forbid you from being good, kind, just, and fair to those who have not fought you because of religion nor driven you from your homeland. Allah loves those who are just. Allah forbids you from giving allegiance to those who have fought you because of religion and have driven you from your homeland, and those who supported your expulsion...❩   *(Qur'an 60: 8-9)*

In addition, the Muslim nation is encouraged to maintain strong military capabilities to promote justice and to deter acts of war and aggression.

❨And make ready for them [their potential aggression] all you can of power, including steeds of war, to deter the enemy of Allah and your enemy, and others besides, whom you may not know but whom Allah knows.❩   *(Qur'an 8: 60)*

The Editor

THE ISLAMIC
VIEWPOINT ON SLAVERY

$\mathcal{S}$lavery existed before the coming of Prophet Muhammad (ﷺ). Islam did not abolish slavery, though it put limits on it and made freeing slaves a highly virtuous act.

In Islam, there is only one way a person may become enslaved and that is by being a non-Muslim among people who have been captured after raising arms and fighting against the Muslim nation. When such people have been conquered, the Muslim ruler has the option of enslaving them or releasing them (with or without ransom), and he makes this decision based upon the best interests and safety of the state. The Prophet (ﷺ) strongly condemned any other means of enslaving a person. Thus, no person may become enslaved due to poverty, debt, kidnapping, committing a crime, voluntarily submitting to slavery, or any other means.

Islam encourages the freeing of slaves and has made the freeing of a slave a form of expiation for sins such as accidental manslaughter, the breaking of a vow, or voiding a fast by engaging in sexual intercourse. The freeing of slaves is also one of the categories upon which the zakâh funds should be spent *(Qur'an 9: 60)*. The Qur'an calls the freeing of a slave an act of righteousness that may be performed at any time:

❴Righteous are those who believe in Allah, the Last Day, the angels, the scripture, and the prophets; and they give money, cheerfully, to the relatives, the orphans, the needy, the wayfarer, the beggars, and to free the slaves.❵   *(Qur'an 2: 177)*

In regards to the treatment of slaves, the Prophet Muhammad (ﷺ) said:

«They are your brothers whom Allah has put under your authority, so if Allah has put a person's brother under his authority, let him feed him from what he eats and clothe him from what he wears, and let him not overburden him with work, and if he does overburden him with work, then let him help him.» (Bukhari)

«Whoever accuses his slave when he is innocent of what he says will be flogged on the Day of Resurrection.» (Bukhari)

«Whoever slaps his slave or beats him, his expiation is to manumit him.» (Muslim)

«If a man had a slave woman whom he fed — and fed her well, and taught her — and taught her well, then he set her free and married her — he will have a double reward.» (Bukhari and Muslim)

The male owner of a female slave has the right to have sexual intercourse with her as long as he, or the slave's previous owner, has not married her to another person. This is a right exclusive to the slave's owner. No one, including the owner's sons, may touch the woman unless the owner marries her to him. If the slave woman bears her owner a child, then her owner may never sell her and she automatically becomes a free woman upon his death, if he has not released her before that.

As can be seen from this evidence, slavery in Islam is far different from the institution of slavery as known in many non-Muslim countries.

The Editor

PUBLISHER'S NOTE

$\mathcal{A}$ll praises and thanks belong to Allah alone, the One, the Almighty, and the All-Merciful. Blessings and peace be upon Prophet Muhammad, the last of His messengers and prophets, and upon his family, his Companions, and all those who follow in his footsteps until the end of time.

In today's predominantly secular environment, business matters and religion are usually perceived to be mutually exclusive. In reality, though, the teachings of Islam are as relevant in the business world as they are in homes, mosques, educational institutes, and, indeed, society at large.

In this book, the author has detailed Islamic teachings as they apply to various aspects of business and finance. He has exerted commendable effort to ensure that business leaders and laypeople know how to follow the Qur'anic verses as well as the Sunnah of Prophet Muhammad (ﷺ) in the day-to-day management of their financial affairs. It is hoped that this work will prove to be beneficial for all individuals, both Muslim and non-Muslim.

May Allah accept the efforts of all those who contributed to the production of this book, and may it be acceptable to Him, *âmeen.*

Muhammad Abdul Mohsin Al-Tuwaijri
Managing Director
International Islamic Publishing House
Riyadh, Saudi Arabia

PREFACE

$\mathcal{A}$ll praise is for Allah (*Subḥânahu wa Ta'âlâ* – Glorified and Exalted is He), Lord of the worlds.

May His peace and blessings be upon Muhammad (*ṣalla Allâhu 'alayhi wa sallam* – blessings and peace be upon him), His slave and His messenger.

As-salâmu 'alaykum wa raḥmatullâhi wa barakâtuhu![1] Peace be upon you, and the mercy and blessings of Allah!

As a teacher of business administration for the last several years, I have constantly faced students' questions about this field – questions such as, "What is meant by the term 'sub-game perfect'?" and "When should firms attempt to innovate?" Of course, in every case I attempted to provide a satisfactory response that was not only correct but also, hopefully, one that they could understand.

American students, aware of my Muslim background, would also ask questions related to Islam. Some questions were more common than others: "Why don't Muslims eat pork?" and "Why do Muslim women wear the hijab (the veil ordained by Allah for believing women)?" The answers would be very simple: "Because Allah forbade us from eating pork," and "Allah commands the Muslim women to observe hijab." These answers would often lead to more discussions

---

[1] Wherever possible, Arabic terms have been translated into English. In cases where we have chosen to retain the Arabic, the transliterated word or phrase is shown in italics the first time it appears in the text; the term is also defined in the Glossary found at the end of this book. (Editor)

on Islam, particularly after students asked follow-up questions like: "Why do you have to do everything that Allah asks you to?"

It was, however, from my Muslim students that I started receiving questions on the issue of Islam in business. The most common questions were all related to *ribâ* (usury).

"Is interest really haram (forbidden according to Islamic law)?"

"Is Islamic banking truly halal (permissible according to Islamic law) or is it only a sugar-coating of conventional banking?"

"Does ribâ refer to usury or to interest?"

"How on earth is it possible to conduct business without interest?"

Despite my knowledge of management, I lacked expertise in economics, finance, *fiqh* (Islamic jurisprudence), and Sharia (Islamic law derived from the Qur'an and the Sunnah), leaving me unsure about the correct responses. In the beginning, I would point them roughly towards the general literature on Islamic banking or Islamic finance. I say 'roughly' because I merely informed them of the existence of such literature, without recommending any specific books or articles to them.

Eventually, I had the same questions myself. Immersed in a typically American environment fascinated with consumerism, I was bombarded with wonderful opportunities to invest, to acquire such consumer goods as cars and computers with zero down and low monthly payments, and to benefit from the convenience of credit cards. Why was I renting and not buying? *Alhamdulillâh* (all praise is for Allah), I could no longer stave off researching the literature on Islamic finance. It was at this time that I stumbled upon Professor Mahmoud El-Gamal's introductory notes and technical pieces on Islamic finance. The exceptional quality of his work made my research quite easy. Very soon, I found myself able to answer my own questions on ribâ. I now knew that I was renting because conventional forms of financing were indeed not permissible.

Handling the students' questions, however, proved to be a little more difficult than answering my own, for at least two reasons.

1) To many, even the simplest Islamic finance concepts seemed contrived; from hard-liners to the non-religious, most people seemed to dismiss these concepts. The former dismissed Islamic finance as a convenient attempt at the Islamization of ribâ, which is declared haram in the Qur'an; they often claimed that banking itself is antithetical to the Islamic social system since the authentic Sunnah (the practice and collected sayings of Prophet Muhammad [ﷺ] that together with the Qur'an forms the basis of Islamic law) does not mention the existence of any formal financial institutions. The latter dismissed Islamic finance as merely placing an artificial façade over conventional interest-based banking in order to exploit the myopia of faith-blind Muslims who believe that interest is the same as ribâ. Generally, these dismissals would come swiftly from both groups.

2) The answers would frequently affect the students at a very personal level. For example, a student seeking employment with a financial institution might ask me to write a recommendation letter. I would have to gently explain that I could not do so because working in banks is haram, and assisting a brother or sister in doing something haram is also forbidden.

Eventually, it became clear that in every case, the task of understanding Islamic finance becomes easier largely through the acquisition of authentic Islamic knowledge. Subsequently, I answered questions by simply presenting the definition of ribâ and highlighting the relevant verses in the Qur'an.

Finance and banking are only portions of business as a whole. Parallel to questions on Islamic banking, there arose many other general questions related to Islam in business, such as, "What happens when you are faced with such ethical dilemmas as whistle-blowing?"

In most cases, I would provide quick explanations and then direct the students to Islam-QA.com, a wonderful online repository of Islamic fatwas (rulings) based on the Qur'an and the authentic Sunnah, available in English and many other languages. It is spearheaded by the eminent *Shaykh* (teacher/mentor) Muhammad al-Munajjid.

Through these simple question-and-answer sessions with my students, I recognized the need for a comprehensive compilation of resources that addresses the most common related topics in business administration and financial management as related to Islamic teachings. From my experience as a professional teacher, I also realized that an effort towards presenting such a compilation in a clear manner would make it easier for readers from diverse backgrounds – Muslim and otherwise – to understand the materials. To my surprise, I could not find a single book written in the English language that directly addressed the general topic of Islam in business administration. Given the relevance of financial issues in modern times, such a book would be quite useful; thus, I began writing a draft for this book.

Early in my writing experience, I faced some of the challenges associated with authoring a book that would offer Islamic guidelines. The fact that I had no requisite knowledge in fiqh-based issues posed the toughest challenge. To abstain from making illegal *ijtihâd* (using one's knowledge of the Qur'an and the Sunnah to derive rulings on matters not specifically mentioned in either source of Islamic law), I have followed a two-pronged approach.

First, I have chosen to focus on presenting verses from the Qur'an, along with authentic narrations of the Prophet (ﷺ), without attempting to directly explain them. Rather, I have simply presented them, with the supplication that they will form the basis of true guidelines. If I have erred in my understanding of the verses and presented them in the wrong context, I beg Allah's mercy. I want to emphasize that I have attempted to limit the severity of my mistakes by abstaining from explanations. I believe it is sufficient to cite a Qur'an verse or an authentic hadith (statement or action of Prophet Muhammad [ﷺ] that was remembered and recorded by his Companions and followers) to support a point.

Secondly, and perhaps more importantly, I have relied heavily on the work of the scholars and students of knowledge of *ahl as-Sunnah wal-jamā'ah* (the people of the Sunnah and the community) who have made the resources of fatwas available in the English language. I also requested that this humble piece be read to a knowledgeable scholar and corrected appropriately.

While researching this book, I discovered an issue related to the authenticity of its content. Admittedly, this issue offers a relatively wide 'grey zone' between correct and incorrect and thus allows multiple opinions. This is largely because the issue relates to philosophy and taste, as I shall highlight below.

When addressing the role of Islam in areas that have developed independently of Islam, under secular or otherwise parochial nurturing, Muslims try to understand how Islam affects those areas. A casual survey reveals that there are at least two approaches.

In one approach, Muslims use a jurisprudence-based point of view. Islam affects a secular, parochial, or scientific field if Islamic laws specify clauses that affect the ideas and operations in those fields. Classical examples are studies related to the origin of the universe. Muslims believe that Allah, as the Creator, originated all creation, whereas a secular approach to science does not adopt such beliefs. Thus, the role of Islam in this case would be simply to highlight the errors in holding beliefs that contradict the divine truth revealed in the Qur'an. This example is useful because it allows one to easily appreciate that such issues are present in many other religions, including Christianity.

In a second approach, Muslims try to discover lessons that Islam offers for other areas that have developed independently. Continuing with our example of the origin of the universe, we know that there are verses in the Qur'an that speak of events that Allah caused as He created the universe. In analogous situations, Muslims could seek lessons that can be learned from Islam on such topics as management, thermodynamics, or sociology.

In this book, I have combined the two approaches, although I leaned more on the first one. Although my choice of methods can be attributed to personal taste, I believe I can also offer some general justifications.

First of all, Islam is comprehensive and therefore offers a combination of both spiritual and practical guidance. I believe the best approach, then, should consider both the Islamic legal aspects for conformance and the lessons that can be learned by analyzing these legal aspects. In addition, fear of Allah is of the highest priority to a Muslim, and it is well known that a major manifestation of this fear of God is in following His commands and avoiding the prohibitions in particular. It can be concluded that knowledge of Islamic jurisprudence with respect to fields that developed in the secular realms is more important than trying to develop those same fields within Islamic spheres.

To highlight this fact, we can consider the role of the Qur'an. It is an important source of prescriptions and legal rulings for all Muslims, but for Muslim scientists in particular, it contains profound intelligence on such topics as embryology.

The result of having selected such an approach is not a book that offers ground-breaking research on financial and business management. Instead, it mainly highlights the issues faced by Muslim practitioners of marketing, finance, management, accounting, and other functions of business administration, as well as those faced by average laypeople.

Due to its generality, the book can prove useful to a wide range of readers. Quite obviously, it can be a gentle reminder to my Muslim brothers and sisters who are involved in business administration. It can also be a source of knowledge for those planning a career in business; it is suitable for use as a textbook for traditional coursework in undergraduate or graduate programs. In today's age of globalization, it may also prove useful for non-Muslims as they attempt to understand the thinking of Muslims and the foreign cultures influenced by Islam. I hope that the book will spark further research in this area so that we can see new developments focusing on Islam in the fields of business administration and finance.

I deliberately tried to keep the book as simple, short, and straightforward as possible. Many of today's readers, particularly those practicing business administration, are extremely busy and cannot spend much time reading a single book. Furthermore, the mode of reading itself has changed over time; online reading requires different skills than traditional book reading. Many references in the book are supplemented with relevant Internet addresses.

The most common criticism of the book is its numerous references to one website: Islam-QA.com. I have noticed, however, that this criticism frequently comes from either those who are proficient in Arabic or those who do not utilize the website. I certainly appreciate these individuals' concern that using a single source too frequently is unscholarly and can result in the introduction of a significant amount of bias. For a variety of reasons, though, I decided to use it extensively whenever there was a need for Islamic rulings or opinions.

Indeed, for English (and generally non-Arabic) speaking Muslims, there is virtually no other source that is comparable in quality (rigour) or size to Islam-QA.com. The website does not merely provide the opinions of one or a few individuals; it is a rich database that offers the fatwas of many scholars. Thus, an answer in Islam-QA.com is not a simple 'yes' or 'no' based on the whims of Shaykh al-Munajjid. Many of the responses are direct quotations from the books of fatwas of prominent shaykhs of the past.

Indeed, what is important is how we use the fatwas. I have read fatwas on Islam-QA.com that I personally believed to be poorly written or even incorrect, but this has not discouraged me in the slightest from continuing to utilize the website for its extremely valuable collection of information. Still, because of the gravity of religion itself, I have tried to be careful when using fatwas from Islam-QA. com. A fatwa from a scholar can certainly be wrong, but it is still a good starting point.

Finally, I deliberately did not mask my reliance on Islam-QA. com, although it would have been very easy to do so since the site offers multiple views. This is because I wanted to encourage all English-speaking Muslims to visit the website. In addition, I see no value in being unscholarly just to appear scholarly.

I have striven to make this text free of errors; nonetheless, there may be mistakes. I request that the readers inform me, through the publisher, of any inaccuracies they find so that they can be corrected in future editions. I beg Allah's mercy and request Him to overlook my mistakes.

ACKNOWLEDGEMENTS

$\mathcal{W}$e must thank Allah first and foremost, for every good thing is a blessing from Him. I would also like to thank all my Muslim brothers and sisters by asking Allah to reward them, for they have helped me to better understand my religion.

Allah has blessed me with a wonderful family, and I ask Him to reward them for their incredible support. I would like to thank Allah for giving me parents who feared Him, reminded me of His mercy, and asked me to fear Him as He should be feared. In particular, I am grateful to my mother, who kept me in check through gentle but strict words of admonishment. I was blessed to be the youngest child of my parents; hence, every member of my family helped me become a better Muslim.

I pray to Allah to reward all those whose works have made my own work shamefully easy. This includes the Companions (*raḍiya Allâhu 'anhum* – may Allah be pleased with all of them) who diligently reported hadiths, as well as such scholars as Shaykh Ibn Taymiyah, Shaykh Ibn Bâz, Shaykh Ibn al-'Uthaymeen, and Shaykh al-Albâni (may Allah have mercy on them all). May Allah reward Shaykh Muhammad al-Munajjid, whose website Islam-QA.com is having a profound effect on non-Arabic-speaking Muslims. In fact, this book would have been unnecessary had enough Muslims visited the website frequently to acquire knowledge.

May Allah reward Dr. Moussa Elbayoumy, a physician and hospital administrator. When I observed him at work, when I was a doctoral student, I realized the value of good business administration. May

Allah reward Brother Wael al-Roumi and Sister Jamila Hakam, whose gentle insistence is the reason that my humble notes are in the process of being published. Finally, may Allah reward the editor for her patient and thorough review of my hard-to-read drafts, which greatly helped to ensure that this piece could be read and understood by readers from diverse backgrounds while being free of errors as much as possible.

INTRODUCTION

$\mathcal{T}$oday, business administration and financial management affect the lives of nearly everyone. Since one in every six human beings is identified as a Muslim, the topic of Islam in financial issues should be quite relevant to many individuals. Let us consider the global financial crisis of 2008, which escalated into the global economic crisis of 2009 and condemned even the largest of the world's economies to recession. While political and economic leaders around the globe struggled to find such solutions as bailouts and stimulus plans, Islamic scholars were well aware of a simple yet profound fact: if Islamic guidelines had been followed in business administration, such a catastrophe would likely never have occurred. Indeed, speculative financial instruments and derivatives have been declared haram because they are founded on both ribâ and *gharar* (uncertainty).[2]

As our first, subtle example of the link between Islam and financial issues, let us consider Egypt's highly lucrative tourism industry. People across the globe recognize Egypt as the home of one of the seven wonders of the ancient world: the Great Pyramid of Giza. Tourists flock there to capture a glimpse of, and to experience the magnificence of, the structures. A practicing Muslim wanting to establish a tour-guide service there would need to reconsider this plan,[3] however, in light of the following evidence:

---

[2] These terms will be discussed further in the chapter on Islamic finance and accounting.

[3] "Obligation to destroy idols," Islam-QA.com, accessed October 23, 2011, http://www.islam-qa.com/en/ref/20894/pyramids.

«When the Messenger of Allah (ﷺ) and his Companions reached *al-Hijr* (the rocky tract where the dwellings of the Thamood were),[4] he admonished his Companions (ﷺ), saying: Do not visit the remains of those who are being punished unless you are weeping, lest something similar befalls you.» (Bukhari and Muslim)[5]

At more micro levels, Islam sometimes appears even more prominently in business administration and financial management. Let us consider the micro-lending model popularized by the Muslim economist from Bangladesh, Professor Muhammad Yunus. Grameen Bank, as he called his model of micro-credit, offers small loans to the poorest entrepreneurs, particularly women, who are not credit-worthy according to conventional banking standards. Many in the Muslim world were overcome with joy when Professor Yunus and Grameen Bank were jointly awarded the 2006 Nobel Peace Prize. Indeed, Grameen Bank is praiseworthy for its efforts in attacking poverty, particularly while many from the wasteful rich communities are busy gambling away their fortunes using haram financial products.

Unfortunately, even a casual analysis of the micro-credit model reveals that micro-credit is based on the exact concept of ribâ that Allah has strongly forbidden in the Qur'an. Consequently, Muslims are not allowed to participate in conventional micro-credit programs by providing loans or even by working in their banks. Quite obviously, Muslims are also not allowed to accept ribâ-based micro-credit loans,

---

[4] The Thamood were the people of Prophet Ṣâliḥ. See *Qur'an 15: 80*. (Editor)

[5] All hadiths in this text have been checked and verified by IIPH's researchers. It is rare, but it does happen that a hadith is not verifiable within the time frame of researching and editing the book. In that case, a decision is made by the editorial board whether or not to include the hadith. It is IIPH's policy not to include weak hadiths or fabricated (fake) hadiths in our publications. If a weak hadith is included in any text, it is only because the author of the book discusses it as a weak hadith. (Editor)

even if they are in difficult circumstances. Allah (ﷻ) has warned in the Qur'an:

﴿ يَمْحَقُ ٱللَّهُ ٱلرِّبَوٰا۟ وَيُرْبِى ٱلصَّدَقَٰتِ ۗ وَٱللَّهُ لَا يُحِبُّ كُلَّ كَفَّارٍ أَثِيمٍ ۝ ﴾

(سورة البقرة: ٢٧٦)

❨Allah will destroy ribâ and will give increase for charity. And Allah likes not the disbelievers, sinners.❩ *(Qur'an 2: 276)*[6]

﴿ يَٰٓأَيُّهَا ٱلَّذِينَ ءَامَنُوا۟ ٱتَّقُوا۟ ٱللَّهَ وَذَرُوا۟ مَا بَقِىَ مِنَ ٱلرِّبَوٰٓا۟ إِن كُنتُم مُّؤْمِنِينَ ۝ فَإِن لَّمْ تَفْعَلُوا۟ فَأْذَنُوا۟ بِحَرْبٍ مِّنَ ٱللَّهِ وَرَسُولِهِۦ ۖ وَإِن تُبْتُمْ فَلَكُمْ رُءُوسُ أَمْوَٰلِكُمْ ۝ ... ﴾

(سورة البقرة: ٢٧٨-٢٧٩)

❨O you who believe! Be afraid of Allah and give up what remains from ribâ, if you are [really] believers. If you do not do it, then take a notice of war from Allah and His Messenger; but if you repent, you shall have your capital sums...❩ *(Qur'an 2: 278-279)*

Knowledge of such issues related to Islam in business administration does not hold Muslims back. On the contrary, it opens doors by providing them with new opportunities to please Allah. They are subsequently inspired to strive in Allah's path and to develop alternatives that comply with Islamic rulings, while carrying on such noble efforts as fighting poverty. As a result of these efforts, Muslim practitioners of business administration, together with Islamic scholars, have developed such alternatives as Sharia-compliant Islamic micro finance.[7]

---

[6] The translations of the meanings of the verses of the Qur'an in this book have been taken (with some changes to the text to clarify meaning) from Khan and al-Hilali, *The Noble Qur'an.*

[7] At the time of this writing, Mahmoud El-Gamal, Economics Department Chair and Professor in Islamic Finance at Rice University, was leading research efforts to collect field data about the implementation of proposed Islamic micro finance models.

At this point, many individuals may begin to question the wisdom behind the apparent blindness of faith. Our example of micro-credit is actually quite illustrative. Even if one acknowledges that conventional micro-credit is indeed based on the prohibited form of interest, does not the end – particularly such a noble one as eradicating poverty – justify the means, which is simply the provision of financial assistance? Indeed, some argue that the issue of halal and haram is not really relevant when the cause is universally accepted as being noble.

Many proponents of ribâ-based micro-credit argue that this model is halal because it involves lending to the poor, without collateral, while charging relatively low interest rates. They base their argument on the principle of emphasizing the 'substance', 'spirit', or 'essence' of the Islamic injunction forbidding ribâ – rather than its form. In particular, they state that since the wisdom behind the prohibition of ribâ is preventing it from being used as a tool for exploitation, then micro-credit is essentially not un-Islamic, even if it involves ribâ, because it is not a tool for exploitation.[8] If one studies Islam, it is easy to discover that this form of rationalizing is not applicable in this case.

Drawing an analogy to highlight this, let us consider the difference between marriage and cohabitation. If we used a similar line of reasoning, we could easily argue that marriage is not a requirement for cohabitation in Islam. One could argue that marriage has been prescribed to ensure mutual rights, and that such alternative arrangements or agreements as 'mutual love' are present in cohabitation; therefore, these rights are ensured and, hence, marriage is not required.

Some go even further in their argument. Many proponents of micro-credit argue that poverty eradication is not possible without the presence of ribâ. Interest, they say, is a **required** element, for it

---

[8] Rozenberg, "Nobel Prizewinner Using Micro-credit for Macro Benefit," *The Times Online*, December 16, 2006, accessed October 23, 2011, http://business.timesonline.co.uk.

tends to eliminate the moral and hazardous problems associated with donations. In other words, interest encourages individuals to be more responsible with money, thereby ensuring the viability of their chosen forms of business. From an Islamic perspective, however, at least one problem arises from this kind of thinking.

Ignoring Islamic guidelines, even when the cause is noble, is antithetical to the essence of Islam. The term 'Islam' is not merely a transliterated name of an ancient religion of the Orient that offers general spiritual guidelines. Rather, Muslims believe that Islam is a complete religion, specified entirely by God. The religion is called 'Islam', which is an Arabic term for 'submission', because it entails complete surrender to God. There are many verses of the Qur'an that highlight the concept of complete submission as the foundation of the Muslim creed:

﴿...ٱلْيَوْمَ أَكْمَلْتُ لَكُمْ دِينَكُمْ وَأَتْمَمْتُ عَلَيْكُمْ نِعْمَتِي وَرَضِيتُ لَكُمُ ٱلْإِسْلَٰمَ دِينًا... ۝﴾ (سورة المائدة: ٣)

❨...This day, I have perfected your religion for you, completed My favour upon you, and have chosen for you Islam as your religion...❩
(Qur'an 5: 3)

﴿إِنَّ ٱلدِّينَ عِندَ ٱللَّهِ ٱلْإِسْلَٰمُ... ۝﴾ (سورة آل عمران: ١٩)

❨Truly, the religion with Allah is Islam...❩ *(Qur'an 3: 19)*

﴿فَإِنْ حَآجُّوكَ فَقُلْ أَسْلَمْتُ وَجْهِيَ لِلَّهِ وَمَنِ ٱتَّبَعَنِ... ۝﴾ (سورة آل عمران: ٢٠)

❨So if they dispute with you [Muhammad], say: I have submitted myself to Allah, and [so have] those who follow me...❩ *(Qur'an 3: 20)*

﴿...أَفَتُؤْمِنُونَ بِبَعْضِ ٱلْكِتَٰبِ وَتَكْفُرُونَ بِبَعْضٍ فَمَا جَزَآءُ مَن يَفْعَلُ ذَٰلِكَ مِنكُمْ إِلَّا خِزْيٌ فِي ٱلْحَيَوٰةِ ٱلدُّنْيَا وَيَوْمَ ٱلْقِيَٰمَةِ يُرَدُّونَ إِلَىٰ أَشَدِّ ٱلْعَذَابِ... ۝﴾

(سورة البقرة: ٨٥)

❨...Then do you believe in a part of the scripture and reject the rest? Then what is the recompense of those who do so among you, except disgrace in the life of this world, and on the Day of Resurrection they shall be consigned to the most grievous torment...❩   *(Qur'an 2: 85)*

﴿ يَـٰٓأَيُّهَا ٱلَّذِينَ ءَامَنُوا۟ ٱدْخُلُوا۟ فِى ٱلسِّلْمِ كَآفَّةً وَلَا تَتَّبِعُوا۟ خُطُوَٰتِ ٱلشَّيْطَـٰنِ ۚ إِنَّهُۥ لَكُمْ عَدُوٌّ مُّبِينٌ ﴾ ۝

(سورة البقرة: ٢٠٨)

❨O you who believe! Enter perfectly in Islam and follow not the footsteps of Satan. Verily, he is to you a plain enemy.❩   *(Qur'an 2: 208)*

From the aforementioned verses, we can learn a few very important lessons: complete submission to Allah, the Creator, is the religion of Islam; complete submission requires us to follow **all** the guidelines specified in Islam; and these guidelines have been specified completely by Allah and His Messenger (ﷺ).

Let us revisit three of the common arguments presented by the proponents of micro-credit.

The first one is that complying with the prohibition of ribâ is not important in these issues. Clearly, this is a violation of the rule of complete submission, as indicated in *Qur'an 2: 85* above.

The second argument is that we have to place greater emphasis on the wisdom behind the rule than on the rule itself, thus letting our wisdom decide what is best. It follows from this argument that if the prohibition of ribâ is based on the principle of poverty eradication, then the ribâ in micro-credit is not significant or haram because micro-credit itself is based on that same principle of poverty eradication. This argument violates the principle that Islam is a complete and perfect religion, as indicated by *Qur'an 5: 3* above.

The basic principle is that the haram becomes halal only in cases of genuine necessity, and specific cases have been mentioned. Consider something that is much simpler than ribâ but that is also generally haram: lying.

And it was narrated that 'Abd-Allaah ibn Mas'ood also said: Lying is not appropriate whether in earnest or in jest. Recite if you wish (interpretation of the meaning): O you who believe! Fear Allaah, and be with those who are true (in words and deeds) (*Soorat al-Tawbah, 9: 119*). Then he said: Do you find any concession allowing that to anyone?[9]

It has also been narrated that the Prophet (ﷺ) said:

«Lying is not good, whether one is serious or joking.» (al-Bayhaqi; a sound hadith according to al-Albâni)

Islam is so complete that it has even specified three cases in which lying is permitted. It was narrated that Asmâ' bint Yazeed (*raḍiya Allâhu 'anhâ* – may Allah be pleased with her) narrated that the Messenger of Allah (ﷺ) said:

«Lies are not appropriate except in three cases: a man speaking to his wife to please her, telling lies at times of war, and lying in order to bring about reconciliation between people.» (at-Tirmidhi; a reliable hadith according to al-Albâni)

In contrast, Islam does not specify **any** situation in which ribâ becomes permissible.

The third argument maintains that we can decide for ourselves whether something that is haram is necessary. To claim that ribâ is necessary for poverty eradication is a serious offense. Poverty was present alongside ribâ at the time of the advent of Islam, yet it was Allah's infinite wisdom that He did not select ribâ as a solution; rather, He specified *zakâh* (obligatory charity) as the solution. Furthermore, He has strongly warned against ribâ, so if we suggest that ribâ is a necessary means to fight poverty, we are violating the basic principle of submission as highlighted in the verses above.

---

[9] "Ruling on lies that do not harm anyone," Islam-QA.com, accessed October 23, 2011, http://www.islam-qa.com/en/ref/105477. See also aṭ-Ṭabari, *Tahdheeb al-Âthâr.*

Knowing the basic principle of submission in Islam, we were able to choose an appropriate title for this book: *Your Money Matters: The Islamic Approach to Business, Money, and Work*. If Islam entails complete submission, then Muslims must submit to Allah in all their endeavours, including business administration.

Unfortunately, many Muslims have gone against the true holistic nature of Islam by separating their professional from their religious lives. This is despite the fact that Islam is a complete, all-encompassing religion: the perfect *deen* (religion) or 'code of life'. It is meant to – and does – affect us in every facet of our lives. This is not surprising, since Allah has mentioned His purpose for creating us:

(سورة الذاريات: ٥٦)   ﴿ وَمَا خَلَقْتُ الْجِنَّ وَالْإِنسَ إِلَّا لِيَعْبُدُونِ ۝ ﴾

﴿And I [Allah] created not the *jinn*[10] and humankind except that they should worship Me [alone].﴾   *(Qur'an 51: 56)*

Too many Muslims pray the five daily prayers, fast the month of Ramadan, pay zakâh, and perform the Hajj (annual pilgrimage to Makkah, if that is obligatory for them), but then 'switch hats' to excel at other tasks, often forgetting their religion completely.

This separation is the reason why there are so many haram activities in many workplaces today, even in those where the workers are exclusively Muslim. True believers try to follow the Creator's commands whenever they are applicable. While the Quraysh mocked the complete nature of the deen, the Companions were busy implementing it from dawn to dusk, in their trade and farming, in their diplomacy and confrontations, in their family lives, and even in their personal hygiene.

---

[10] jinn (sg. *jinni*): non-human, rational beings created by Allah from fire, often referred to as 'demons' or 'devils'. They have free will like humans: some are Muslims whereas others are disbelievers; some are obedient to Allah whereas others are disobedient.

«At the time of the Prophet (ﷺ), one of the polytheists said to Salmân al-Fârisi (*raḍiya Allâhu 'anhu* – may Allah be pleased with him) mockingly: Your Prophet has taught you everything, even how to defecate?

Salmân replied with pride: Yes indeed! He forbade us from facing the direction of prayer (Makkah, which all Muslims face when praying) when urinating or defecating.» (Muslim and at-Tirmidhi)

True believers accept Islam entirely, for several reasons. Their goals are to seek Allah's pleasure and to succeed in the hereafter. There is no hypocrisy in them, and they are not two-faced. They realize that the separation of religious and professional lives comes at a heavy price.

﴿ وَإِذَا قِيلَ لَهُمْ ءَامِنُواْ كَمَآ ءَامَنَ ٱلنَّاسُ قَالُوٓاْ أَنُؤْمِنُ كَمَآ ءَامَنَ ٱلسُّفَهَآءُ أَلَآ إِنَّهُمْ هُمُ ٱلسُّفَهَآءُ وَلَٰكِن لَّا يَعْلَمُونَ ۝ وَإِذَا لَقُواْ ٱلَّذِينَ ءَامَنُواْ قَالُوٓاْ ءَامَنَّا وَإِذَا خَلَوْاْ إِلَىٰ شَيَٰطِينِهِمْ قَالُوٓاْ إِنَّا مَعَكُمْ إِنَّمَا نَحْنُ مُسْتَهْزِءُونَ ۝ ﴾ (سورة البقرة: ١٣-١٤)

⟨And when it is said to them [hypocrites]: Believe as the people have believed – they say: Shall we believe as the fools have believed? Verily, they are the fools, but they know not. And when they meet those who believe, they say: We believe – but when they are alone with their devils, they say: Truly, we are with you; verily we were but mocking.⟩ (Qur'an 2: 13-14)

Therefore, it is imperative for a Muslim to submit unconditionally to Allah when engaged in any endeavour, including one related to business and finance. This book highlights some of the obligations, challenges, and opportunities that Muslims may face when carrying out marketing, management, accounting, and various other tasks of business administration and financial management. Since ignorance is the main cause of the unfortunate separation between religious and professional lives at the expense of one's hereafter, this book can help by quickly highlighting some aspects of the Islamic code that apply when managing a business; this will, inshallah (God willing), encourage reflection and further research on relevant topics.

The chapters in this book can be classified into three parts. The first part introduces the topic and explains the foundation and epistemological stances associated with the scholarship of the book. It also explains the approach used in subsequent chapters with regard to direct and inferential reasoning on Islamic principles.

The second part introduces some Islamic principles that directly affect business administration. It reflects the conventional modularity of coursework in a standard business administration academic program; thus, there are chapters related to such traditional undergraduate or graduate business sub-fields as marketing, finance, operations, and human resource (HR) management. This is an ideal approach for at least two reasons.

1. It provides students, practitioners, and educators with standard points of reference to easily understand Islamic principles in the context of business administration.

2. It allows this book to be used in a variety of settings, including academia. It is obvious that while most courses in business programs deal with topics that feature prominently in Islamic guidelines and rules, Islamic issues are rarely discussed in those courses.

Finally, the third part concludes the book by addressing the special topic of business ethics as well as discussing the road ahead.

As we shall discuss at length in the following chapter, there has been a long association between business and religion. Even the wisest business owners know that they can only do so much to ensure any success at all, let alone sustain the performance of their businesses. History is full of cases in which large business houses eventually faded into oblivion, while small businesses that started in garages made convincing cases for 'luck' as a determinant of success. Consequently, some Muslim business managers use the services of 'holy-men inter-cessors' to improve their luck. Non-Muslim managers even cater to such superstitions, turning to such practices as numerology.

This book, however, is not a metaphysical panacea for ailing busi-nesses and their managers. In fact, application of the Islamic principles in this book may even lead to an overall apparent **decrease** in the profitability of a business after the haram elements are eliminated. This can prove to be a profitable exercise of the most sublime form, though, because it will ensure the highest reward from the Creator, along with His pleasure, which will manifest itself in the form of blessings in other areas of one's life – both here on the earth and, more importantly, in the hereafter.

PART ONE

PART ONE

CHAPTER ONE

ISLAM

$\mathcal{A}$cross the globe, business communities in predominantly Muslim cultures tend to know that there is a relationship between Islam and business administration. This relationship manifests itself in various forms in different parts of the world.

For example, at the inception of many Muslim-owned businesses on the Indian subcontinent, innovated ceremonies are performed in an effort to ensure the eventual prosperity of the business. These include the *meelâd*[1] and another gathering where each individual recites one section of the Qur'an, so that the complete Qur'an is recited as many times as possible for extra blessings. (Surprisingly, even businesses that are considered to be haram in Islam, such as conventional banks and insurance companies, often begin this way.) Many firms continue the stream of 'religious' activities throughout the lifetime of the business, even inviting stakeholders and well-wishers to annual meelâd and Qur'an reading sessions.

Some companies build working relationships with pirs,[2] who provide business-related and spiritual advice. Doorways to the

---

[1] *meelâd:* a ceremonial chanting session to praise Prophet Muhammad (ﷺ); some of the poetic verses recited in his honour border on *shirk* (associating partners with Allah). Professional reciters are called to conduct these sessions. (Editor)

[2] pirs: specially-trained Sufi (mystic) holy men whom some believe to be exceptionally close to God and able to seek the intercession of saints. (Editor)

businesses are often adorned with religious inscriptions, including narrations of the Prophet (ﷺ) or even some verses of the noble Qur'an. Many businesses go to elaborate lengths, displaying extravagant inscriptions of verses in gold filigree or engraving. All these are efforts to please their Creator, for they acknowledge that He controls their destiny with His strong grip on their forelocks.

A closer inspection of those situations, however, reveals an ironic twist: Some Muslim businesspeople seek the blessings of the Creator while they are actively engaging in activities known to displease Him.

Indeed, activities such as the meelâd are regarded as *bid'ah*: reprehensible innovations in religion, or attempts to worship Allah in ways that were not taught and practiced by the Prophet (ﷺ). Some ignorant Muslim businesspeople believe that the soul of the Prophet (ﷺ) descends to attend the meelâd and similar events; others believe that some Sufi pirs can communicate with dead 'saints', which makes them exceptional 'business advisors' due to their supposed knowledge of the unseen. Such beliefs go against the true essence of Islam that attributes divinity only to one God – a concept known as *tawheed* (pure monotheism).

The paradoxical practice of seeking Allah's blessing while failing to follow His commands is not limited to the Indian subcontinent with its non-Arab population. Let us look at the Arab region, where the religion of Islam has its roots and has played a very dominant role in shaping the culture.

Affluent Muslim business owners in the Arab Gulf countries are often quite sensitive to matters of halal and haram and to Muslim sentiments. Many businesses are inaugurated with ribbon-cutting ceremonies that start quite beautifully with a remembrance of Allah, often through recitation from the noble Qur'an; they avoid such bid'ah practices as the meelâd. In sharp contrast to the shabby meelâd arrangements of the Indian subcontinent, these professionally-managed, gorgeous events in the Gulf can easily cost thousands of dollars.

The cost is readily justified; like advertising or other big-ticket operational expenditures, these events are said to be necessary to compete in the contemporary business climate.

Unfortunately, despite having strong 'Islamic' themes, the lavish launch ceremonies of many halal businesses are more examples of business activities that are paradoxical, not least because the noble religion of Islam forbids extravagance and wastefulness. Keeping in mind images of hungry Muslim children in Bangladesh, Pakistan, Afghanistan, Somalia, Sudan, and many other countries today, **any** Muslim should be ashamed to engage in such wasteful spending.

Our third example of the paradoxical practices of many Muslim-owned businesses is the most grievous, for it involves Muslims starting and operating businesses that are categorically haram. In almost every Muslim country, one can find the contradictory practice of Muslims working in ribâ-based conventional banks as a way of seeking bounties and blessings, all of which come from Allah. This is quite ironic when one considers the severity of Allah's warning against ribâ:

﴿ يَٰٓأَيُّهَا ٱلَّذِينَ ءَامَنُواْ ٱتَّقُواْ ٱللَّهَ وَذَرُواْ مَا بَقِيَ مِنَ ٱلرِّبَوٰٓاْ إِن كُنتُم مُّؤۡمِنِينَ ۝ فَإِن لَّمۡ تَفۡعَلُواْ فَأۡذَنُواْ بِحَرۡبٖ مِّنَ ٱللَّهِ وَرَسُولِهِۦۖ وَإِن تُبۡتُمۡ فَلَكُمۡ رُءُوسُ أَمۡوَٰلِكُمۡ ... ۝ ﴾

(سورة البقرة: ٢٧٨-٢٧٩)

﴿O you who believe! Be afraid of Allah and give up what remains [due to you] from ribâ, if you are believers. If you do not do it, then take notice of war from Allah and His Messenger; but if you repent, you shall have your capital sums...﴾   *(Qur'an 2: 278-279)*

Many argue that such mistakes are trivial when made by Muslim businesses and that they should be overlooked in favour of the noble intentions behind those actions. They even cite as evidence the

following hadith in which 'Umar ibn al-Khaṭṭâb (رضي الله عنه) narrated that
the Prophet (ﷺ) said:

«Actions are only by intentions, and every person will have (be
rewarded for) what he intended. Whoever migrated for Allah and His
Messenger, his migration is for Allah and His Messenger. Whoever
migrated for worldly benefits he can acquire or for a woman he will
marry, his migration will be for that for which he migrated.» (Bukhari
and Muslim)

There are at least two problems with this kind of reasoning. As we
have already seen in the previous chapter, Islam is a complete religion
and therefore Allah has already decided which mistakes are trivial
and which ones are serious. Furthermore, even when the intentions
are noble, ignorance cannot be used indefinitely as an excuse.

An-Nu'mân ibn Basheer narrated that he heard Allah's Messenger
(ﷺ) saying:

«Both legal and illegal things are evident; however, in between them
are doubtful (suspicious) things, and most of the people have no
knowledge about them. Whoever saves himself from these suspicious
things saves his religion and his honour; whoever indulges in these
suspicious things is like a shepherd who grazes (his animals) near
the private pasture of someone else and at any moment he is liable
to enter it. (O people!) Beware! Every king has a private pasture,
and the private pasture of Allah on the earth constitutes the actions
that he has forbidden. Beware! There is a piece of flesh in the body;
if it becomes good (reformed), the whole body becomes good, but
if it gets spoilt, the whole body gets spoilt. That piece of flesh is the
heart.» (Bukhari)

Perhaps even more profound is Allah's warning:

﴿قُلْ هَلْ نُنَبِّئُكُم بِٱلْأَخْسَرِينَ أَعْمَٰلًا ۝ ٱلَّذِينَ ضَلَّ سَعْيُهُمْ فِى ٱلْحَيَوٰةِ ٱلدُّنْيَا وَهُمْ يَحْسَبُونَ أَنَّهُمْ
يُحْسِنُونَ صُنْعًا ۝ أُوْلَٰٓئِكَ ٱلَّذِينَ كَفَرُواْ بِـَٔايَٰتِ رَبِّهِمْ وَلِقَآئِهِۦ فَحَبِطَتْ أَعْمَٰلُهُمْ فَلَا نُقِيمُ لَهُمْ
يَوْمَ ٱلْقِيَٰمَةِ وَزْنًا ۝﴾   (سورة الكهف: ١٠٣-١٠٥)

❬Say [O Muhammad]: Shall We tell you the greatest losers in respect to [their] deeds? Those whose efforts have been wasted in this life while they thought that they were acquiring good by their deeds. They are those who deny the signs of their Lord and the meeting with Him. So their works are in vain, and on the Day of Resurrection, We shall assign no weight for them.❭   *(Qur'an 18: 103-105)*

Muslim scholars have clarified that two basic conditions must be fulfilled for the acceptance of righteous deeds. Firstly, the intention must be to perform those deeds for Allah's sake alone, without any showing off or desire to gain praise or fame. Secondly, such deeds must be performed in accordance with the Sunnah of Allah's Messenger, Muhammad ibn 'Abdullâh (ﷺ), the last of the prophets. 'Â'ishah (﵂) narrated that Allah's Messenger (ﷺ) said:

«If somebody innovates something which is not present in our religion (of Islamic monotheism), that thing will be rejected.» (Bukhari)

'Â'ishah (﵂) also narrated that the Prophet (ﷺ) said:

«Whoever performs a (good) deed which we have not ordered (anyone) to do (or is not in accordance with our religion of Islamic monotheism), that deed will be rejected and will not be accepted.» (Bukhari)

Perhaps what is most disheartening is that many continue with practices that are known to displease Allah, even after they receive gentle reminders based on evidence similar to that mentioned above. In the next chapter, we have included a special section on *da'wah* (calling people to the straight path) that may prove useful under such circumstances. Meanwhile, one is left to wonder whether the remarkable endurance of such practices is the result of true religious conviction or merely superstition, particularly since superstition has been a common element in business administration. It has permeated a range of communities of different religions, cultures, and times. The idol-worshipping Quraysh used to practice the throwing of arrows:

﴿حُرِّمَتْ عَلَيْكُمُ ٱلْمَيْتَةُ وَٱلدَّمُ وَلَحْمُ ٱلْخِنزِيرِ وَمَآ أُهِلَّ لِغَيْرِ ٱللَّهِ بِهِۦ وَٱلْمُنْخَنِقَةُ وَٱلْمَوْقُوذَةُ وَٱلْمُتَرَدِّيَةُ وَٱلنَّطِيحَةُ وَمَآ أَكَلَ ٱلسَّبُعُ إِلَّا مَا ذَكَّيْتُمْ وَمَا ذُبِحَ عَلَى ٱلنُّصُبِ وَأَن تَسْتَقْسِمُوا۟ بِٱلْأَزْلَٰمِ ذَٰلِكُمْ فِسْقٌ ٱلْيَوْمَ يَئِسَ ٱلَّذِينَ كَفَرُوا۟ مِن دِينِكُمْ فَلَا تَخْشَوْهُمْ وَٱخْشَوْنِ ٱلْيَوْمَ أَكْمَلْتُ لَكُمْ دِينَكُمْ وَأَتْمَمْتُ عَلَيْكُمْ نِعْمَتِى وَرَضِيتُ لَكُمُ ٱلْإِسْلَٰمَ دِينًا فَمَنِ ٱضْطُرَّ فِى مَخْمَصَةٍ غَيْرَ مُتَجَانِفٍ لِّإِثْمٍ فَإِنَّ ٱللَّهَ غَفُورٌ رَّحِيمٌ ٣﴾

(سورة المائدة: ٣)

﴿Forbidden to you are: the dead animals, blood, the flesh of swine, and the meat of that which has been slaughtered as a sacrifice for others than Allah, or has been slaughtered for idols, and so on, or on which Allah's name has not been mentioned while slaughtering, and that which has been killed by strangling, or by a violent blow, or by a headlong fall, or by the goring of horns – and that which has been [partly] eaten by a wild animal – unless you are able to slaughter it [before its death] – and that which is sacrificed on stone altars. [Forbidden] also is to use arrows seeking luck or decision; [all] that is disobedience of Allah and sin. This day, those who disbelieved have given up all hope of your religion, so fear them not, but fear Me. This day, I have perfected your religion for you, completed My favour upon you, and have chosen for you Islam as your religion. But as for him who is forced by severe hunger, with no inclination to sin, then surely, Allah is Oft-Forgiving, Most Merciful.﴾   (Qur'an 5: 3)

﴿يَٰٓأَيُّهَا ٱلَّذِينَ ءَامَنُوٓا۟ إِنَّمَا ٱلْخَمْرُ وَٱلْمَيْسِرُ وَٱلْأَنصَابُ وَٱلْأَزْلَٰمُ رِجْسٌ مِّنْ عَمَلِ ٱلشَّيْطَٰنِ فَٱجْتَنِبُوهُ لَعَلَّكُمْ تُفْلِحُونَ ٩٠﴾

(سورة المائدة: ٩٠)

﴿O you who believe! Intoxicants, gambling, animals that are sacrificed on stone altars for idols, and arrows for seeking luck or decision are abominations of Satan's handiwork. So avoid that in order that you may be successful.﴾   (Qur'an 5: 90)

Pre-Islamic Arabs used arrows to seek better fortunes. More than 1400 years later, it is not uncommon to find talismans in the offices of senior executives in the largest corporations, or at least a Magic 8 Ball for occasional consultation.[3]

At the other end of the spectrum is business administration that is practiced in a completely secular manner. This approach may be rational and somewhat more organic, since the field of business administration arose largely within a secular domain, but this approach is certainly not Islamic.

There is clearly a need to establish exactly what constitutes a truly Islamic approach to business administration and financial management – one that will please Allah, the Creator. The first step in defining such an approach involves a correct understanding of Islam. In many ways, Islam needs no introduction, because 'Islam' has become a very familiar term these days. It is known generally to be an originally Middle Eastern (Arab) religion that spread to the four corners of the globe. Consequently, there are many different people who identify themselves as Muslim.

The vast majority of Muslims were born within Muslim cultures or sub-cultures, often with specific versions of Islam practiced quite comfortably over centuries. For example, many areas of the Indian subcontinent have had a strong Muslim heritage ever since the Mughal presence. Many Muslims of Indian, Pakistani, and Bangladeshi origin today continue centuries-old 'Islamic' traditions, observing such 'Muslim' holidays as the Prophet's birthday, *shab-e-barât* (middle of Sha'bân), and Ramadan. Shiite Muslims observe the Islamic month of Muḥarram as a month for grieving;[4] Sunni Muslims, on the other

---

[3] The Magic 8 Ball is a toy used for fortune telling. (Editor)

[4] In some countries, mourning is observed because it is believed that Ḥusayn ibn 'Ali (the Prophet's grandson) was martyred on the tenth of Muḥarram in Karbala, Iraq. (Editor)

hand, commemorate *'Âshoorâ'* (the tenth of Muḥarram) as a happy remembrance of the day on which Prophet Moses (ﷺ) and the Israelites were saved. Sunni Muslims in the Arab Gulf countries are largely opposed to celebrating the Prophet's birthday or shab-e-barât, but they strictly observe Ramadan. Thus, different versions of Islam co-exist with each other as well as with other religions and cultures.

With drastic increases in the movement of people and ideas, largely due to technological advances in communications and transportation, regional demographics today reflect much more diversity. For example, when Muslims from around the world congregate, they find variations in the way that prayers are offered by their brothers and sisters from different regions. Diversity obviously offers strength, but it can also lead to disagreement; indeed, Islam is now becoming synonymous with conflict. Keeping this in mind, the following few simple facts should be of interest to Muslims and non-Muslims alike.

The first fact is that Islam is still spreading 1400 years after its founding; this is taking place largely in non-Arab populations, including those in prosperous Western countries such as the United States.

A second truth is that many people believe that Islam and its adherents preach intolerance, since there appear to be many Muslim extremists who engage in anti-social activities targeting non-Muslims and even fellow Muslims.

Third, those who follow Islam differ drastically in their level of adherence to Islamic principles. At one end of the spectrum are individuals who call themselves Muslims but who completely forsake Islamic practices. The 'centre-left' is populated by Muslims who appreciate an occasional taste of Islam but are not consumed by it; in contrast, the 'centre-right' is populated by Muslims who want Islam to affect every conceivable aspect of their lives. Then there are hard-liners and extremists at the right end of the spectrum, who will not shy away from resorting to the toughest means, including violence, to punish even the slightest deviation from Islamic teachings.

Various think tanks have been established around the globe to attempt to understand and even modify Muslim behaviour. This is not surprising if one considers the many regions of the world embroiled in conflict, and its often violent consequences, where Muslims are involved. A major source of the conflict is that the ideologies held by a variety of Muslims worldwide appear to be at odds with such Western values and principles as the separation of church and state, democracy, and women's rights.

It is therefore an extremely useful task today, by definition for Muslims and by relevance for non-Muslims, to understand Islam. The remainder of this chapter will introduce and explain the basic principles of Islam.

What is Islam?

Islam is a religion, and its followers are called Muslims. A religion usually acknowledges divinity, offers a philosophy, and prescribes a way of life based on that philosophy. What are the principles of Islam and the Islamic philosophy? What is the truly Islamic way of life? How is Islam unique from other religions?

From our discussion above, it is quite clear that if one were to ask these questions today, different respondents would give many different and often contradictory answers. The questioner would have the complex task of determining which answers are correct or even wondering if there exists a single correct answer to any given question. We offer a simple and logical approach as a method of resolution. Since the religion of Islam was preached by Prophet Muhammad (ﷺ), it is most useful to investigate how he defined Islam. Ibn 'Umar (ﷺ) narrated that Allah's Messenger (ﷺ) said:

«Islam is based on (the following) five (principles):

To testify that none has the right to be worshipped but Allah and that Muhammad (ﷺ) is Allah's messenger, to offer the (compulsory congregational) prayers dutifully and perfectly, to pay zakâh, to perform Hajj, and to fast during the month of Ramadan.» (Bukhari)

Abu Hurayrah (رضي الله عنه) narrated:

«One day while the Prophet was sitting in the company of some people, (the angel) Gabriel came and asked: What is faith?

Allah's Messenger (ﷺ) replied: Faith is to believe in Allah, His angels, His revealed books, His messengers, and (the process of) resurrection.

Gabriel further questioned: What is Islam?

Allah's Messenger (ﷺ) answered: To worship Allah alone and no one else, to offer prayers perfectly, to pay the zakâh, and to fast during the month of Ramadan.

He inquired: What is *ihsân* (excellence)?

Allah's Messenger (ﷺ) responded: To worship Allah as if you see Him, and if you cannot achieve this state of devotion, you must consider that He sees you...» (Bukhari)

Thus, Islam is a religion based on complete submission to one God – Allah, the Creator and Lord of the worlds. Islam is manifested through five pillars:

1. *shahâdatayn* (dual testimony of faith)
2. *salâh* (obligatory formal prayers)
3. zakâh
4. fasting in the month of Ramadan
5. Hajj

The foundation of Islam is the Qur'an and then the Sunnah.

Very few Muslims can or will argue about the above definition; they only argue about the implications. Since we are talking about business administration, we can use that context to illustrate this fact.

An, easy albeit naïve, statement, after considering this definition of Islam, is that Islam and business administration are not related at all. One can argue that Islam clearly affects religious issues related to worship, such as mandatory prayer, charity, fasting, and pilgrimage. Worship is the manifestation of one's spiritual conviction, which is highly personal in essence; it seems unrelated to such worldly tasks as those in business administration.

The argument that Islam and business administration are not related is dismissed if one considers a bit more closely the first pillar of Islam, which involves testifying to the oneness of Allah. The rationale is extremely straightforward: **if Allah has specified rules that affect any activity in business administration, ignoring such rules contradicts one's testimony that Allah is the one true God.** We will explain this principle below as we begin our discussion of each pillar individually.

Pillar I: The *shahâdatayn*

Shahâdah is an Arabic term that can be translated as 'testimony', and shahâdatayn means 'two testimonies'. In the context of Islam, it means to testify that there is none worthy of worship other than Allah and that Muhammad (ﷺ) is His slave and messenger. The shahâdatayn constitute the first pillar of Islam, as Prophet Muhammad (ﷺ) mentioned the shahâdatayn first on the list. Reflecting on the greatness of this statement, one can easily appreciate its meaning.

The statement of shahâdatayn is the most distinctive characteristic of the adherents to the Muslim faith. In other words, only Muslims state that they believe in Allah alone as one God, to the exclusion of any other being or entity that claims to be God or is deified, and that they believe in Muhammad (ﷺ) as Allah's messenger. Jews, for example, believe in only one God but not in the prophethood of Muhammad (ﷺ).[5]

---

[5] The term 'prophethood' is not in the English dictionary but is an invented term, formed along the pattern of 'childhood' and 'motherhood', as a=

Pronouncing the shahâdatayn offers Muslims both purpose and guidance. In other words, those who have embraced Islam by declaring the shahâdatayn need to validate this statement with appropriate actions; otherwise, their testimony would degenerate into mere lip service. Individuals cannot state that they believe in Allah as God and then refuse to obey His commands. Similarly, they must believe in the truthfulness of the messenger selected by Allah and therefore follow the commands given by this messenger of Allah (ﷺ).

The shahâdatayn lays the foundation for the other pillars. The second pillar, prayer, can only be valid if one knows to whom one is praying and how to perform the prayer. The order of the five pillars can be inferred from the well-known hadith related to da'wah. Ibn 'Abbâs (رضي الله عنه) narrated that when the Prophet (ﷺ) sent Mu'âdh to Yemen, he said to him:

«You are going to a nation of the People of the Scripture; the first thing to which you should invite them is the oneness of Allah. If they learn that, tell them that Allah has enjoined on them five prayers to be offered in one day and one night. If they pray, tell them that Allah has enjoined on them the zakâh of their properties; it has to be taken from their rich and given to their poor. If they agree to that, take from them the zakâh, but avoid the best property of the people.» (Bukhari)

The declaration of the shahâdatayn is more universal than the other pillars in more than one sense. Obligatory prayers, for example, are performed only five times a day, and fasting is obligatory in only one out of the twelve months in the year. The pillar of shahâdatayn is more enduring because declaring Allah's lordship will affect every

---

=noun reflecting a particular state of being. It is meant to translate the meaning of the Arabic word *nubuwwah*, which has no one-word equivalent in English, but which could be translated as meaning 'the state of being a prophet' and is also used to refer to 'all things that have to do with being a prophet'. The term 'prophethood' has become common in English-language Islamic discourse. (Editor)

moment of the rest of one's life, and it affects more issues than the other pillars. It is the basis of the link between Islam and any other aspect of life, including business administration, as we will explain later in the chapter.

Tawḥeed

The first part of the shahâdatayn is a testimony about God, or more precisely, the oneness of God. This concept of pure monotheism is known in Islam as tawḥeed. Many statements by Allah in the Qur'an lay down the foundation of this principle of tawḥeed; indeed, all of *Soorat* (chapter) *al-Ikhlâṣ* is dedicated to this concept.

﴿قُلْ هُوَ ٱللَّهُ أَحَدٌ ۝ ٱللَّهُ ٱلصَّمَدُ ۝ لَمْ يَلِدْ وَلَمْ يُولَدْ ۝ وَلَمْ يَكُن لَّهُۥ كُفُوًا أَحَدٌ ۝﴾ (سورة الإخلاص: ١-٤)

﴾Say [O Muhammad]: He is Allah, [the] One. Allah – the Self-Sufficient Master, Whom all creatures need. He begets not, nor was He begotten. And there is none co-equal or comparable unto Him.﴿

(Qur'an 112: 1-4)

﴿إِيَّاكَ نَعْبُدُ وَإِيَّاكَ نَسْتَعِينُ ۝﴾ (سورة الفاتحة: ٥)

﴾You [Alone] we worship, and You [Alone] we ask for help.﴿

(Qur'an 1: 5)

﴿يَٰٓأَيُّهَا ٱلنَّاسُ ٱعْبُدُوا۟ رَبَّكُمُ ٱلَّذِى خَلَقَكُمْ وَٱلَّذِينَ مِن قَبْلِكُمْ لَعَلَّكُمْ تَتَّقُونَ ۝﴾ (سورة البقرة: ٢١)

﴾O humankind! Worship your Lord [Allah], Who created you and those who were before you so that you may become pious.﴿

(Qur'an 2: 21)

﴿وَإِلَٰهُكُمْ إِلَٰهٌ وَٰحِدٌ لَّآ إِلَٰهَ إِلَّا هُوَ ٱلرَّحْمَٰنُ ٱلرَّحِيمُ ۝﴾ (سورة البقرة: ١٦٣)

﴾And your God is one God [Allah]; there is none who has the right to be worshipped but He, the Most Gracious, the Most Merciful.﴿

(Qur'an 2: 163)

When a Muslim embraces Islam and pronounces the shahâdatayn, stating that there is no God but Allah and that Muhammad (ﷺ) is His slave and messenger, he or she needs to understand the implications of this mighty statement.

To help illustrate this point, we shall use a simple example. When a man announces his agreement to marry a woman, that statement has certain implications. He has rights over her, and she has rights over him. In Islam, he must pay her the agreed-upon dowry, provide for her, fulfil her marital rights, and live honourably with her. She must be faithful to him, bear his children, and protect his household.

Similarly, once an individual becomes a Muslim by stating the shahâdatayn, he or she has certain rights and responsibilities; likewise, Allah has rights over him or her. Mu'âdh (ﷺ) narrated:

«Once I was riding with the Prophet (ﷺ) on a donkey called 'Ufayr. The Prophet asked: O Mu'âdh! Do you know what Allah's rights on His slaves are and what the slaves' rights on Him are?

I replied: Allah and His Messenger know better.

The Prophet (ﷺ) explained: Allah's right on His slaves is that they should worship Him (alone) and should not worship anyone besides Him. The slave's right on Allah is that He should not punish the one who worships none besides Him.

I exclaimed: O Allah's Messenger! Should I not inform the people of this good news?

He said: Do not inform them, lest they depend on it (absolutely).» (Bukhari)

To better understand the rights of Allah, we must start by reflecting upon the shahâdatayn itself. In particular, what does it mean to acknowledge the lordship of Allah alone? We can divide that question into two parts. First, what is meant by the term 'God'? Second, what is the implication of acknowledging Allah as the one and only God?

'God' is quite simply the term used to refer to a being or entity that is worshipped. In many faiths, this being is also the Originator, the Creator of all creation. Worship is the highest form of obedience; if you claim to worship God, you cannot obey some other entity (or perhaps even your own desires) more than you are obeying God. The statement of the shahâdatayn says that there is no God but Allah. Thus, you are allowed to worship only Allah, and you cannot disobey Him through your obedience to anyone or anything else.

﴿أَفَرَءَيْتَ مَنِ ٱتَّخَذَ إِلَٰهَهُۥ هَوَىٰهُ وَأَضَلَّهُ ٱللَّهُ عَلَىٰ عِلْمٍ وَخَتَمَ عَلَىٰ سَمْعِهِۦ وَقَلْبِهِۦ وَجَعَلَ عَلَىٰ بَصَرِهِۦ غِشَٰوَةً فَمَن يَهْدِيهِ مِنۢ بَعْدِ ٱللَّهِ أَفَلَا تَذَكَّرُونَ ۝﴾ (سورة الجاثية: ٢٣)

❨Have you seen him who takes his own lust as his god? And Allah knowing [him as such], left him astray, and sealed his hearing and his heart, and put a cover on his sight. Who then will guide him after Allah? Will you not then remember?❩ (Qur'an 45: 23)

﴿ ٱتَّخَذُوٓا۟ أَحْبَارَهُمْ وَرُهْبَٰنَهُمْ أَرْبَابًا مِّن دُونِ ٱللَّهِ وَٱلْمَسِيحَ ٱبْنَ مَرْيَمَ وَمَآ أُمِرُوٓا۟ إِلَّا لِيَعْبُدُوٓا۟ إِلَٰهًا وَٰحِدًا لَّآ إِلَٰهَ إِلَّا هُوَ سُبْحَٰنَهُۥ عَمَّا يُشْرِكُونَ ۝﴾ (سورة التوبة: ٣١)

❨They [the Jews and the Christians] took their rabbis and their monks to be their lords besides Allah and the Messiah, son of Mary, while they were commanded [in the Torah and the Gospel] to worship none but one God [Allah]. None has the right to be worshipped but He. Praise and glory be to Him [; far above is He] from having the partners they associate [with Him].❩ (Qur'an 9: 31)

Once, while Allah's Messenger (ﷺ) was reciting this verse:

«'Adiyy ibn Ḥâtim said: O Allah's Messenger, they do not worship them (the rabbis and the monks).

Allah's Messenger (ﷺ) stated: They certainly do. They (the rabbis and the monks) declared lawful things to be unlawful and unlawful things to be lawful, and they (the Jews and the Christians) followed them – and this was akin to worshipping them.» (at-Tirmidhi; a reliable hadith according to al-Albâni)

Thus, even by blindly following desires, one may elevate them to the degree of worship. From the verses quoted above, it is easy to appreciate that understanding tawḥeed – true monotheism – requires reflection. To facilitate understanding, scholars have traditionally classified tawḥeed into three recognizable essences.[6]

1. *Tawḥeed ar-ruboobiyah* (oneness of the divine Lordship): There is only one supreme Lord. He is the Creator and the Most High.

2. *Tawḥeed al-uloohiyah* (oneness of the divine nature): He is the only One Who can be worshipped.

3. *Tawḥeed al-asmâ' waṣ-ṣifât* (oneness of the divine names and attributes): Only Allah can be described as He has described Himself in the Qur'an. For example, Allah is the Most Merciful, the Most Forgiving, the Most Wise, the Lawmaker, the Fairest Judge, and the Most Kind. There are ninety-nine names that Allah has used for Himself in the Qur'an. These names, in their form and essence, cannot be used for any other being or entity.

Since tawḥeed emphasizes oneness, its opposite signifies multitude. In Islam, the opposite of tawḥeed is known as *shirk,* which means 'associating partnership'. The only way a human being can negate the concept of tawḥeed, which attributes divinity to only one God – Allah – is by attributing divinity to some other entity. Shirk can take many forms. It is a very serious issue in Islam, primarily because Allah has warned that He will never forgive shirk:

﴿ إِنَّ ٱللَّهَ لَا يَغۡفِرُ أَن يُشۡرَكَ بِهِۦ وَيَغۡفِرُ مَا دُونَ ذَٰلِكَ لِمَن يَشَآءُ ۚ وَمَن يُشۡرِكۡ بِٱللَّهِ فَقَدِ ٱفۡتَرَىٰٓ إِثۡمًا عَظِيمًا ﴾

(سورة النساء: ٤٨)

---

[6] For more information, see "What is the evidence for dividing Tawheed into three categories?" Islam-QA.com, accessed October 23, 2011, http://www.islam-qa.com/en/ref/26338.

《Verily, Allah forgives not that partners should be set up with Him, but except that, He forgives [anything else] to whom He wills; and whoever sets up partners with Allah in worship, he has indeed invented a tremendous sin.》 *(Qur'an 4: 48)*

It is important to remember that, as with the case of *kufr* (disbelief), the Muslim creed does not allow extremism in the stance on shirk. There are many different forms of shirk, and they are classified into two main groups: minor shirk and major shirk.[7]

The Prophet (ﷺ) taught his Companions (رضي الله عنهم) about shirk, saying:

«Shirk among you will be more subtle than the footsteps of an ant, but I will teach you something through which both minor and major shirk will be kept away from you. Say: *Allâhumma inni a'oodhu bika an ushrika bika wa anâ a'lam wa astaghfiruka limâ lâ a'lam* (O Allah, I seek refuge with You from associating anything with You knowingly, and I seek Your forgiveness for that of which I am unaware).» (Bukhari)

Major shirk means to ascribe to someone other than Allah something that belongs only to Allah, such as lordship (ruboobiyah), divinity (uloohiyah), or divine names and attributes (al-asmâ' waṣ-ṣifât). It can be overt, for instance in the form of grave worshipping, or remain covert, as when people hide their hypocrisy of not trusting Allah.

One type of major shirk that is proving to be quite a trial for Muslims today takes the form of a belief:

...that there is someone else who must be obeyed absolutely besides Allaah, so they follow him [the mentor/professor and so

---

[7] Detailed information on this topic is available from such rulings as "What is the true meaning of shirk and what are its types?"Islam-QA.com, accessed October 23, 2011, http://www.islam-qa.com/en/ref/34817.

on] in regarding as permissible or forbidden whatever he wants, even if that goes against the religion of the Messengers.[8]

An example of this in the context of business administration is a student who chooses to believe an eminent professor's or mentor's view of what is wonderful or important – say, speculative financial instrument-like derivatives – without paying heed to the rules already established by Allah. As a result of an exclusively secular business education, some Muslims blindly implement erroneous business advice. Interestingly, this kind of shirk is not necessarily limited to negating Allah's divinity altogether or even partially. One can commit shirk by granting others – besides Allah – the right to be worshipped. (May Allah protect us from such evil actions.)

﴾ وَمِنَ ٱلنَّاسِ مَن يَتَّخِذُ مِن دُونِ ٱللَّهِ أَندَادًا يُحِبُّونَهُمْ كَحُبِّ ٱللَّهِ ... ﴿١٦٥﴾ ﴾

(سورة البقرة: ١٦٥)

﴿And of humankind are some who take [for worship] others besides Allah as rivals [to Him]. They love them as they love Allah...﴾

(Qur'an 2: 165)

Minor shirk constitutes anything and everything that may lead to major shirk, although it is not as serious as major shirk.

«The Messenger of Allah (ﷺ) said: The thing I fear most for you is minor shirk.

The Companions asked: O Messenger of Allah, what is minor shirk? He replied: Showing off – for Allah will say on the day when people are recompensed for their actions: Go to those to whom you were showing off with your deeds in the world and see what reward you find with them.» (Aḥmad and al-Haythami; a sound hadith according to al-Albâni)

---

[8] See "What is the true meaning of shirk and what are its types?" Islam-QA. com, accessed October 23, 2011, http://www.islam-qa.com/en/ref/34817.

The Prophet (ﷺ) also said:

«Incantations, amulets, and love spells are shirk.» (Abu Dâwood; al-Albâni graded it as sound)

The difference between major and minor shirk is that major shirk puts a person beyond the fold of Islam; the one who commits it is judged to have apostatized from Islam and is considered to be a disbeliever. Although minor shirk does not put a person beyond the folds of Islam, it is still a major sin.

Being a Muslim

The definition of Islam combines both belief and practice. In Islam, the Arabic terms for belief and practice are *eemân* (faith) and *'aml* (actions), respectively. Individuals first become Muslims by believing; then they remain Muslims by letting their eemân guide their actions based on correct knowledge. Those who become Muslim without believing, or who call themselves Muslim without having any eemân, earn the dangerous label of 'hypocrite'. Those who become Muslims sincerely, with eemân, but do not practice according to it – should reassess their *'aqeedah* (creed). A Muslim having a sound eemân is referred to as a believer.

Sa'd (﵁) narrated:

«Allah's Messenger (ﷺ) distributed (zakâh) amongst (a group of) people while I was sitting there, but he left out a man whom I thought was the best of the lot.

I asked: O Allah's Messenger! Why have you left that person out? By Allah, I regard him as a faithful believer.

The Prophet (ﷺ) commented: Or merely a Muslim...» (Bukhari)

We have discussed how Islam is distinct because it attributes divinity to only one God in the purest sense. A problem that frequently arises when using this definition is extremism.

In one extremist school of thought, a very simple logic is deployed: those who knowingly commit sins have chosen to undermine the divinity of the one God in favour of pleasing themselves or someone else; thus they have violated the very definition of their religion and can no longer be considered Muslims.

At the opposite end of the spectrum is another form of extremism: that belief is purely in the heart, so one's actions can never render void one's belief in the oneness of God.

Clearly a middle course is the best, and that is the Sunnah of the Prophet (ﷺ), as we shall see further below.

For the sake of simplicity, we will just mention now that Allah and His Prophet (ﷺ) have told us that believers will sin and that they are encouraged to repent for that. This negates the argument of the first type of extremists, who equate committing sins with apostasy. As for the claim that belief is completely distinct from actions, it has little merit since actions (or sometimes the lack thereof) reflect the state of belief (or possibly the lack thereof).

We can read an excerpt from a fatwa from Shaykh 'Abd-Allaah al-Ghunaymaan:

> Kufr takes different forms. The Murji'ah and other followers of bid'ah (reprehensible innovation) say that kufr is only based on disbelief. But this view is contrary to the evidence and contrary to the truth. It is known that the Messengers were sent with miracles and proof to which hearts submitted. It is rare indeed that people believed that what the Prophets brought was false; most instances of kufr stemmed from arrogance, rejection and stubbornness. Allaah mentioned that Quraysh did not disbelieve the Prophet (peace and blessings of Allaah be upon him),
>
> "but it is the Verses (the Qur'aan) of Allaah that the Zaalimoon (polytheists and wrongdoers) deny" [al-An'aam 6: 33]
>
> This happens very often. Hence the scholars divided kufr into various types: the kufr of negligence and not caring; the kufr of

arrogance and pride; the kufr of disbelief; the kufr of hypocrisy; the kufr of doubt. There is a great deal of evidence to that effect in the Book of Allaah and the Sunnah of His Messenger (peace and blessings of Allaah be upon him). The story of Abu Taalib and the Prophet (peace and blessings of Allaah be upon him) is clear; he believed in him and he used to say: Our son does not tell lies, but he was still a kaafir, because he never made a statement of faith or followed it up with actions.[9]

We can highlight the interrelationships among obedience through action, sincerity of belief, and the belief system of the Islamic creed by using the particular case of ṣalâh (prayer), which is a fundamental pillar of Islam.[10]

Suppose you have three people with the following views:

Person A says, "I believe in one God, Allah, but I do not believe that prayer is necessary."

Person B says, "I believe in one God, Allah, and I understand that I am required to perform the prayers, but I am not regular in performing them."

Person C says, "I believe in one God, Allah, and I never deliberately miss prayers."

All three people call themselves Muslim, and all three claim that they believe in one God, Allah, but they differ when it comes to Islam's second pillar, the ṣalâh. It is quite easy to see that the three

---

[9] See "The misguidance of those who believe that kufr only means disbelief," Islam-QA.com, accessed October 23, 2011, http://www.islam-qa.com/en/ref/12811.

[10] Ibn al-'Uthaymeen has formally discussed this in *Liqâ' al-Bâb al-Maftooḥ*, no. 45. "Reconciling between the hadeeth which says that whoever says Laa ilaaha ill-Allaah will enter Paradise and the idea that the mushrikeen will abide in Hell forever," Islam-QA.com, accessed October 23, 2011, http://www.islam-qa.com/en/ref/21683.

people are really part of a spectrum, where A is the least religious and C is the most religious.

There are two main questions that can be asked about Muslims with respect to this spectrum. Where do they lie on the spectrum? What is their belief about the validity of a version of Islam represented in the spectrum?

The first question is quite easy for individuals to answer for themselves, but the second question is much harder to answer precisely. For example, scholars of ahl as-Sunnah have debated the validity of the Islam practiced by Person B.[11] However, there has been consensus regarding Person A, not least because this person is denying one of the pillars of the religion that Allah has established.[12] While Person A believes that Allah is the one God, he or she is expressing through actions and statements that there is categorically no need to worship Allah. Based on what we have mentioned previously, Person A is in effect denying divinity to Allah in favour of granting it to some other entity, be it desire or the founder of a human-made philosophy such as secularism.

Let us look at the following excerpt from *Fatâwâ Samâhat al-Imâm 'Abdullâh ibn Ḥumayd*, which explains that abandoning ṣalâh negates one's Islam.

---

[11] "A person's believing his haraam action to be permitted is not always a condition for denouncing him as a kaafir," Islam-QA.com, accessed October 23, 2011, http://www.islam-qa.com/en/ref/10095. The following is an excerpt from this fatwa:

But there are some differences among the imaams of the madhhabs [the scholars of the different schools of Islamic jurisprudence] concerning the kufr of one who does not pray. Some said that he does not become a [non-Muslim] in a complete sense so long as he does not deny that prayer is obligatory.

[12] See the section below on the second pillar; it lists verses and hadiths that directly address this topic.

Praise be to Allaah.

Prayer is the greatest pillar of Islam after the Shahaadatayn.

The Messenger of Allaah (peace and blessings of Allaah be upon him) said: "Between a person and kufr and shirk stands the abandonment of prayer."

(Narrated by al-Tirmidhi, 2766. Classed as saheeh by Ibn Maajah, 1078, and by al-Albaani).

Salaah is so called because it is a connection (silah) between a person and his Lord. Whoever does not pray, his zakaah, fasting, Hajj, jihaad, enjoining of what is good, forbidding of what is evil, reading of Qur'aan and upholding of family ties will not be accepted. Indeed, all his good deeds will be rejected if he does not pray. The scholars, including Imaam Ahmad, said that whoever does not pray should be executed as a kaafir, and his body should not be washed or shrouded, the funeral prayer should not be offered over him, he should not be buried in the Muslims' graveyard and his Muslim heirs cannot inherit from him.[13]

Of course, there are many who question the authority of any human being, even a scholar, to definitively label an individual a disbeliever after he or she has stated the shahâdatayn. We can refer to Shaykh Ibn al-'Uthaymeen's comments on the topic:

The Shahaadatayn must be spoken with sincerity. Listen to what Allaah says concerning the munaafiqeen (interpretation of the meaning):

"And when they [the hypocrites] stand up for As-Salaah (the prayer), they stand with laziness and to be seen of men, and they do not remember Allaah but little" [*al-Nisa' 4: 142*]

---

[13] See Ibn Ḥumayd, *Fatâwâ Samâḥat al-Imâm 'Abdullâh ibn Ḥumayd,* 86, quoted in "Ruling on one who reads Qur'aan but does not pray," Islam-QA. com, accessed November 2, 2011, http://www.islam-qa.com/en/ref/10094.

In the same passage, Allaah says (interpretation of the meaning):

"Verily, the hypocrites will be in the lowest depth (grade) of the Fire; no helper will you find for them" [*al-Nisa' 4: 145*]

And Allaah says of them (interpretation of the meaning):

"When the hypocrites come to you (O Muhammad), they say: 'We bear witness that you are indeed the Messenger of Allaah'" [*al-Munaafiqoon 63: 1*]

This is merely verbal testimony, but:

"Allaah knows that you are indeed His Messenger, and Allaah bears witness that the hypocrites are liars indeed" [*al-Munaafiqoon 63: 1*]

i.e., that they are lying when they say, "We bear witness that you are indeed the Messenger of Allaah". For they mention Allaah and bear witness to His Messenger, but their hearts are devoid of that which is uttered by their lips.[14]

The second question asks whether one considers all the persons, A through C, to be Muslims. The implications of the second question are even harder to handle and require considerable wisdom. To illustrate that, examine Person C. He appears to be a Muslim in terms of both belief and practice. Interestingly, however, he may nullify his own belief if he believes that Person A is not committing disbelief in the light of the evidence given above. We list this and some other implications below.

The validity of one's own belief system depends upon one's belief about the validity of others' belief systems. A Muslim cannot believe, for example, that someone who is directing worship to other than Allah, the Creator, will be forgiven after dying in this state, because that contradicts the Qur'an. Therefore Person C, who has embraced the valid

---

[14] "Reconciling between the hadeeth which says that whoever says Laa ilaaha ill-Allaah will enter Paradise and the idea that the mushrikeen will abide in Hell forever," Islam-QA.com, accessed October 23, 2011, http://www.islam-qa.com/en/ref/21683.

beliefs and practices of Islam, cannot believe that Person A is a Muslim, since it is clear from the Islamic teachings that abandoning the prayer takes one out of the folds of Islam. While the position of Person A is clear, there is a gray area regarding Person B.

Also, just because a self-proclaimed Muslim like Person A does not have the right 'aqeedah, this does not mean that it is automatically the duty of ordinary Muslims to attack this individual, for that would be considered extremism. Instead, they must resort to the approach prescribed by Allah and advocated by the Prophet (ﷺ); this includes an attempt to educate the concerned individuals about the errors they are making. Muslims all across the spectrum should try to improve themselves while protecting themselves from extremism. In other words, a Muslim who does not regularly perform the prayers should try hard to become like the one who does.

The length of our discussion on the first pillar of Islam (the shahâdatayn) should not be surprising if one considers that the Prophet (ﷺ) spent much of the first decade of his prophethood preaching the concept of the oneness of God. Islamic monotheism, or tawḥeed as it is referred to in the Islamic sciences, is the basis for all Islamic beliefs and practices. There is a chapter in the Qur'an on tawḥeed; it is called Soorat *al-Ikhlâṣ* and is regarded as being one-third of the Qur'an in essence and in importance.[15]

The failure to understand tawḥeed is an easy trap used by Satan to cause turmoil or discord. It can lead people to adopt extremist views: either to abandon Islam and commit acts of disbelief or to carry out such extremist actions as wrongfully harming people whom they deem to be disbelievers. It can also lead people to utter inaccurate statements about Islam without realizing the gravity of those statements.

---

[15] For further information, see al-Munajjid, "The virtues of Soorat al-Ikhlaas, etc.," Islam-QA.com, accessed November 2, 2011, http://www.islam-qa.com/en/ref/2241.

Today, many Muslims try to reconcile Islam with secular Western philosophies and value systems. Muslims should realize that Islam has been perfected by Allah and prescribed for all humankind until the Day of Judgement. There can be no more modifications to Islam from the prophets (because Muhammad [ﷺ] was the last of Allah's prophets), let alone modification by ordinary human beings.

Islam, the religion prescribed by the Creator, has a universal appeal to all His creation; there are Muslims from virtually every culture, society, continent, and country who have recognized its truth. Still, Muslims should realize that despite Islam's universal appeal, there are some who will never be able to recognize its truth and accept its message – but this is not a reason to make changes to Islam. It has been this way since the Prophet (ﷺ) preached his message, and it will continue to be this way until the end of time. Those who attempt to alter Islam to make it seem more appealing to modern society will lose – with respect to their religion as well as to other people.

﴿عَمَّ يَتَسَآءَلُونَ ۝ عَنِ ٱلنَّبَإِ ٱلۡعَظِيمِ ۝ ٱلَّذِى هُمۡ فِيهِ مُخۡتَلِفُونَ ۝ كَلَّا سَيَعۡلَمُونَ ۝ ثُمَّ كَلَّا سَيَعۡلَمُونَ ۝﴾

(سورة النبأ: ١-٥)

❝What are they asking one another about? About the great news about which they are in disagreement. Nay, they will come to know! Nay, again, they will come to know!❞   *(Qur'an 78: 1-5)*

The Sunnah

In the second part of the shahâdatayn, Muslims testify that Muhammad (ﷺ) is Allah's slave and messenger. This act of testifying has implications as well. Our Prophet Muhammad (ﷺ) dedicated twenty-three years of his prophethood to teaching the religion as it should be followed. True Muslims who have acknowledged Allah as the one God should respond to this call from Allah's Messenger (ﷺ). They should strive to learn the Sunnah (way) of Prophet Muhammad (ﷺ) and to implement that Sunnah while following the true form of Islam.

There are at least two sets of arguments used frequently by those Muslims who fail to recognize the importance of adhering to the Sunnah. In the first set, many Muslims argue that a practical approach to following Islam in the modern day is to follow the general guidelines offered by the Qur'an and select only some of the Sunnah. They argue that many aspects of the Sunnah were part of social norms in the sixth and seventh centuries and are neither feasible nor appropriate in the twenty-first century.

For example, they argue that while it may have been quite normal at the advent of Islam for women to be covered from head to toe and for the society to practice segregation, those same practices may raise eyebrows or even foment resentment among non-Muslims today. This argument is overused, and Muslim beards and hijabs have been replaced by symbolic goatees and cover-all, body-hugging suits that are more acceptable in terms of contemporary fashion standards. At first glance, these arguments seem to have some strength; indeed, few people ride camels nowadays. However, the following points highlight the flaws in this kind of reasoning:

1) Excluding the details given in the Sunnah, and choosing instead to take general guidelines from the Qur'an only, is an approach that contradicts the instructions in the Qur'an itself:[16]

$$ \text{﴿ قُلْ إِن كُنتُمْ تُحِبُّونَ ٱللَّهَ فَٱتَّبِعُونِي يُحْبِبْكُمُ ٱللَّهُ وَيَغْفِرْ لَكُمْ ذُنُوبَكُرْ ... ﴿٣١﴾ ﴾} $$

(سورة آل عمران: ٣١)

---

[16] A formal presentation by Shaykh Muhammad al-Munajjid refutes the arguments of those who follow only the Qur'an and exclude the Sunnah. See al-Munajjid, "Justification for following the Sunnah," Islam-QA. com, accessed November 2, 2011, http://www.islam-qa.com/en/ref/604.

❰Say: If you love Allah, then follow me, Allah will love you and forgive you your sins...❱   *(Qur'an 3: 31)*

﴿قُلْ أَطِيعُواْ ٱللَّهَ وَأَطِيعُواْ ٱلرَّسُولَ فَإِن تَوَلَّوْاْ فَإِنَّمَا عَلَيْهِ مَا حُمِّلَ وَعَلَيْكُم مَّا حُمِّلْتُمْ وَإِن تُطِيعُوهُ تَهْتَدُواْ وَمَا عَلَى ٱلرَّسُولِ إِلَّا ٱلْبَلَٰغُ ٱلْمُبِينُ ﴾ ۝   (سورة النور: ٥٤)

❰Say: Obey Allah and obey the Messenger, but if you turn away, he is only responsible for the duty placed on him and you for that placed on you. If you obey him, you shall be on the right guidance. The Messenger's duty is only to convey [the message] in a clear way.❱
(Qur'an 24: 54)

The Prophet (ﷺ) said:

«Whoever obeys me obeys Allah, and whoever disobeys me disobeys Allah.» (Bukhari and Muslim)

«The Prophet (ﷺ) said: All of my Ummah (the Muslim nation) will enter paradise except those who refuse.

He was asked: O Messenger of Allah, who are those who refuse?

He said: Whoever obeys me will enter paradise, and whoever disobeys me has refused.» (Bukhari)

2) It is not even possible to become or remain a Muslim if one excludes the Sunnah. This argument should not surprise Muslims at all, because if this were possible, then there would have been no need for a messenger in the first place. The fact that the Prophet (ﷺ) was sent as a messenger to teach Muslims the religion is evidence that it is not possible to exclude the Sunnah if one is to be a Muslim.

Let us consider the prayer as an example. In the Qur'an, Allah commands all Muslims to pray five times a day, but He does not specify how to actually pray, which is found only in the Sunnah of the Prophet (ﷺ).

The Sunnah does not merely reflect the desires of the Prophet (ﷺ); it also highlights the following command from Allah:

﴿ وَمَا يَنطِقُ عَنِ ٱلْهَوَىٰ ۝ إِنْ هُوَ إِلَّا وَحْيٌ يُوحَىٰ ۝ ﴾ (سورة النجم: ٣-٤)

﴿Nor does he speak of [his own] desire. It is only a revelation that is revealed.﴾ *(Qur'an 53: 3-4)*

3) Many Islamic prescriptions were not part of the social norm at the time they were revealed. In fact, if they had been, Islam would not have caused such a stir among the local Arab population. The Arabs in the seventh century were highly surprised by some of the Islamic prescriptions taught by the Prophet (ﷺ), but the first generation of Muslims remained steadfast nonetheless.

It was narrated from al-Miqdâm ibn Ma'di Karb (ﷺ) that the Messenger of Allah (ﷺ) said:

«Verily, I have been given the Qur'an and something similar to it along with it. But soon there will come a time when a man will be reclining on his couch with a full stomach, and he will say: You should adhere to this Qur'an; what you find that it says is permissible, take it as permissible, and what you find it says is forbidden, take it as forbidden. But indeed, whatever the Messenger of Allah forbids is like what Allah forbids.» (at-Tirmidhi; al-Albâni graded it as reliable)

Al-'Irbâd ibn Sâriyah (ﷺ) reported:

«The Messenger of Allah (ﷺ) led our prayer one day; then he turned to us and exhorted us strongly. He said: Pay attention to my Sunnah and the way of the Rightly-Guided Caliphs after me; adhere to it and hold fast to it.» (Abu Dâwood; the grade of this hadith is acceptable)

4) The religion of Allah is complete and is meant to be followed until the Day of Judgement. Allah Himself has prescribed the Sunnah as part of the religion:

﴿ فَلَا وَرَبِّكَ لَا يُؤْمِنُونَ حَتَّىٰ يُحَكِّمُوكَ فِيمَا شَجَرَ بَيْنَهُمْ ثُمَّ لَا يَجِدُوا فِي أَنفُسِهِمْ حَرَجًا مِّمَّا قَضَيْتَ وَيُسَلِّمُوا تَسْلِيمًا ۝ ﴾ (سورة النساء: ٦٥)

❴But no, by your Lord, they can have no faith until they make you [Muhammad] judge in all disputes between them, and find in themselves no resistance against your decisions, and accept [them] with full submission.❵   *(Qur'an 4: 65)*

«There will come a day when a Muslim holding fast to his deen will be like he who is gripping a hot coal.» (An authentic hadith recorded by at-Tirmidhi)

Another set of arguments concerns the definition of the Sunnah. Many Muslims argue that while the Qur'an is accessible and guaranteed by Allah to be authentic, there is considerable doubt regarding the definition of the Sunnah. They further argue that the Sunnah cannot be authenticated because some of its records may have been lost over time.

Interestingly, there is some degree of truth in those arguments. Allah has indeed stated that He would protect the Qur'an, and it is quite remarkable that it has remained intact over the last 1400 years and that billions of copies around the world all match each other exactly. It is also true that Allah has not made any direct statement about the Sunnah as such, yet we have already seen in the Qur'an that Muslims are commanded by Allah to follow the Sunnah. Thus, it is imperative on us to believe that the authentic Sunnah exists and must be accessible.

We can look at an excerpt from Ibn Ḥazm's commentary on this topic in *al-Iḥkâm*:

Allaah says (interpretation of the meaning):

"Verily, it is We Who have sent down the Dhikr and surely, We will guard it (from corruption)" Al Qur'an, s. 15 (al-Hijr), v. 9

"Say (O Muhammad): "I warn you only by the Revelation (from Allaah and not by the opinion of the religious scholars and others). But the deaf (who follow the religious scholars and others blindly) will not hear the call, (even) when they are warned [i.e. one should follow only the Qur'an and the Sunnah (legal ways, orders, acts of worship, and the statements of Prophet Muhammad, as the Companions of the Prophet did)]" Al Qur'an, s. 21 (al-Anbiyâ), v. 45

Allaah tells us that the words of His Prophet (peace and blessings of Allaah be upon him) are all Wahy (revelation), and Wahy is undoubtedly Dhikr, and Dhikr is preserved according to the text of the Qur'aan. Thus it is correct to say that his words (peace and blessings of Allaah be upon him) are all preserved by Allaah, may He be glorified and exalted, and He has promised that none of them will be lost to us, because that which Allaah preserves can certainly not be lost at all; it has all been transmitted to us and Allaah has established proof and left us with no excuse.[17]

Authenticity of Hadith: Nearly all Muslims are aware of the secondary source of knowledge known as the Hadith, which is the record of the Sunnah of the Prophet (ﷺ). Of course, the question of whether or not hadiths can be authenticated is – and should be – of concern to Muslims. The scholars have recommended that Muslims follow the guidelines provided by authentic hadiths only, in order to follow the true Islam. Authentic hadiths are referred to as 'sound' or 'reliable'. Hadiths that cannot be judged to be authentic may or may not be correct and are generally classified as 'weak'. In some cases, evidence points to them being less authentic, or even fabricated, and they are classified as such.

There is a large body of literature on the science of Hadith, and we praise Allah for this blessing, because the Muslims were the first nation to engage in this effort to ensure the authenticity of their religious scriptures. The scriptures of other religions, including Christianity and Judaism, have been changed and distorted; this has resulted in their followers deviating from the path of pure monotheism. We

---

[17] Ibn Ḥazm's *al-Iḥkâm*, 1:95. See "The saheeh Sunnah is wahy (Revelation) from Allaah," Islam-QA.com, accessed November 2, 2011, http://www.islam-qa.com/en/ref/77243.

can observe some interesting facts regarding the soundness of the science and methodology of Hadith.[18]

First, the modern scientific approach of maintaining the authenticity and credibility of a report through an exercise of proper citation was firmly in place among Hadith scientists over 1400 years ago.

Second, the science of Hadith authentication uses strong logic; it considers such factors as the quality of the narrator's memory, the length of time he or she was with the Prophet's Companions (ﷺ), and his or her overall character. It also entails cross-checking narrations with facts and well-known events.

Third, Hadith scientists maintained a high degree of objectivity due to two factors:

1. the gravity of attributing something to the Prophet (ﷺ) that he did not actually say or do
2. the knowledge that Allah is the Protector of His final revelation, of which the Sunnah is a part

Fourth, hadiths were not authenticated simply because they offered seemingly good advice, and they were not confirmed simply because they were transmitted by relatives. Even the consensus of scholars was not considered to be authoritative enough to authenticate a weak hadith or to invalidate a sound hadith.

While it is obvious that Muslims should follow the guidance found in sound hadiths because of the fundamental importance of following the Sunnah, what should Muslims do regarding the hadiths that are weak? On one hand, it is a serious offense in Islam to attribute something to the Prophet (ﷺ) that he did not say or do. On the other, a weak hadith is not necessarily incorrect. The general guideline is to ensure that at least three conditions are fulfilled:

---

[18] Islam Q&A, "The methodology of the muhadditheen is just and fair," Islam-QA.com, accessed November 2, 2011, http://www.islam-qa.com/en/ref/82365.

1. The hadith is not so weak that it is likely to be fabricated,

2. The hadith deals with such general principles as virtuous deeds, and

3. One does not believe it to be highly authentic, since it has not been authenticated. [19]

Imam Aḥmad states:

When we narrate hadith concerning halal and haram, we are very strict; but when we narrate reports about acts of virtue, we are more lenient, because no rulings depend on reports about acts of virtue; rather they are like the virtue of fasting, jihad, prayer and so on.[20]

If a weak hadith contradicts a sound hadith, it is clear that one must follow the sound hadith because sound hadiths are part of the proven Sunnah, which in turn is part of the revelation from Allah.

Over time, many practices have been introduced into Islam, often out of ignorance or in an attempt to make it more compatible with current norms. These practices are classified as bid'ah (innovations in religion).

Shaykh Muhammad ibn al-'Uthaymeen defined bid'ah as:

Worshipping Allaah in ways that Allaah has not prescribed, or worshipping Allaah in ways that are not those of the Prophet (peace and blessings of Allaah be upon him) or his rightly guided successors (al-khulafaa' al-raashidoon).

The evidence for the above is given in the following hadith.

I urge you to adhere to my way (the Sunnah) and the way of the rightly-guided successors (al-khulafaa' al-raashidoon) who come after me. Hold fast to it and bite onto it with your eyeteeth [i.e.,

---

[19] From the fatwa on the permissibility of following weak hadiths from Ibn Jibreen. "Is following da'eef hadeeths regarded as shirk?" Islam-QA.com, accessed October 23, 2011, http://www.islam-qa.com/en/ref/142939.

[20] Ibn Ḥajar al-'Asqalâni, *al-Qawl al-Musaddad fee Musnad Aḥmad*, 11.

cling firmly to it], and beware of newly-invented matters. (An acceptable hadith recorded by Abu Dâwood)[21]

There are many practices that constitute bid'ah. For example, many Shiite Muslims flagellate or otherwise physically punish themselves quite severely in the month of Muḥarram. In addition to being harmful, such actions have no basis in the Qur'an or the Sunnah. They are thus bid'ah and should not be practiced.

Some practices of bid'ah appear to be harmless. Consider the celebration on the night midway through the Islamic month of Sha'bân. Many Muslims around the world believe that this is when one's fate for the following year is determined, so they spend the entire night in prayer, hoping that the coming year will be fruitful.

Other examples of bid'ah include celebrating the Prophet's birthday, determining the beginning of the lunar months in the Islamic calendar by calculation instead of by moon-sighting, and, in modern times, celebrating holidays such as Thanksgiving.

Each of these examples might seem to be a virtuous action. Their proponents argue that they are "good bid'ah", not unlike the innovations of using acoustic systems and motor vehicles to facilitate worship and pilgrimage in modern times. The problem with these analogies is that secular innovations that can be used to promote good are allowed and welcome, but innovations in religion are not permitted. Allah completed and perfected His religion at the time of Prophet Muhammad (ﷺ), and no one but He can add to it, alter it, or make something in it obsolete. One can ride a donkey or a car to reach the place of the congregational prayer, but one cannot introduce a new act in the prayer itself. In terms of the religion, there is no such thing as a 'good' bid'ah; all bid'ah is deviation.

---

[21] Ibn al-'Uthaymeen, *Majmoo' Fatâwâ wa Rasâ'il Ibn 'Uthaymeen*, 2:291, quoted in "Detailed discussion of bid'ah and shirk," Islam-QA. com, accessed October 23, 2011, http://www.islam-qa.com/en/ref/10843.

When viewed in this context, hadiths that might seem to support 'good innovations' are not actually supporting innovations at all. On the contrary, they are encouraging the revival of actions that are already part of the Sunnah, not new actions or alterations to the Sunnah.

We have already seen that the mere existence of a hadith does not make it authentic. Due to the severity of the warnings against bid'ah and the warnings against attributing something to the Prophet (ﷺ) that he did not say or do, Muslims should avoid hadiths that cannot be authenticated. The Prophet (ﷺ) said:

«Every bid'ah is going astray, and every going astray is in hellfire.» (An authentic hadith recorded by an-Nasâ'i)

If we acknowledge the severity of the warnings against practicing bid'ah, it is clear that the only valid excuse for doing so is ignorance. However, even ignorance cannot be excused indefinitely, because Muslims are required to acquire knowledge as part of their sincere efforts to practice Islam.

Sadly, though, many Muslims persist in engaging in bid'ah, even after receiving admonition. Two of the most common excuses are:

1. "Even if it is bid'ah, it is a 'good' and 'wholesome' activity."

   The problem with this kind of reasoning is that it reveals impurities in intentions. If the intention is to please Allah, Muslims must strive to do what pleases Him and avoid what displeases Him. If bid'ah is displeasing to Allah, Muslims should abstain from it even if it appears to be harmless or even wholesome.

   This kind of rationale should not be new to Muslims. For example, Muslims offer only two prostrations in each unit of prayer. Almost all Muslims will agree that it is wrong to increase worship by adding a third prostration, since that is not the prescribed way.

2. "Some narrations and hadiths support these bid'ah practices."

As explained above, when viewed in this context, so-called 'good innovations' that are supported in hadiths are in fact simply the revival of actions that are already part of the Sunnah and hence are not innovations at all. Muslims should ensure that the hadiths and narrations that are attributed to the Prophet (ﷺ) are authenticated, leaving no room for the 'good innovations' debate.

In concluding our discussion on the shahâdatayn, we can summarize by saying that Islam features in every aspect of a Muslim's life, including business administration. Through this first pillar, there are two ways in which business administration is affected:

1. The shahâdatayn require a Muslim to acknowledge Allah as God, the supreme authority, and to respect the boundaries that He has established.

2. In acknowledging Prophet Muhammad (ﷺ) as Allah's Messenger, a Muslim follows Islam as Allah prescribed it through His Messenger (ﷺ).

«The Messenger of Allah (ﷺ) said: The Jews were divided into seventy-one groups, the Christians were divided into seventy-two, and my Ummah will be divided into seventy-three, all of which will be in the fire except one.

The Companions asked: Who are they (the saved group), O Messenger of Allah?

He said: They are those who are on the like of what my Companions and I are on.» (A reliable hadith recorded by at-Tirmidhi)

Pillar II: *Ṣalâh*

Ṣalâh, or prayer, is the second pillar of Islam. Like all the other pillars, it is indispensable. While many religions prescribe prayer, the Muslim prayer is unique because it is dedicated to Allah alone, without any intercessor, and it is performed in a manner that is consistent with Allah's direct instructions and the practices of Allah's Messenger (ﷺ).[22]

Every able Muslim must perform prayers five times a day: at early dawn, at mid-day, at mid-afternoon, just after sunset, and later in the evening. Before performing prayers, Muslims must purify themselves ritually by washing at least their heads, arms, hands, and feet.

Prayer in congregation is preferable over prayer performed individually (for men). The uniformity of actions in ṣalâh and their performance in unison during congregational prayers are symbolic of unity and, in turn, true monotheism, which is the essence of Islam. The importance of ṣalâh cannot be overstated. The Prophet (ﷺ) is reported to have said:

«The difference between us and them (the disbelievers) is ṣalâh. Whoever neglects it (the prescribed prayer) is a disbeliever.» (Recorded by Aḥmad and the authors of *Sunan* with a sound chain of narrators)

Ṣalâh cannot be delayed deliberately without a valid reason. The status of ṣalâh is evident when one acknowledges the allowances given by Allah to minimize the obstacles to performing ṣalâh on time. Someone who is sick may pray sitting, lying down, or even through concentration if unable to move. If someone is suffering from incontinence, the ritual purity is not nullified. If someone cannot use water for purification, he or she may use the earth for dry ablution.

Knowing the importance of ṣalâh is imperative for Muslims to realize the route to salvation. To understand the behaviour of Muslims,

---

[22] There are many detailed resources on ṣalâh, one of the best being a treatise by Shaykh Muhammad Nâṣir ad-Deen al-Albâni (may Allah have mercy on him), which is widely available, in print and online, under titles such as "The Prophet's Prayer".

it is helpful for non-Muslims to be instructed about the position that prayer holds in the lives of Muslims. Regrettably, it is not uncommon to see Muslims who have been forced to miss or arrive late for meetings because these meetings were held during prayer times. If prayer time comes during working hours, it will usually be necessary for Muslims to take short breaks to perform their prayers.

Pillar III: *Zakâh*

Zakâh is the pillar of Islam that requires Muslims to donate a fixed percentage of excess wealth every year. The word 'zakâh' is based on a root word that means 'purification'. It essentially helps to purify Muslims' wealth, which is seen as a trust from Allah, by returning the amount that Allah has asked to be given to the poor. Zakâh is also regarded as a means of purification because it helps to purify society by removing the social ills that result from poverty.

The wealth retained by two percent of the world's wealthiest individuals could completely eliminate poverty from the entire world. Since there are many Muslims who are extremely wealthy, it is not difficult to gauge the impact that zakâh could have on global poverty. In general, Allah asks that Muslims who own more than a minimum amount (the value of eighty-five grams of gold, which is approximately US$7,000 or 3000 Euros at this writing) pay zakâh at a rate of 2.5 per cent of their wealth.

It is extremely unfortunate that many Muslims have decided to abandon this pillar in favour of micro-credit models that are based on ribâ. Little do those Muslims realize that their Islam cannot remain intact if they deny a pillar or they make permissible that which is actually impermissible.

There are some interesting opportunities in business administration arising from zakâh. In addition to zakâh fund management firms, many commercial firms are weaving zakâh into their corporate social responsibility (CSR) activities.

Pillar IV: Fasting

Fasting is the pillar of Islam that requires Muslims to fast (abstain from food, drink and marital relations from dawn until sunset) throughout the month of Ramadan every year. Ramadan is the ninth month in the Islamic calendar and is one of the holiest times for Muslims. The Qur'an was first revealed during this month on a special night known as 'The Night of Destiny'; Allah has specifically mentioned that worship during this night is equivalent to the worship of a thousand months.

Fasting is extremely significant for the Muslims because its prescription itself was a mercy from Allah. Ramadan is an opportunity for Muslims to cleanse themselves of sins they committed in the past. Allah guides Muslims to the right way and makes it particularly easy for His slaves to engage in self-improvement, for the devils are chained during this month. Muslims recognize the opportunity and also find fasting easier in Ramadan than in other months. Thus, they gain a much-needed 'push' toward progress.

A negative trend is the promotion of Ramadan as a cultural and commercial celebration rather than a holy month to be spent in increased worship. In many Muslim countries, advertising expenses increase and retailers try to tempt Muslims into increased indulgence. Instead of taking opportunities to improve spiritually through prayer during such great nights as The Night of Destiny, some Muslims waste time and other resources on extravagant feasts that result in wastage; they also spend their time, money, and effort acquiring material goods for the Eid celebration that takes place when Ramadan ends. Abstention from food through fasting is replaced by a mere shift in food-intake timings and increased gluttony.

Of course, there is nothing to suggest that commerce is haram during Ramadan. However, Muslim businesses and chambers of commerce should refrain from distracting their brothers and sisters from the invaluable opportunities for worship during the precious, limited time in Ramadan.

Pillar V: Hajj

Hajj is the fifth pillar of Islam; it is the pilgrimage to Makkah, mandatory at least once in a lifetime for those who have the financial means as well as the physical ability. It is a very significant event because it has the potential to erase all of one's previous sins. In order for their Hajj to be accepted by Allah, Muslims should attempt to perform it as perfectly as possible after purifying their intentions.

Islam is a religion that always lightens the burdens of its followers, and it allows pilgrims to engage in trade even as they go on the Hajj pilgrimage. Of course, Muslims should follow Islamic guidelines entirely. While we appreciate the noteworthy efforts of our hosts in meeting the extremely difficult challenge of handling the logistics and safety of all the pilgrims, and thereby making the Hajj easier, it is sad to observe how the Hajj has become a luxury retreat for many.

Once again, it is recommended that Hajj companies balance their offer of convenience against tempting Muslims to engage in excessive extravagance and waste. With a huge attendance of up to three million Muslims, the Hajj is the largest annual congregation in the world.

This has great economic significance, and not surprisingly, many companies have taken advantage of this fact. For example, Huawei, one of the world's largest manufacturers of telecommunications equipment, has used the Hajj as an event to boost future revenues. As a Chinese competitor to existing European giants like Ericsson, Huawei was facing considerable challenges in proving the quality of its products; even their lower prices could not convince customers to switch from Huawei's competitors. In order to convince customers of the high quality and dependability of its products, Huawei publicized the fact that their products consistently supported communication during the Hajj in three consecutive years.

Summary and conclusion

Islam is a great religion with over one billion followers. We have seen that the true Islam, as preached by Prophet Muhammad (ﷺ), involves complete submission to one God: Allah. Islam is defined by its five pillars, each of which is indispensable. The first and most important pillar of Islam is the shahâdatayn, which tie all worldly tasks, including business administration, to religion. The shahâdatayn require Muslims to accept Allah unconditionally as God and to follow the path of Allah's Messenger, Prophet Muhammad (ﷺ). Thus, Muslims refer to two sources: the Qur'an and the authentic Hadith, which records the Sunnah of the Prophet (ﷺ). The way of Islam is balanced and eschews extremism in all aspects.

Following Islam is a means of achieving peace in today's con-flict-filled world. In fact, one of the meanings of the root word of Islam is 'peace', for indeed the creation can only be at peace after full submission to its Creator. Understanding true Islam will allow both Muslims and non-Muslims to chart paths that will reduce conflicts in the world and promote harmony.

In a world that is already tense, many people are adding fuel to existing fires of fury or fanning flames of conflict, and this is largely due to ignorance. Such actions are often taken without understand-ing Muslim sentiment; they increase the feelings of resentment and sometimes lead individuals to adopt extreme and dangerous views.

For example, in 2010, Belgium passed a law banning the face veil. The arguments offered in the Belgian parliament were that the face veil creates a security threat by concealing a woman's identity and also that it is oppressive to women.[23] When one studies Islam, one discovers that there can be no compulsion in religion. Furthermore, a Muslim woman will feel more oppressed when she is forced to abandon her choice to cover her face or to follow any other Islamic recommendation or prescription.

In a country like Belgium, Muslim women cannot be forced to wear the face veil because their 'freedom of choice' is guaranteed by the constitution; thus, the argument that it is a sign of oppression is rendered completely baseless. Ironically, forcing a woman to take it off is actually a direct violation of the same freedom of choice that Belgium is claiming to protect. Meanwhile, according to one report, there are only about thirty women in Belgium who even wear the face veil.[24]

While it may be true that security may improve by banning face coverings, it is also true that banning them may cause even more resentment in an already volatile global community, eventually leading to more conflict and threats to security.

If one is going to deal with Muslims, it is better to first study Islam to understand them.[25] Not only will this help to sustain harmony, but it often offers other benefits, too.

---

[23] "Belgian lawmakers pass burka ban," *BBC News*, April 30, 2010, accessed October 23, 2011, http://news.bbc.co.uk/2/hi/8652861.stm.

[24] "Belgian lawmakers pass burka ban," *BBC News*, April 30, 2010, accessed October 23, 2011, http://news.bbc.co.uk/2/hi/8652861.stm.

[25] In an opinion piece titled "America's Muslims: Guilty Until Proven Innocent?", published on the CBS News website on May 24, 2010, Stephan Salisbury explains that the Rand Corporation analyzed terrorist attacks since the World Trade Center strikes and concluded that the threat was serious but greatly exaggerated. According to Rand researchers, the forty-six cases of American citizens or longtime residents plotting to commit acts of terrorism since September 11 involved a total of one hundred and twenty-five people (and most of these attempts failed).=

A classic example is the growth of Islamic finance. Many of the world's largest conventional banks – for example, HSBC – now offer special Islamic banking services that cater to Muslim sentiments; this simultaneously helps the firm perform better.

=Salisbury writes:

Think about that number for a moment: it averages out to about six cases of purported radicalization and terrorism a year. Faisal Shahzad's utterly inept effort in Times Square would make incident 47. In the 1970s, the report points out, the country endured, on average, around 70 terrorist incidents a year. From January 1969 to April 1970 alone, the U.S. somehow managed to survive 4,330 bombings, 43 deaths, and $22 million of property damage. The Rand report, "Would-Be Warriors: Incidents of Jihadist Terrorist Radicalization in the United States since September 11, 2001," argues that ham-handed surveillance and aggressive police investigations can be, and often are, counter-productive, sowing a deep-seated fear of law enforcement and immigration authorities throughout Muslim communities – whose assistance is vital in coping with the threat of Islamic terrorism, tiny as it is here.

CHAPTER TWO

BUSINESS ADMINISTRATION

$\mathcal{W}$hen asked what his or her profession is, a business professor must often endure unspoken scepticism after providing the answer. The uncomfortable reason is the inexplicable choice of a profession... Professors are not known to be wealthy, so would it not be better for business professors to engage in commerce rather than teach it? Business professors should not be the only academics who experience this discomfort, but great basketball coaches are somehow not expected to be great athletes. Indeed, teaching and performing are not the same.

Perhaps this discrimination has been brought on by a general lack of knowledge about business administration. What exactly is business administration? Is it the same as management or commerce? Is it any different from economics? If these questions are not readily answered, it may prove difficult for an individual to understand why a business professor, even an excellent one, is not necessarily wildly successful at business.

What is business administration?

The easiest way to think about business administration is to consider a business as a box containing a production engine that delivers products, which are in turn sold in exchange for revenues. Running the production engine requires resources and raw materials, so the business incurs costs. If the revenues exceed the costs, the business makes a profit; otherwise, it incurs losses. Our highly simplistic box model of a business is shown in Figure 2.1.

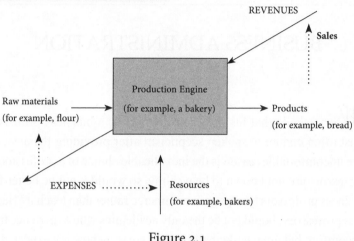

Figure 2.1

The diagonal arrows indicate the flow of money into and out of the business. If revenues typically exceed expenses, the business is profitable.

To improve and sustain a business's profitability, its performance needs to be managed well. Business administration involves all the tasks executed for that purpose. There are three categories of business administration tasks, which are quite easy to understand:

1. **Marketing** helps to improve sales. It involves the identification of buyers' needs, assistance with product design, and (generally) a reduction of the gap between the demand for the products and the business' supply of them.

2. **Finance** helps to procure and efficiently manage financial resources, which in turn can be used to acquire other resources.

3. **Operations management** is the broad set of activities that ensure that the production engine runs as a happy, well-oiled machine.

There are other categories of tasks in business administration. Accounting helps with record-keeping, which allows monitoring and reporting. Newer categories include information systems, which roughly refers to the tasks involving the use of information technology to facilitate business administration. Many other categories, such as HR (Human Resource) management, are self-explanatory.

A business administration education program, at both the undergraduate and graduate levels, helps to instil models of the best practices among current and future managers. Business administration professors investigate those best practices in their research.

Acknowledging the nature of business administration in practice and in academia, it is easy to understand why a business professor is not necessarily a living oxymoron. Just because someone is an expert in marketing does not mean that he or she needs to know how to make money, or even knows every aspect of business administration, for that matter. In fact, the rich diversity of tasks and the large numbers of employees needed for running many businesses means that it is simply not possible for every good business professor to be good at business or to prove that fact (which should come as quite a relief to the thousands of business professors around the world).

Our last statement is quite useful for reflecting upon current trends in business administration. Although by definition **any** business requires business administration, the importance of management differs across contexts.

Let us compare a private practice, a clinic, and a large hospital. At a certain level, all of them may offer similar procedures by providers who may have nearly identical qualifications. It is easy to comprehend nonetheless that a business administration task like finance plays a more mission-critical role at a large hospital than it does at a private practice.

Despite the fact that business administration is most often considered to be wholly a support function, it can actually be more important than direct production. Although a furniture maker, a scientist, a surgeon, a teacher, or a chef may be involved most directly with production at IKEA (a Scandinavian home furnishings company), Pfizer (a multinational pharmaceutical corporation), Kaiser Permanente (a health care consortium), Harvard University, or The Olive Garden (a chain of restaurants) respectively, the role of the CEOs (Chief Executive Officers) at these companies is arguably more crucial. In general, the functionality of virtually all other fields depends upon effective business administration. Indeed, medical practices can thrive only when effective management helps establish an ideal platform. Even business administration research within academic settings is profoundly affected by the quality of administration at those institutions.

The role and importance of business administration becomes quite clear if one looks at history. After the mid-1930s, businesses began to grow in size, and it was widely acknowledged that large corporations were too complex to be handled in the same way as small businesses. To tackle the complexity, companies adopted policies of decentralization, creating functional divisions such as accounts and marketing. The importance of these divisions for the overall health of the company attracted researchers to consider the best practices within these domains. Meanwhile, large companies began to diversify, seeking better profit opportunities by entering new markets. As larger companies essentially turned into diverse collections of smaller companies, administration became even more important to ensure the viability of those smaller companies.

In the 1970s, these portfolio-holding firms began realizing the problems that come with handling too many diverse operations, and they opted for a balanced approach that would yield synergy. In the 1980s, this trend, combined with increasing competition, resulted in a greater focus upon developing high-performing companies. At the same time, research in the field of business administration skyrocketed.

The business landscape became even more competitive and complicated in the 1990s, with the emergence of globalization and the adoption of information technology. By the 2000s, it was recognized that two major success factors, which could not be replaced by scale economies resulting from capital investment, were knowledge and the productivity of knowledge workers.

Today's business administration programs throughout the world prepare students to become knowledge workers. Not surprisingly, the MBA (Master of Business Administration) degree has become one of the most sought-after qualifications around the world.

The field and practice of business administration continues to evolve and increase in importance in its recursive relationship with business and industry models. For example, complex management practices are now commonly used for supply chains supporting gigantic retail chains that offer a variety of products made thousands of miles away in Chinese or Bangladeshi factories.

Within marketing, the field of customer relations management has emerged. It alone has generated a multi-billion dollar industry as complex software and hardware are developed to enable firms to succeed amidst fierce competition.

Because economic growth is directly tied to business performance, there is considerable impetus for sustaining quality business administration education programs all over the world. In the United States, for example, earning an MBA from a prestigious business school can cost more than $100,000. Still, the demand for the degree is exceptionally strong; this is often fuelled by the belief that such a qualification is a 'sure ticket', offering a giant leap on the career trajectory. Consequently, the demand for business academics is also strong, and business professors are paid considerably more than their counterparts in most other departments and schools.[1]

---

[1] Most interestingly, business professors are, on average, paid significantly more than professors of economics.

It is important to understand the academic structure of a business administration program, because we will be borrowing from it to present our analysis of the role of Islam in the field. From our discussion earlier in this chapter, one can easily (and correctly) guess that a typical business administration program involves coursework dedicated to most categories of tasks in the field. In most schools following the guidelines of the Association to Advance Collegiate Schools of Business (AACSB), the largest and most respected accrediting body among business education programs, a typical undergraduate or graduate program in business administration has a core set of common courses in management, accounting, finance, marketing, and information systems. In addition, students then select from a variety of higher or specialized courses, and they declare majors or concentrations. Coursework is frequently supported by fieldwork in the forms of internships, research projects, or laboratory consulting.

The content of business administration offers both theory and practical examples. Theories are developed and tested by business administration professors active in research. The foundations of theory in business administration borrow from three primary areas: economics, mathematics, and psychology. Business administration theory is distinct from its foundation fields, primarily due to its emphasis on practice. For example, economics courses about financial markets might analyze market dynamics, whereas their counterpart courses in business administration might place greater emphasis on tools for financial analysis.[2]

A particularly strong motivation for writing this book is my desire to show that practicing or teaching business administration can, inshallah, be a profession that is full of righteous acts for the believer who follows the rights, commands, and limits established in Islam.

---

[2] This may provide one explanation for the significant difference in salaries earned by business administration professors as compared to Economics or Psychology professors.

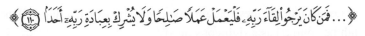

﴾ ... فَمَن كَانَ يَرْجُواْ لِقَآءَ رَبِّهِ فَلْيَعْمَلْ عَمَلًا صَٰلِحًا وَلَا يُشْرِكْ بِعِبَادَةِ رَبِّهِۦٓ أَحَدَۢا ﴿١١٠﴾ ﴾

(سورة الكهف: ١١٠)

﴾...So whoever hopes for the meeting with his Lord, let him work righteousness and associate none as a partner in the worship of his Lord.﴾ *(Qur'an 18: 110)*

Ibn Katheer (may Allah have mercy on him) says:

So whoever hopes for the Meeting with his Lord, means his reward; let him work righteousness means, that which is in accordance with the laws of Allaah; and associate none as a partner in the worship of his Lord; this means seeking the Face of Allaah alone, with no partner or associate. These two conditions are the basis of acceptable deeds, which must be sincerely for the sake of Allaah alone and correct according to the sharee'ah of the Messenger of Allaah (peace and blessings of Allaah be upon him).[3]

We see from the above that any task that fulfils the two conditions mentioned (righteousness and not associating partners with Allah) has the potential to be considered a righteous deed. The vastness of business administration makes it a rich platform from which a Muslim can conduct righteous deeds. In fact, this is the role of Islam in business administration. As we shall see in subsequent chapters, in almost every major functional area of business administration, there are issues concerning which Allah has prescribed rules. When Muslims who are engaged in business administration follow those rules for the sake of pleasing Allah, they can also hope for a reward from Allah, the Most Gracious.

Let us consider marketing as an example. Islam prohibits lewd music, wanton ways, or using sex to promote sales. If a Muslim marketing manager refrains from designing or approving marketing

---

[3] al-Munajjid, "Conditions of righteous deeds," Islam-QA.com, accessed November 2, 2011, http://www.islam-qa.com/en/ref/13830.

materials that use these haram elements to boost sales, that will inshallah be counted as a righteous deed.

﴿ يُؤْمِنُونَ بِاللَّهِ وَالْيَوْمِ الْأَخِرِ وَيَأْمُرُونَ بِالْمَعْرُوفِ وَيَنْهَوْنَ عَنِ الْمُنكَرِ
وَيُسَٰرِعُونَ فِي الْخَيْرَٰتِ وَأُوْلَٰئِكَ مِنَ الصَّٰلِحِينَ ۝ ﴾   (سورة آل عمران: ١١٤)

﴿They believe in Allah and the Last Day; they enjoin what is right and forbid what is wrong; and they hasten in good works; and they are among the righteous.﴾   *(Qur'an 3: 114)*

Another justification for considering the role of Islam in business administration is the popularity of the field. It is not uncommon for universities around the world to charge higher tuition for their business schools than for other schools, in a reflection of the stronger demand for business programs. Throughout the world, a large number of Muslims choose business administration as their field of study. For example, in Bangladesh (a largely Muslim country), admission statistics indicate that the most popular major in the top few private universities is business administration.

Business administration may be viewed quite favourably because it supports business, and businesses often involve investments and transactions that can benefit a large portion of the Ummah. As such, it is somewhat antithetical to hoarding wealth, which is criticized severely in Islam. An individual who spends all his wealth before it has been held for a year is exempt from paying zakâh, regardless of his or her original financial position.[4]

In Islam, working to support oneself is superior to being dependent, and business administration involves a lot of work. Perhaps most importantly, establishing and running businesses has been encouraged in Islam through the hadith of the Prophet Muhammad (ﷺ) in which

---

[4] Of course, Islam discourages extravagance; optional charity is also a means of seeking Allah's pleasure at any time.

he said that a good, halal sale is one of the two best forms of earning a halal income. It was narrated that Râfi' ibn Khadeej (ﷺ) said:

«The Prophet (ﷺ) was asked: O Messenger of Allah, what kind of earning is best?

He replied: For a man to work with his hands and every honest transaction.» (Bukhari and Aḥmad)

Thus, business administration is an ideal task for a Muslim, since it involves labour and can be a means to support honest transactions. [5]

Following Chapters

Each of the chapters ahead addresses a major functional area of business administration. While it is possible for a reader to jump to the chapter which is most relevant to him or her, it is recommended that the entire book be read from beginning to end at least once; it has been written with this reading approach in mind. It is particularly important that one reads the introduction to Islam (in the previous chapter) first, because it lays out the foundation of the Islamic approach according to the Qur'an and the Sunnah.

The first business administration task that we will consider is setting up a business. Even though most business practitioners might never be engaged in establishing a business, we have placed it in the beginning because it highlights the importance of applying Islamic teachings right from the foundation. It also involves knowledge that

---

[5] It can be argued that the hadith refers to physical labour and that the work of business executives in glossy offices hardly fits that definition. Nonetheless, one should not forget that:

Much of business administration does not involve gloss.

It is acknowledged that in today's competitive labour markets, most employees have to work very hard, and work-related stress is becoming an epidemic.

Employees are not the owners; hence, they are workers.

is important for Muslims to have before beginning any managerial work, not least because it allows them to choose the right places to work. As a topic, it also comes first chronologically.

Next, we consider finance and accounting. Although the two are distinct fields in business administration theory, they are related in practice. In particular, finance-related activities are facilitated through standard accounting practices. In Islam, the major topics of finance are ribâ and contracts, which are also important in accounting.

Following that, two chapters deal with human behaviour. It is easy to assume that the links between Islam and human behaviour in business organizations will be readily apparent, for Islam has been prescribed as a religion based on both belief and deeds. We consider HR management first, followed by its mother discipline of organizational behaviour, because the former is closer to application and managers can relate to it more easily.

We follow the chapter on organizational behaviour with one on marketing. This progress is quite natural, since there is a significant body of marketing literature concerning what is known as consumer behaviour; it uses findings from organizational behaviour and, more generally, from psychology. Interestingly, though, Islam features most prominently in marketing in terms of Islamic jurisprudence and not with respect to consumer behaviour. We continue on that theme and introduce operations management in the next part.

In the chapter on operations, we have attempted to highlight the most salient, common topics, although it is challenging to adequately cover this area because operations tend to vary significantly across companies.

The most general term used to describe many business administration tasks is 'management'; most practitioners of business administration either are, or eventually become, managers. The brevity of our discussion of this vast topic may seem surprising, but it can be explained by two factors.

First of all, many aspects of management have already been discussed, albeit implicitly, in the other chapters that address specific topics. Secondly, there is already a rich, in-depth discussion of Islam and management in another book, which I will recommend.

In the tenth chapter, we present our final discussion of a major topic: business ethics. In some ways, one might expect ethics to be the most obvious conduit connecting religion and business administration; for a Muslim manager, Islam replaces any arbitrarily-decided universal code of ethics. Islam is distinct from other religions in at least two ways. First, the ethical standards of Muslim businesses and their administration are not only the result of spiritual guidelines; rather, they are the implementation of Islamic principles. Secondly, Islam features prominently in a variety of ways other than ethics.

PART TWO

PART TWO

CHAPTER THREE

MANAGERIAL ASSETS

*E*arlier, we identified superstition as a popular but false link between Islam and business administration, and one can observe the same link between businesses and many other religions in the past and in the present. Muslims do not find this fact remarkable, in light of the innate human behaviour described in the Qur'an as follows:

﴿ هُوَ ٱلَّذِى يُسَيِّرُكُمْ فِى ٱلْبَرِّ وَٱلْبَحْرِ حَتَّىٰٓ إِذَا كُنتُمْ فِى ٱلْفُلْكِ وَجَرَيْنَ بِهِم بِرِيحٍ طَيِّبَةٍ وَفَرِحُوا۟ بِهَا جَآءَتْهَا رِيحٌ عَاصِفٌ وَجَآءَهُمُ ٱلْمَوْجُ مِن كُلِّ مَكَانٍ وَظَنُّوٓا۟ أَنَّهُمْ أُحِيطَ بِهِمْ دَعَوُا۟ ٱللَّهَ مُخْلِصِينَ لَهُ ٱلدِّينَ لَئِنْ أَنجَيْتَنَا مِنْ هَٰذِهِۦ لَنَكُونَنَّ مِنَ ٱلشَّٰكِرِينَ ﴾

(سورة يونس: ٢٢)

﴿He it is Who enables you to travel through the land and the sea, until when you are in the ships and they sail with them with a favourable wind, and they rejoice, then comes a stormy wind and the waves come to them from all sides, and they think that they are encircled therein. Then they invoke Allah, making their faith pure for Him Alone, saying: If You deliver us from this, we shall truly be of the grateful.﴾
(Qur'an 10: 22)

Human beings, as creations of Allah, have an inborn tendency to acknowledge divinity when they are forced to admit their limitations. What they generally refer to as luck can be a severely limiting factor facing them as they attempt to be productive. For example, a student trying to learn art may need to work much harder than the one who is regarded as a born artist. It is generally accepted that success in business is a function of at least two factors: management and 'luck'. In Islam, there is no such thing as luck. To understand the Islamic perspective, we should first analyze the roots and pervasiveness of the concept of luck in business administration.

While good management can improve the likelihood of success, it is certainly not sufficient to ensure it. History is full of examples in which businesses, even those having poor management, became successful for reasons outside their control. Typically, such success has been attributed to luck, or the concept of unexpected outcomes due to factors that cannot be controlled. The driving force behind the apparent role of luck is of course uncertainty, because luck cannot be foreseen. Since it is impossible to perfectly forecast demand, business conditions, or the development of new production technologies, the role of luck in business administration is readily acknowledged, even by the agnostic.

A considerable amount of effort is spent in trying to decrease the perceived effect of luck to thereby increase the effectiveness of good management practices. All the largest American firms, for example, spend millions of dollars annually on forecasting activities, deploying teams of brilliant, doctoral-trained decision scientists, physicists, and mathematicians to develop and implement complex models using powerful information processing systems. They are faced nonetheless with two challenges. The increasing complexity of management leaves fewer opportunities to rely on luck alone, but while it may be reduced through improved planning, the effect of luck apparently cannot be eliminated from the equation completely. As luck prevails, so does superstition; not surprisingly, we see the enduring practices of horoscopes, numerology, and even blind religiosity among business managers.

Unfortunately, owing primarily to ignorance, even Muslims are not immune to this trap. Some Muslims, for example, pray hundreds of units of prayer hoping that a certain stock price will rise and allow for windfall profits. Many businesses continue such bid'ah practices as starting every workday with a recitation from the Qur'an, played on office-wide acoustic systems to which workers pay little attention, in the hope that it will bring luck. Even worse is soliciting the services of self-proclaimed Islamic holy men who claim to have knowledge of the unseen; this action constitutes shirk.

True Muslims are blessed because their religion completely liberates them from superstition. They know that in Islam, there is simply no such concept as luck. Everything is in the hands of Allah, Who decrees what He wills for humankind. He gives to some and withholds from others; both situations can be the means of blessings, tests, or even destruction. The goal of true Muslims is to please their Creator, Who controls all their affairs; they achieve this goal by striving to follow the Sunnah of the Prophet (ﷺ), by trusting in Allah, and by avoiding actions like bid'ah, which displease Allah.

The approach of true Muslims in following their religion in business administration is different from that of others in at least two ways.

1) Muslims do not follow their religion only in the uncertain parts of the business equation, as others do. Because they recognize that Islam requires complete submission, Muslims follow their religion in both parts of the success equation: the acts of management that they can control and the uncertainties that they cannot. They follow the guidelines related to management; they trust Allah and acknowledge His dominion.

2) Muslims do not expect Allah to automatically compensate them for their submission through increased business revenues or other bonuses. They understand that the immediate effect of implementing Islamic principles and eliminating haram ones may even be a reduction of wealth. Nonetheless, they are pleased to do this because they know that true success lies only in pleasing Allah.

In this chapter, we present four priceless practices from which Muslims performing business administration can benefit:

1. *taqwâ* (righteousness)
2. *tawakkul* (trusting Allah) and patience
3. *istikhârah* (prayer for guidance) and *shoorâ* (consultation)
4. da'wah

Taqwâ

There are at least two reasons why Muslim managers today will frequently encounter situations that test the strength of their eemân.

The study of business administration as a field emerged within largely secular, or at least non-Muslim, circles. Consequently, many practices that are already well established in non-Muslim businesses actually contradict Islamic principles. A classic example is conventional banking practices, which violate the Islamic prohibition of ribâ. Similarly, there are many HR principles that contradict Islamic rules of social interaction (such as restrictions on men and women mingling).

In addition, it is well known that Western nations, particularly the United States, have a tendency to impose – both passively and actively – Western practices and values that are often at odds with Islamic teachings. This situation has worsened as many Muslims blindly accept these foreign ways without properly assessing the true costs or interests. Something that works well in the consumerism-based economies of the West may have grave consequences for a Muslim's personal relationship with Allah. If we recognize the Judeo-Christian foundations of Western civic philosophies, we can easily appreciate the profoundness of the following verse:

﴿وَلَن تَرْضَىٰ عَنكَ ٱلْيَهُودُ وَلَا ٱلنَّصَرَىٰ حَتَّىٰ تَتَّبِعَ مِلَّتَهُمْ قُلْ إِنَّ هُدَى ٱللَّهِ هُوَ ٱلْهُدَىٰ وَلَئِنِ ٱتَّبَعْتَ أَهْوَآءَهُم بَعْدَ ٱلَّذِى جَآءَكَ مِنَ ٱلْعِلْمِ مَا لَكَ مِنَ ٱللَّهِ مِن وَلِيٍّ وَلَا نَصِيرٍ ۝﴾

(سورة البقرة: ١٢٠)

﴿Never will the Jews or the Christians be pleased with you [O Muhammad] until you follow their religion. Say: Verily, the guidance of Allah is the [only] guidance. And if you were to follow their desires after what you have received of knowledge, then you would have against Allah neither any protector nor any helper.﴾   *(Qur'an 2: 120)*

The eminent scholar of Islam, Shaykh Ibn Taymiyah, says:

In *al-Saheehayn* [the two authentic collections of Bukhari and Muslim] it is narrated in the hadeeth of Abu Sa'eed (may Allaah be pleased with him) that the Prophet (peace and blessings of Allaah be upon him) said: You will follow the path of those who came before you step by step, so that even if they entered the hole of a lizard, you will enter it too. They said, O Messenger of Allaah, do you mean the Jews and Christians? He said, Who else? This report is confirmed by the aayah (interpretation of the meaning):

So enjoy your portion (awhile) as those before you enjoyed their portion (awhile); and you indulged in play and pastime (and in telling lies against Allaah and His Messenger Muhammad) as they indulged in play and pastime *(Qur'an 9: 69)*.[1]

It is reasonable to assume that Muslim managers face this dilemma when selecting the Sharia-compliant alternative when it involves an apparent reduction in profit. Profit is broadly defined here, to include such non-pecuniary factors as pleasing managers and shareholders or even purely personal preferences. After reading in the previous

---

[1] "He wants something that will guide him in his worldly and religious affairs," Islam-QA.com, accessed October 23, 2011, http://www.islam-qa.com/en/ref/21982.

chapters about the comprehensiveness of Islam, one should no longer wonder why Muslims would forgo seemingly innocuous opportunities to make good profits; nor should one regard their devotion to Islam as blind and irrational religious conviction. In fact, two simple concepts make it easy to see why the Muslim approach is very logical indeed: taqwâ and reward.

$$ \left\{ ... \ \text{وَلَقَدْ وَصَّيْنَا الَّذِينَ أُوتُوا الْكِتَبَ مِن قَبْلِكُمْ وَإِيَّاكُمْ أَنِ اتَّقُوا اللَّهَ} \ ... ﴾ (١٣١) \right\} $$

(سورة النساء: ١٣١)

﴾...And verily, We have recommended to the People of the Scripture before you, and to you, that you fear Allah and keep your duty to Him...﴿

(Qur'an 4: 131)

Islam is submission, and this submission has two aspects: Muslims must strive to do whatever pleases Allah, and they must avoid whatever angers Allah. They can achieve these objectives only if they have taqwâ – which can be translated as righteousness, God-consciousness, or fear of Allah due to His position over us.

$$ \left\{ \text{يَـأَيُّهَا الَّذِينَ ءَامَنُوا اتَّقُوا اللَّهَ حَقَّ تُقَاتِهِ وَلَا تَمُوتُنَّ إِلَّا وَأَنتُم مُّسْلِمُونَ} (١٠٢) ﴾ \right\} $$

(سورة آل عمران: ١٠٢)

﴾O you who believe! Fear Allah as He should be feared, and die not except in a state of Islam.﴿

(Qur'an 3: 102)

When the Prophet (ﷺ) sent Mu'âdh (ﷺ) to Yemen, he advised him:

«O Mu'âdh, fear Allah wherever you are. Follow up a bad deed with a good deed, and it will wipe it out; treat people in a kind manner.» (Aḥmad and at-Tirmidhi; a reliable hadith according to al-Albâni)

Allah mentions fear before prohibition in the following verse:

$$ \left\{ \text{يَـأَيُّهَا الَّذِينَ ءَامَنُوا اتَّقُوا اللَّهَ وَذَرُوا مَا بَقِىَ مِنَ الرِّبَوٰا إِن كُنتُم مُّؤْمِنِينَ} (٢٧٨) ﴾ \right\} $$

(سورة البقرة: ٢٧٨)

《O you who believe! Be afraid of Allah and give up what remains [is due to you] from ribâ, if you are believers.》   *(Qur'an 2: 278)*

We can also see from this verse that Allah has termed fear of Him as a condition for true belief. Muslims are extremely fortunate because fearing Allah will not only testify to their faith but will also allow them to hope for a reward. In fact, true faith, with its fundamental component of taqwâ, is the only route to the sole real form of success, which is success in the afterlife. All the forms of rewards and profits that this life can offer will fade away, whereas the rewards in the afterlife are permanent.

A comparison between the rewards in the two lives shows that a reward that will endure forever is clearly better than **any** short-lived temporal reward. Thus, a true Muslim does not find it disconcerting in any way to give up a profit, however large, for the purpose of avoiding anything that will anger Allah. Despite its simplicity, this fact may not be easily understood by human beings who have a weak psyche. Praise is to Allah, who has provided many words of encouragement in the Qur'an:

﴿ زُيِّنَ لِلنَّاسِ حُبُّ ٱلشَّهَوَٰتِ مِنَ ٱلنِّسَآءِ وَٱلْبَنِينَ وَٱلْقَنَٰطِيرِ ٱلْمُقَنطَرَةِ مِنَ ٱلذَّهَبِ وَٱلْفِضَّةِ وَٱلْخَيْلِ ٱلْمُسَوَّمَةِ وَٱلْأَنْعَٰمِ وَٱلْحَرْثِ ذَٰلِكَ مَتَٰعُ ٱلْحَيَوٰةِ ٱلدُّنْيَا وَٱللَّهُ عِندَهُۥ حُسْنُ ٱلْمَـَٔابِ ﴾ (سورة آل عمران: ١٤)

《Beautified for men is the love of things they covet: women, children, much of gold and silver [wealth], branded beautiful horses, cattle and well-tilled land. This is the pleasure of the present world's life; but Allah has the excellent return with Him.》   *(Qur'an 3: 14)*

﴿ إِنَّا جَعَلْنَا مَا عَلَى ٱلْأَرْضِ زِينَةً لَّهَا لِنَبْلُوَهُمْ أَيُّهُمْ أَحْسَنُ عَمَلًا ﴾ (سورة الكهف: ٧)

《Verily! We have made that which is on earth as an adornment for it, in order that We may test them [humankind] as to which of them are best in deeds.》   *(Qur'an 18: 7)*

﴿ ... وَمَن يَتَّقِ ٱللَّهَ يَجْعَل لَّهُۥ مَخْرَجًا ۝ وَيَرْزُقْهُ مِنْ حَيْثُ لَا يَحْتَسِبُۚ وَمَن يَتَوَكَّلْ عَلَى ٱللَّهِ فَهُوَ حَسْبُهُۥٓۚ إِنَّ ٱللَّهَ بَٰلِغُ أَمْرِهِۦۚ قَدْ جَعَلَ ٱللَّهُ لِكُلِّ شَىْءٍ قَدْرًا ۝ ﴾ (سورة الطلاق: ٢-٣)

﴾...And whosoever fears Allah and keeps his duty to Him, He will make a way for him to get out [from every difficulty], and He will provide him from [sources] he never could imagine. And whosoever puts his trust in Allah, then He will suffice him. Verily, Allah will accomplish his purpose. Indeed Allah has set a measure for all things.﴿

(Qur'an 65: 2-3)

There are two important reminders in the aforementioned verses. First of all, Islam advocates a perfectly balanced approach. Allah does not command Muslims to give up this world entirely; we are only asked to give up the haram and to seek halal bounties instead. Allah has prohibited neither trade nor sale; He only requires that we fear Him and respect His commands while engaging in them. He mentions:

﴿رِجَالٌ لَّا تُلْهِيهِمْ تِجَٰرَةٌ وَلَا بَيْعٌ عَن ذِكْرِ ٱللَّهِ وَإِقَامِ ٱلصَّلَوٰةِ وَإِيتَآءِ ٱلزَّكَوٰةِ ۙ يَخَافُونَ يَوْمًا تَتَقَلَّبُ فِيهِ ٱلْقُلُوبُ وَٱلْأَبْصَٰرُ ۝ ﴾ (سورة النور: ٣٧)

﴾Men whom neither trade nor sale [business] diverts from the remembrance of Allah, nor from performing the prayer, nor from giving the zakâh. They fear a day when hearts and eyes will be overturned.﴿

(Qur'an 24: 37)

And more generally:

﴿ ... رَبَّنَآ ءَاتِنَا فِى ٱلدُّنْيَا حَسَنَةً وَفِى ٱلْءَاخِرَةِ حَسَنَةً وَقِنَا عَذَابَ ٱلنَّارِ ۝ ﴾ (سورة البقرة: ٢٠١)

﴾...Our Lord! Give us in this world what is good and in the hereafter what is good, and save us from the torment of the fire.﴿

(Qur'an 2: 201)

This call for a balanced approach is a sharp blow both to those who equate Islam with extreme asceticism and to those who claim that it is impossible to follow Islam in modern times.

The Prophet (ﷺ) said:

«Do not acquire land (for farming) lest you become too attached to worldly matters.» (Recorded and classed as reliable by at-Tirmidhi)

The second reminder is offered directly in the following verse:

$$﴿ ... وَيَرْزُقْهُ مِنْ حَيْثُ لَا يَحْتَسِبُ وَمَن يَتَوَكَّلْ عَلَى اللَّهِ فَهُوَ حَسْبُهُ ۚ ﴿٣﴾ ﴾$$

(سورة الطلاق: ٣)

﴿And He will provide for him from [sources] he never could imagine. Whosoever puts his trust in Allah, then He will suffice him...﴾

(Qur'an 65: 3)

Allah asks us to have trust in Him (*tawakkul*) after we give up something for Him.

Tawakkul and patience

When faced with a test of faith, human beings must overcome two great challenges: pride and a failure to trust Allah. In order to pass the test of faith, human beings must be sufficiently humble when thinking about the Creator. There is no room for created beings to show pride or arrogance in front of their Creator, since it is only through Him that they have been given everything they have. Pride was the fatal mistake made by the accursed Satan; it led him to deny the command of his Creator. May Allah protect us from such a grievous mistake.

Soorat *al-Kahf* gives an example of a man ruining his blessings through pride:

$$﴿ وَدَخَلَ جَنَّتَهُ وَهُوَ ظَالِمٌ لِّنَفْسِهِ قَالَ مَا أَظُنُّ أَن تَبِيدَ هَٰذِهِ أَبَدًا ﴿٣٥﴾ وَمَا أَظُنُّ السَّاعَةَ قَائِمَةً وَلَئِن رُّدِدتُّ إِلَىٰ رَبِّي لَأَجِدَنَّ خَيْرًا مِّنْهَا مُنقَلَبًا ﴿٣٦﴾ قَالَ لَهُ$$

صَاحِبُهُ وَهُوَ يُحَاوِرُهُ أَكَفَرْتَ بِالَّذِى خَلَقَكَ مِن تُرَابٍ ثُمَّ مِن نُّطْفَةٍ ثُمَّ سَوَّىٰكَ رَجُلًا

لَّٰكِنَّا۠ هُوَ ٱللَّهُ رَبِّى وَلَآ أُشْرِكُ بِرَبِّىٓ أَحَدًا ٣٨ وَلَوْلَآ إِذْ دَخَلْتَ جَنَّتَكَ قُلْتَ ٣٧

مَا شَآءَ ٱللَّهُ لَا قُوَّةَ إِلَّا بِٱللَّهِ إِن تَرَنِ أَنَا۠ أَقَلَّ مِنكَ مَالًا وَوَلَدًا ٣٩ فَعَسَىٰ رَبِّىٓ أَن

يُؤْتِيَنِ خَيْرًا مِّن جَنَّتِكَ وَيُرْسِلَ عَلَيْهَا حُسْبَانًا مِّنَ ٱلسَّمَآءِ فَتُصْبِحَ صَعِيدًا زَلَقًا

٤٠ أَوْ يُصْبِحَ مَآؤُهَا غَوْرًا فَلَن تَسْتَطِيعَ لَهُۥ طَلَبًا ٤١ وَأُحِيطَ بِثَمَرِهِۦ فَأَصْبَحَ يُقَلِّبُ

كَفَّيْهِ عَلَىٰ مَآ أَنفَقَ فِيهَا وَهِىَ خَاوِيَةٌ عَلَىٰ عُرُوشِهَا وَيَقُولُ يَٰلَيْتَنِى لَمْ أُشْرِكْ بِرَبِّىٓ أَحَدًا ٤٢

(سورة الكهف: ٣٥-٤٢)

❨And he went into his garden while in a state [of pride and disbelief], unjust to himself. He said: I think not that this will ever perish, and I think not the hour will ever come, and if indeed I am brought back to my Lord [on the Day of Resurrection], I surely shall find better than this when I return to Him. His companion said to him during the talk with him: Do you disbelieve in Him Who created you out of dust, then out of mixed semen drops of male and female discharge, then fashioned you into a man? But as for my part, [I believe] that He is Allah, my Lord, and none shall I associate as partner with my Lord. It was better for you to say, when you entered your garden: What Allah wills [will come to pass]! There is no power but with Allah! If you see me less than you in wealth and children, it may be that my Lord will give me something better than your garden, and will send on it torment from the sky, then it will be as a barren, slippery earth. Or the water thereof [of the gardens] becomes deep-sunken [underground] so that you will never be able to seek it. So his fruits were encircled [with ruin]. And he remained clapping his hands [with sorrow] over what he had spent upon it, while it was all destroyed on its trellises, and he could only say: Would that I had ascribed no partners to my Lord!❩

(Qur'an 18: 35-42)

Too often, human beings forget that it is Allah Who controls all affairs.

﴿ءَأَمِنتُم مَّن فِى ٱلسَّمَآءِ أَن يَخْسِفَ بِكُمُ ٱلْأَرْضَ فَإِذَا هِىَ تَمُورُ ۝﴾ (سورة الملك: ١٦)

﴿Do you feel secure that He Who is over the heaven [Allah] will not cause the earth to sink with you, and then it should quake?﴾

(Qur'an 67: 16)

﴿۞ وَعِندَهُۥ مَفَاتِحُ ٱلْغَيْبِ لَا يَعْلَمُهَآ إِلَّا هُوَ وَيَعْلَمُ مَا فِى ٱلْبَرِّ وَٱلْبَحْرِ وَمَا تَسْقُطُ مِن وَرَقَةٍ إِلَّا يَعْلَمُهَا وَلَا حَبَّةٍ فِى ظُلُمَٰتِ ٱلْأَرْضِ وَلَا رَطْبٍ وَلَا يَابِسٍ إِلَّا فِى كِتَٰبٍ مُّبِينٍ ۝﴾ (سورة الأنعام: ٥٩)

﴿And with Him are the keys of the unseen; none knows them but He. He knows whatever there is in [or on] the earth and in the sea; not a leaf falls, but He knows it. There is not a grain in the darkness of the earth nor anything fresh or dry, but it is written in a clear record.﴾

(Qur'an 6: 59)

Realizing Allah's supreme power, our best action is to depend upon him solely.

﴿...وَعَلَى ٱللَّهِ فَتَوَكَّلُوٓاْ إِن كُنتُم مُّؤْمِنِينَ ۝﴾ (سورة المائدة: ٢٣)

﴿...and depend upon [trust in] Allah, if you are truly believers.﴾

(Qur'an 5: 23)

﴿إِنَّمَا ٱلْمُؤْمِنُونَ ٱلَّذِينَ إِذَا ذُكِرَ ٱللَّهُ وَجِلَتْ قُلُوبُهُمْ وَإِذَا تُلِيَتْ عَلَيْهِمْ ءَايَٰتُهُۥ زَادَتْهُمْ إِيمَٰنًا وَعَلَىٰ رَبِّهِمْ يَتَوَكَّلُونَ ۝﴾ (سورة الأنفال: ٢)

﴿The believers are those who, when Allah is mentioned, feel a tremor in their hearts, and when His verses are recited to them, they increase their faith and they put their trust in their Lord.﴾   *(Qur'an 8: 2)*

﴿... وَمَن يَتَوَكَّلْ عَلَى ٱللَّهِ فَهُوَ حَسْبُهُۥٓ إِنَّ ٱللَّهَ بَٰلِغُ أَمْرِهِۦ قَدْ جَعَلَ ٱللَّهُ لِكُلِّ شَىْءٍ قَدْرًا ۝﴾ (سورة الطلاق: ٣)

❨...And whosoever puts his trust in Allah, then He will suffice him. Verily, Allah will accomplish his purpose. Indeed Allah has set a measure for all things.❩   *(Qur'an 65: 3)*

﴿وَٱلَّذِينَ قَالَ لَهُمُ ٱلنَّاسُ إِنَّ ٱلنَّاسَ قَدْ جَمَعُوا لَكُمْ فَٱخْشَوْهُمْ فَزَادَهُمْ إِيمَٰنًا وَقَالُوا حَسْبُنَا ٱللَّهُ وَنِعْمَ ٱلْوَكِيلُ ۝﴾

(سورة آل عمران: ١٧٣)

❨Those [believers] to whom the people said: Verily, the people [pagans] have gathered against you [a great army], so fear them. But it only increased their faith, and they said: Allah [alone] is sufficient for us, and He is the best disposer of affairs.❩   *(Qur'an 3: 173)*

Some scholars have stated that tawakkul is the dependence of one's heart on Allah; it is equivalent to half of the religion. (The other half is repenting to Allah). Tawakkul is a command from Allah, and at the same time it is a blessing and a great mercy to humankind from Him. Indeed, the Creator has been generous enough to allow humankind to rely directly upon Him, the One Who controls all affairs. Clearly, tawakkul is particularly important because of its close link to tawheed.

It is important to remember that tawakkul does not preclude taking precautions. In fact, true faith requires both tawakkul and precautions.

Ibn al-Qayyim states that one cannot attain true tawheed without taking the means (created by Allah) that lead to the ends. He further emphasizes:

> Neglecting the means undermines the essence of putting one's trust in Allah and undermines the divine command and wisdom, because the one who neglects them thinks that this is a sign of stronger trust in Allah. But neglecting them is a sign of helplessness that contradicts putting one's trust in Allah, the essence of which is the heart's dependence on Allah to acquire that which will benefit a person in both religious commitment and worldly affairs, and will ward off that which will harm the person in both religious commitment and worldly affairs. Along with this dependence, one must take

the means; otherwise he or she will be ignoring the wisdom and command of Allah. We should not regard helplessness as putting our trust in Allah, or putting our trust in Allaah as helplessness.[2]

«One day Prophet Muhammad (ﷺ) noticed a Bedouin leaving his camel without tying it to something, so he asked the Bedouin: Why did you not tie your camel?

The Bedouin answered: I put my trust in Allah.

The Prophet (ﷺ) said: Tie your camel first, then put your trust in Allah.» (A sound hadith recorded by Ibn Ḥibbân)

Business managers will find the concept of tawakkul extremely useful.[3] It relieves them of the unreasonable pressure that is characteristic of corporate positions around the globe, exemplified by such contemporary ills as *karoshi,* the Japanese term for stress-related deaths caused by overwork. At the same time, the balanced view of tawakkul allows managers to take appropriate measures to reduce the risks to which shareholders are exposed.

In addition to the general measures of precaution, Muslims in business administration are encouraged to fully utilize three other tools: patience and forbearance, istikhârah, and shoorâ.

Too often, a person's judgement fails in the face of short-sightedness and impatience. The failure to become Muslim is perhaps the saddest example of that fact; many people forget the rewards and punishment of the afterlife and are too eager for immediate gratification, making the fatal choice of disbelief over eemân. It is not surprising that patience and perseverance are integral to one's faith.

(سورة الأنفال: ٤٦)

﴾... إِنَّ ٱللَّهَ مَعَ ٱلصَّـٰبِرِينَ ﴿٤٦﴾﴿

﴿...Surely, Allah is with those who are the patient.﴾ *(Qur'an 8: 46)*

---

[2] al-Jawziyah, *Zâd al-Ma'âd,* 4:15.

[3] Naceur Jabnoun has offered an excellent discussion on tawakkul in his book *Islam and Management.*

﴿...وَلَئِن صَبَرْتُمْ لَهُوَ خَيْرٌ لِّلصَّٰبِرِينَ ۝﴾   (سورة النحل: ١٢٦)

﴿...But if you endure patiently; verily, it is better for the patient.﴾

(Qur'an 16: 126)

﴿وَٱسْتَعِينُوا بِٱلصَّبْرِ وَٱلصَّلَوٰةِ وَإِنَّهَا لَكَبِيرَةٌ إِلَّا عَلَى ٱلْخَٰشِعِينَ ۝﴾

(سورة البقرة: ٤٥)

﴿And seek help in patience and the prayer and truly, it is extremely heavy and hard except for the true believers – those who obey Allah with full submission, fear much from His punishment, and believe in His promise and in His warnings.﴾   *(Qur'an 2: 45)*

Umm Salamah (رضي الله عنها) reported that she heard the Messenger of Allah (ﷺ) say:

«Allah will compensate, with something better, every Muslim who is stricken with a calamity and says what Allah has enjoined: Verily to Allah we belong, and to Him is our return. O Allah, reward me for my affliction and compensate me with something better.» (Muslim)

Istikhârah and shoorâ

Effective business administration largely involves making good decisions, but this is difficult when managers have to choose from several alternatives with a considerable degree of uncertainty. Muslim managers are blessed with the special option of istikhârah, which is a prescribed method of seeking Allah's guidance in making a decision.

Jâbir ibn 'Abdullâh as-Salâmi (رضي الله عنه) said:

«The Messenger of Allah (ﷺ) used to teach his Companions to make istikhârah in all things, just as he used to teach them soorahs from the Qur'an. He said: If any you is concerned about a decision he has to make, let him pray two units of non-obligatory prayer and say:

Allâhumma inni astakheeruka bi 'ilmika wa astaqdiruka bi qudratika, wa as'aluka min faḍlik al-'adheem, fa innaka taqdiru wa lâ aqdir, wa ta'lamu wa lâ a'lam, wa anta 'allâm ul-ghuyoob. Allâhumma in kunta ta'lamu anna hâdhal-amra (then the matter should be mentioned by name) *khayrul-lee fee deeni wa ma'âshi wa 'âqibati amri* (or: *fee 'âjil amree wa âjilihi*) *faqdurhu lee wa yassirhu lee thumma bârik lee feeh. Allâhumma wa in kunta ta'lamu annahu sharrul-lee fee deeni wa ma'âshi wa 'âqibati amri* (or: *fee 'âjili amri wa âjilihi*), *faṣrifhu 'annee, waṣrifnee 'anhu, waqdir lee al-khayra ḥaythu kâna thumma arḍinee bih.*

(O Allah, I seek Your guidance (in making a choice) by virtue of Your knowledge, and I seek ability by virtue of Your power, and I ask You of Your great bounty. You have power; I have none. You know, while I know not. You are the Knower of the unseen. O Allah, if in Your knowledge, this matter (then it should be mentioned by name) is good for me in my religion, my livelihood, and my affairs (or: for me, both in this world and in the hereafter), then ordain it for me, make it easy for me, and bless it for me. And if in Your knowledge, it is bad for me and for my religion, my livelihood, and my affairs (or: for me, both in this world and the next), then turn me away from it (and turn it away from me), and ordain for me the good, wherever it may be, and make me pleased with it.)» (Bukhari)

The eminent scholar an-Nawawi, author of the famous compilation of Hadith, *Riyâḍ aṣ-Ṣâliḥeen*, states:

It is recommended but not obligatory, before praying istikhârah, to consult someone whom you know is sincere, caring and has experience, and who is trustworthy with regard to their religious commitment and knowledge.[4]

Muslims at all levels are encouraged to use shoorâ when making decisions; this involves consulting others and considering their points of view. Allah has mentioned:

---

[4] "Istikhaarah prayer," Islam-QA.com, accessed November 2, 2011, http://www.islam-qa.com/en/ref/11981/consultation.

﴿...وَشَاوِرْهُمْ فِي ٱلْأَمْرِ فَإِذَا عَزَمْتَ فَتَوَكَّلْ عَلَى ٱللَّهِ إِنَّ ٱللَّهَ يُحِبُّ ٱلْمُتَوَكِّلِينَ ١٥٩﴾

(سورة آل عمران: ١٥٩)

﴿...and consult them in the affairs. Then when you have taken a decision, put your trust in Allah; certainly Allah loves those who put their trust [in Him].﴾ *(Qur'an 3: 159)*

Da'wah

Our last section in this chapter deals with a task that is specific to Muslims. In today's diverse world, it is inevitable that a Muslim manager will deal with colleagues who are unaware of, or who oppose, the role of Islam in business administration. In any case, Muslims have an obligation to call others to the way of Allah. Praise be to Allah, Who has given us a complete religion to follow and has perfected it. Islam offers guidelines related to da'wah:[5]

﴿وَمَنْ أَحْسَنُ قَوْلًا مِّمَّن دَعَا إِلَى ٱللَّهِ وَعَمِلَ صَٰلِحًا وَقَالَ إِنَّنِي مِنَ ٱلْمُسْلِمِينَ ٣٣﴾

(سورة فُصِّلَت: ٣٣)

﴿And who is better in speech than he who invites to Allah, and does righteous deeds, and says: I am one of the Muslims.﴾ *(Qur'an 41: 33)*

﴿وَلْتَكُن مِّنكُمْ أُمَّةٌ يَدْعُونَ إِلَى ٱلْخَيْرِ وَيَأْمُرُونَ بِٱلْمَعْرُوفِ وَيَنْهَوْنَ عَنِ ٱلْمُنكَرِ وَأُوْلَـٰئِكَ هُمُ ٱلْمُفْلِحُونَ ١٠٤﴾

(سورة آل عمران: ١٠٤)

﴿Let there arise out of you a group of people inviting to all that is good [Islam], enjoining what is right and forbidding what is wrong. It is they who are the successful.﴾ *(Qur'an 3: 104)*

The Prophet (ﷺ) said:

«Convey from me even if it is (only) one verse.» (Bukhari)

---

[5] Interested readers may refer to Mobabaya, *Da'wah According to the Qur'an and Sunnah.*

Islam also offers guidelines on the manner of da'wah.

﴿ ٱدۡعُ إِلَىٰ سَبِيلِ رَبِّكَ بِٱلۡحِكۡمَةِ وَٱلۡمَوۡعِظَةِ ٱلۡحَسَنَةِ وَجَٰدِلۡهُم بِٱلَّتِي هِيَ أَحۡسَنُ إِنَّ رَبَّكَ هُوَ أَعۡلَمُ بِمَن ضَلَّ عَن سَبِيلِهِۦ وَهُوَ أَعۡلَمُ بِٱلۡمُهۡتَدِينَ ﴿١٢٥﴾ ﴾

(سورة النحل: ١٢٥)

❨Invite to the way of your Lord with wisdom and fair preaching, and argue with them in a way that is better. Truly, your Lord knows best who has gone astray from His path, and He is the best knower of those who are guided.❩   *(Qur'an 16: 125)*

﴿ فَبِمَا رَحۡمَةٍ مِّنَ ٱللَّهِ لِنتَ لَهُمۡ وَلَوۡ كُنتَ فَظًّا غَلِيظَ ٱلۡقَلۡبِ لَٱنفَضُّواْ مِنۡ حَوۡلِكَ فَٱعۡفُ عَنۡهُمۡ وَٱسۡتَغۡفِرۡ لَهُمۡ وَشَاوِرۡهُمۡ فِي ٱلۡأَمۡرِ... ﴿١٥٩﴾ ﴾   (سورة آل عمران: ١٥٩)

❨And by the mercy of Allah, you [Muhammad] dealt with them gently. Had you been severe and harsh-hearted, they would have broken away from about you; so pass over [their faults], and ask [Allah's] forgiveness for them; and consult them in the affairs...❩

(Qur'an 3: 159)

Given the deep-rooted Western (secular or Judeo-Christian) philosophies of modern business administration, the following verses may offer valuable guidelines.

﴿ ۞ وَلَا تُجَٰدِلُوٓاْ أَهۡلَ ٱلۡكِتَٰبِ إِلَّا بِٱلَّتِي هِيَ أَحۡسَنُ إِلَّا ٱلَّذِينَ ظَلَمُواْ مِنۡهُمۡ وَقُولُوٓاْ ءَامَنَّا بِٱلَّذِيٓ أُنزِلَ إِلَيۡنَا وَأُنزِلَ إِلَيۡكُمۡ وَإِلَٰهُنَا وَإِلَٰهُكُمۡ وَٰحِدٌ وَنَحۡنُ لَهُۥ مُسۡلِمُونَ ﴿٤٦﴾ ﴾   (سورة العنكبوت: ٤٦)

❨And argue not with the People of the Scripture, unless it be in [a way] that is better, except with such of them as do wrong; and say [to them]: We believe in what has been revealed to us and revealed to you; our God and your God is One [that is, Allah], and to Him we have submitted [as Muslims].❩   *(Qur'an 29: 46)*

﴿ فَٱصۡبِرۡ إِنَّ وَعۡدَ ٱللَّهِ حَقٌّ وَلَا يَسۡتَخِفَّنَّكَ ٱلَّذِينَ لَا يُوقِنُونَ ۝ ﴾

(سورة الروم: ٦٠)

﴿So be patient [O Muhammad (ﷺ)]. Verily, the promise of Allah is
true; and let not those who have no certainty of faith discourage you
from conveying Allah's message.﴾   *(Qur'an 30: 60)*

Conclusion

In this chapter, we have highlighted standard practices in Islam that
can strongly benefit Muslims in the field of business administration:
taqwâ, tawakkul, patience, shoorâ, istikhârah, and da'wah. These are
all highly commendable approaches to dealing with business administration. They stand in sharp contrast to the false 'religious' practices
that are based on superstition: for instance, seeking the intercession
of saints through supplications made at their tombs, using good luck
charms, or seeking the opinions of 'holy men' who claim knowledge
of the unseen.

The six practices that we have discussed help to highlight the
completeness of Islam in many ways. The interrelationships among
these practices reveals that Muslims are supported by Islam in every
facet of their professional lives in business administration.

Muslim managers are guided by fear of Allah (taqwâ). This is a
beneficial fear in that it encourages them to seek the halal and eschew
the haram, and Allah has promised a great reward for that. Muslim
managers need to rely on Allah only. This is a beautiful reliance, for
Allah is the Greatest, the One Who controls destiny; still, the Muslims
themselves must do their part and must not be negligent.

Muslim managers practice patience and have no regrets, having
sought Allah's guidance in every affair through shoorâ and istikhârah.
They can continue the noble mission of spreading the message of
Islam by utilizing the guidelines in the Qur'an. Such a complete

religion entails complete submission, which is the true essence of Islam.

A striking aspect of Islam is that it liberates Muslims through submission. When Muslims ignore their religion and choose to confine themselves to the traditional ethos of business administration, they risk incurring Allah's anger; this is often for the sake of work that is pointless from an Islamic perspective. Proponents of conventional banking, which is based on ribâ and other un-Islamic transactions, argue that it is necessary in modern day business administration. Muslims, however, realize that Allah is the source of sustenance; they are liberated from such illogical thinking because they know that Allah's power is unimaginable.

While our religion is beautifully simple, our success depends upon our devotion to Allah alone and upon keeping ourselves free of shirk; it also depends upon our conviction and resolve, sincerity, and fear of Allah. Muslim managers must reflect upon the importance of faith and the purpose of life. Allah has created us to worship Him alone. Career advancement, financial success, fame, and other worldly goals are always secondary and cannot contradict our worship. Ideally, these goals should be the means to achieve our primary objective of worshipping only Allah.

Many of us will be tested in our careers. Many Muslim women have had to give up brilliant careers, not because of any glass ceiling but to avoid mingling with men. Many women and men have sacrificed high-paying banking careers to avoid the abhorred ribâ, and many more have given up windfall profit opportunities in order to avoid bribes. All those sisters and brothers were successful, inshallah, because abandoning wrongdoing leads to true success in both this life and the hereafter.

Muslim managers can prepare themselves – with the right knowledge, and by strengthening their eemân and fearing Allah – to face such tests when they are engaged in business administration. With

Allah's help, they will be able to make the right choices, even if those choices appear to contradict common practices.

We must remember that Allah is our source of strength, that we believers belong to Allah, and that He provides us with our sustenance and our wealth. We must fully trust Him and follow His commands.

To conclude, let us consider what happened to Prophet Joseph (ﷺ).[6]

﴿ وَلَقَدْ هَمَّتْ بِهِۦ وَهَمَّ بِهَا لَوْلَآ أَن رَّءَا بُرْهَٰنَ رَبِّهِۦ ۚ كَذَٰلِكَ لِنَصْرِفَ عَنْهُ السُّوٓءَ وَٱلْفَحْشَآءَ ۚ إِنَّهُۥ مِنْ عِبَادِنَا ٱلْمُخْلَصِينَ ﴿٢٤﴾ ﴾   (سورة يوسف: ٢٤)

﴿And indeed she did desire him, and he would have inclined to her desire had he not seen the evidence of his Lord. Thus it was that We might turn away from him evil and illegal sexual intercourse. Surely, he was one of Our chosen, guided slaves.﴾   *(Qur'an 12: 24)*

﴿ قَالَ رَبِّ ٱلسِّجْنُ أَحَبُّ إِلَىَّ مِمَّا يَدْعُونَنِىٓ إِلَيْهِ ۖ وَإِلَّا تَصْرِفْ عَنِّى كَيْدَهُنَّ أَصْبُ إِلَيْهِنَّ وَأَكُن مِّنَ ٱلْجَٰهِلِينَ ﴿٣٣﴾ فَٱسْتَجَابَ لَهُۥ رَبُّهُۥ فَصَرَفَ عَنْهُ كَيْدَهُنَّ ۚ إِنَّهُۥ هُوَ ٱلسَّمِيعُ ٱلْعَلِيمُ ﴿٣٤﴾ ثُمَّ بَدَا لَهُم مِّنۢ بَعْدِ مَا رَأَوُا۟ ٱلْءَايَٰتِ لَيَسْجُنُنَّهُۥ حَتَّىٰ حِينٍ ﴿٣٥﴾ ﴾

(سورة يوسف: ٣٣-٣٥)

﴿He said: O my Lord! Prison is dearer to me than that to which they invite me. Unless You turn their plot away from me, I will feel inclined towards them and be one of the ignorant. So his Lord answered his invocation and turned their plot away from him. Verily, He is the All-Hearer, the All-Knower. Then it occurred to them, after they had

---

[6] The story of Prophet Joseph is told in full in Chapter 12 of the Qur'an, which is named Joseph. After having been thrown down a well by his brothers, he was found by members of a caravan and taken to Egypt, where he was sold as a slave to a wealthy man called 'Azeez. When Joseph had grown into a handsome young man, the wife of 'Azeez tried to seduce him, and although Joseph rejected her advances, he was punished. (Editor)

seen the proofs [of his innocence], to imprison him for a time.⟩

(Qur'an 12: 33-35)

Joseph (﷽) told his fellow prisoners:

﴿...إِنِّى تَرَكْتُ مِلَّةَ قَوْمٍ لَّا يُؤْمِنُونَ بِٱللَّهِ وَهُم بِٱلْأَخِرَةِ هُمْ كَٰفِرُونَ ۝ وَٱتَّبَعْتُ مِلَّةَ ءَابَآءِىٓ إِبْرَٰهِيمَ وَإِسْحَٰقَ وَيَعْقُوبَ مَا كَانَ لَنَآ أَن نُّشْرِكَ بِٱللَّهِ مِن شَىْءٍ ذَٰلِكَ مِن فَضْلِ ٱللَّهِ عَلَيْنَا وَعَلَى ٱلنَّاسِ وَلَٰكِنَّ أَكْثَرَ ٱلنَّاسِ لَا يَشْكُرُونَ ۝﴾

(سورة يوسف: ٣٧-٣٨)

﴿...Verily, I have abandoned the religion of a people that believe not in Allah, and are disbelievers in the hereafter. And I have followed the religion of my fathers – Abraham, Isaac, and Jacob, and never could we attribute any partners whatsoever to Allah. This is from the grace of Allah to us and to humankind, but most men thank not.⟩

(Qur'an 12: 37-38)

Allah has further mentioned:

(سورة يوسف: ٥٧)   ﴿وَلَأَجْرُ ٱلْأَخِرَةِ خَيْرٌ لِّلَّذِينَ ءَامَنُوا۟ وَكَانُوا۟ يَتَّقُونَ ۝﴾

﴿And verily, the reward of the hereafter is better for those who believe and used to fear Allah and keep their duty to Him.⟩ *(Qur'an 12: 57)*

﴿...إِنَّهُۥ مَن يَتَّقِ وَيَصْبِرْ فَإِنَّ ٱللَّهَ لَا يُضِيعُ أَجْرَ ٱلْمُحْسِنِينَ ۝﴾

(سورة يوسف: ٩٠)

﴿...Verily, he who fears Allah with obedience to Him, and is patient, then surely, Allah makes not the reward of the good-doers to be lost.⟩

(Qur'an 12: 90)

Indeed, an excellent example can be seen in Prophet Joseph (﷽). He faced a test and chose the more difficult option because he knew that it would please Allah. He feared Allah, remembered Him, and sought His help. He engaged in tawakkul and patience, and he persisted in inviting others to the right path. Allah then helped Prophet Joseph (﷽), who would otherwise have been unsuccessful, given the weak resolve of human beings. In the end, Allah gave him authority and provision in this life as a reward for his obedience and devotion.

CHAPTER FOUR

SETTING UP A BUSINESS

$\mathcal{S}$etting up a business is a specialized task of entrepreneurship; it is not a commonly-encountered task of business administration. In fact, most managers will not have been involved in setting up the business they help manage. Nonetheless, we have chosen to discuss this topic now - before the more common tasks of finance, marketing, and operations management - in order to underscore an important idea.

Muslims should realize that the sooner they consider Islam in the lifetime of the business, the easier it will be to implement business practices that are consistent with their religious beliefs. Muslim investors, for example, may seize a particular business opportunity but only later discover that the relevant business models are typically sustained by haram elements. If they continue to engage in that business with its haram aspects, they will clearly be harming themselves. Even if they extract themselves, and as much of their original investment as possible, their net gain is almost always negative, particularly if one considers the opportunity cost of bogus investment activities.

Let us consider the case of Muslim investors who initially do not realize that coeducation is generally not halal (because it violates the commandment to lower the gaze and results in prohibited intermingling between men and women).[1] They decide to engage in the

---

[1] See "He wants to marry a girl but she wants to go to university and they live in a corrupt society," Islam-QA.com, accessed November 2, 2011, http://www.islam-qa.com/en/ref/5384.

noble effort of establishing a private school, which can be a good, halal business. They strive to offer a high quality education, but due to ignorance, they choose to make the school coeducational.

After two years, their school begins to operate profitably. At this time, one Muslim investor realizes the problem with coeducation. He is faced with multiple dilemmas and a great deal of resistance, but if he continues as before, he risks his own religion.

﴿ إِنَّهُمْ إِن يَظْهَرُوا۟ عَلَيْكُمْ يَرْجُمُوكُمْ أَوْ يُعِيدُوكُمْ فِى مِلَّتِهِمْ وَلَن تُفْلِحُوٓا۟ إِذًا أَبَدًا ۝ ﴾ (سورة الكهف: ٢٠)

﴿For, if they come to know of you, they will stone you or turn you back to their religion; and in that case you will never be successful.﴾

(Qur'an 18: 20)

If the school separates the boys and the girls so he can stay, they risk upsetting the market. If he withdraws his investment and sells his share, the school is placed under considerable risk. Even if the school is not at risk, our protagonist Muslim still apparently loses at the end of the day, for several reasons.

For one thing, the transaction costs associated with investment and pulling out are not recoverable. Had he invested elsewhere, he could have enjoyed a profit rather than sacrificing it. Still, it is better for him to withdraw for the sake of obeying Allah, and he is even promised a reward for doing so.[2]

---

[2] The world is a complicated place, and issues are not always black and white. There is a difference between what is prescribed in Islam (which this book is trying to portray) and what an individual's response should be or how one will be judged according to the circumstances in which they find themselves. Prescriptions are made in Islam, and Muslims must make sacrifices to try to fulfil them; they must increase their faith and trust in Allah to be able to meet their goals. In the case of coeducation, for example, persons studying under such a system should seek a way out if they possibly can.

﴿ ...وَمَن يَتَّقِ اللَّهَ يَجْعَل لَّهُ مَخْرَجًا ۝ وَيَرْزُقْهُ مِنْ حَيْثُ لَا يَحْتَسِبُ... ۝ ﴾

(سورة الطلاق: ٢-٣)

﴾...And whosoever fears Allah and keeps his duty to Him, He will make a way for him to get out [from every difficulty]. And He will provide him from [sources] he could never imagine...﴿

(Qur'an 65: 2-3)

In general, Islam has always placed strong emphasis upon establishing solid foundations for future sustainability. Let us consider the following examples:

- The first pillar, the testimony of faith, is an all-inclusive foundation, as we have already discussed in detail. There are significant lessons to be learned from this. We can see, for example, how ṣalâh and other pillars are possible only because of the establishment of the foundation: the concept of the shahâdatayn. If it is established from the beginning that Muslims will set up business organizations that do not contradict Islamic guidelines, then Muslim managers, stakeholders, and patrons will continue to benefit from the founding and growth of such business houses.

- The basic principles were preached for a long time before the rules were prescribed. During the first half of his prophethood, the Prophet (ﷺ) preached tawḥeed in order to establish the necessary foundation among the early Muslims. Muslim laws that are known popularly (hijab, for example) were prescribed only after tawḥeed was established.

- We know from the biography of the Prophet (ﷺ) that when he and his followers migrated to Madinah, his very first task was the construction of a mosque. The Prophet (ﷺ) rode into Madinah and proceeded until his camel came to a stop and knelt down; he then designated that spot as the location for the new mosque. Before taking care of his own personal needs, the Prophet (ﷺ)

felt it was his duty to begin building a religious and social services headquarters for the Muslims.

From its inception, the Prophet's Mosque was built upon good, solid physical and spiritual foundations, with the aim of establishing and propagating the religion of Allah. The site was cleaned and levelled, trees were planted around it, and the Prophet (ﷺ) himself participated in laying the bricks for the walls.[3]

- The construction of this mosque can be contrasted with the construction of one known as the Mosque of Harm. The hypocrites, wishing to manipulate the religion to achieve their own aims, erected this mosque to serve as the headquarters for their activities. To achieve legitimacy, they invited the Prophet (ﷺ) to come and pray in their mosque, but Allah warned him away; later, the Prophet (ﷺ) sent a group of his followers to destroy the building. This mosque is mentioned in the Qur'an:

﴿وَٱلَّذِينَ ٱتَّخَذُواْ مَسْجِدًا ضِرَارًا وَكُفْرًا وَتَفْرِيقًا بَيْنَ ٱلْمُؤْمِنِينَ وَإِرْصَادًا لِّمَنْ حَارَبَ ٱللَّهَ وَرَسُولَهُۥ مِن قَبْلُ وَلَيَحْلِفُنَّ إِنْ أَرَدْنَآ إِلَّا ٱلْحُسْنَىٰ وَٱللَّهُ يَشْهَدُ إِنَّهُمْ لَكَٰذِبُونَ ۝ لَا تَقُمْ فِيهِ أَبَدًا لَّمَسْجِدٌ أُسِّسَ عَلَى ٱلتَّقْوَىٰ مِنْ أَوَّلِ يَوْمٍ أَحَقُّ أَن تَقُومَ فِيهِ فِيهِ رِجَالٌ يُحِبُّونَ أَن يَتَطَهَّرُواْ وَٱللَّهُ يُحِبُّ ٱلْمُطَّهِّرِينَ ۝ أَفَمَنْ أَسَّسَ بُنْيَٰنَهُۥ عَلَىٰ تَقْوَىٰ مِنَ ٱللَّهِ وَرِضْوَٰنٍ خَيْرٌ أَم مَّنْ أَسَّسَ بُنْيَٰنَهُۥ عَلَىٰ شَفَا جُرُفٍ هَارٍ فَٱنْهَارَ بِهِۦ فِي نَارِ جَهَنَّمَ وَٱللَّهُ لَا يَهْدِى ٱلْقَوْمَ ٱلظَّٰلِمِينَ ۝﴾ (سورة التوبة: ١٠٧–١٠٩)

﴿And as for those who put up a mosque by way of harming and disbelief, and to disunite the believers, and as an outpost for those who warred against Allah and His Messenger [Muhammad] before, they will indeed swear that their intention is nothing but

---

3 al-Mubarakpuri, *The Sealed Nectar*, 227.

good. Allah bears witness that they are certainly liars. Never stand in it [to pray]. Verily, the mosque whose foundation was laid from the first day on piety is more worthy that you stand in it [to pray]. In it are men who love to clean and to purify themselves. And Allah loves those who make themselves clean and pure. Is it then he, who laid the foundation of his building on piety to Allah and His good pleasure, [who is] better, or he who laid the foundation of his building on an undetermined brink of a precipice ready to crumble down, so that it crumbled to pieces with him into the fire of hell? And Allah guides not the wrong-doers.❯ (Qur'an 9: 107-109)

From these examples, we can see that Islam has always placed great emphasis upon strong, pure foundations. Similarly, Muslim businesses should be established from the very beginning with a strong foundation of submission to Allah.

We can classify the issues that arise at the inception of any business into two broad headings: Halal and haram businesses and legal issues.

Halal and haram businesses

At the core of complying with the Sharia is determining whether or not the business is halal in the first place. The best way to answer this question is to have a qualified Islamic scholar review the detailed business plan and give a fatwa regarding its permissibility. In any case, it may prove useful to consider the following four categories of businesses.

1. Businesses that earn their revenue by selling haram products or services

Businesses that earn their revenue from haram products or services such as pork, gambling, alcohol, or prostitution are undoubtedly haram. Many Muslims fool themselves by arguing that although they sell alcohol in their liquor stores, they do not consume it themselves;

that they sell to non-Muslims only; or that they do not compel anyone to purchase it. In fact, it has been reported that the Prophet (ﷺ) said: «When Allah forbids a thing, He forbids its price.» (Aḥmad and Abu Dâwood; al-Albâni graded it as sound)

Muslims should completely avoid such businesses, instead of trying to find ways to rationalize their involvement in them.

2. Businesses that contaminate their revenues by selling a few haram products

There are numerous examples of businesses that taint a generally halal business model with a few products that are forbidden in Islam. We will list a few for the sake of illustration:

- A hotel that sells alcoholic drinks. While providing room and board can be a halal source of revenue, this is ruined by allowing a bar in the hotel to sell alcohol.

- A mobile phone company that offers additional value-added services like daily horoscope readings. Connectivity can be a great service and a wonderful source of halal income. Unfortunately, most operators of mobile networks are susceptible to temptation, targeting additional revenues by offering haram services over their networks.

- A university that teaches haram forms of music. As we shall discuss later, Islam forbids many forms of music.

- A supermarket that sells pork or liquor (even if it is in a section designated for non-Muslims), or that sells haram forms of music.

- A newspaper or a television station that runs haram advertisements, including those with provocative pictures evoking sinful desires.

- A coffee shop that plays music to entertain its patrons.

- A barbershop that offers shaving (of men's beards).[4]

---

[4] Adapted from the rulings of Shaykh Ibn Bâz, *Majmoo' Fatâwâ*, 8:372.

Among today's major *fitan* (turmoils) is the widespread notion among business managers and owners that some level of haram is inevitable. They argue that they are part of a system that is already entrenched in haram, and hence it is impossible for them, as individual players, to go against the norm. They cite examples from Muslim countries of bars in airports and of flag-carrying airlines serving alcohol on their planes. Even if ordinary citizens and patrons can do little to physically change these systems, they can voice their opinions and educate their fellow Muslims. Those who have been entrusted with positions of authority must be admonished concerning the gravity of their passive acceptance and implementation of the haram. They must be reminded to fear Allah and to rely upon Him alone.

3. Businesses that sell items that may be used either for halal or haram purposes

Often, businesses sell items that can be used in halal ways but that unfortunately can also be used in explicitly haram ways. There are many contemporary examples in this category, of which we can cite a few:

- An mp3 player can be used to listen to Islamic lectures, or it can be used to listen to lewd music.
- Using cosmetics is a permissible way for women to feel more beautiful when they are with their husbands or among female friends, but the same makeup can be used to corrupt society by shamefully attracting the attention of non-*mahram*[5] men.
- The Internet and many of its applications, like Facebook, can be used for acquiring Islamic knowledge, spreading Islam, or simply interacting with others in a halal manner. With the profusion of pornography on the Internet, though, it is easy to see how the same technologies can be used for haram means.
- A hotel room can be used for lodging by travellers, but it can also be utilized for illegal activities.

---

[5] non-*mahram*: a man whom a woman is allowed to marry and vice versa.

- Selling cars or real estate may encourage potential buyers to seek ribâ-based financing.

Generally, a sale is haram if the seller knows that a product will be used in haram ways.[6] Allah has mentioned:

﴿...وَتَعَاوَنُوا۟ عَلَى ٱلْبِرِّ وَٱلتَّقْوَىٰ ۖ وَلَا تَعَاوَنُوا۟ عَلَى ٱلْإِثْمِ وَٱلْعُدْوَٰنِ ۚ وَٱتَّقُوا۟ ٱللَّهَ ۖ إِنَّ ٱللَّهَ شَدِيدُ ٱلْعِقَابِ ۞﴾   (سورة المائدة: ٢)

﴿...Help one another in virtue, righteousness and piety, but do not help one another in sin and transgression. And fear Allah. Verily, Allah is severe in punishment.﴾   *(Qur'an 5: 2)*

For example, a taxi driver should not knowingly drive a fellow Muslim to a concert, even though the service being provided (transportation) is not haram in itself. If a young Muslim attempts to purchase an mp3 player, the seller should assess the likelihood of his using it for haram versus halal purposes. If the buyer appears to want the mp3 player for halal reasons, it is allowed to sell it to him, inshallah.

One particular concern with this approach is that it can generate considerable controversy because those selling products or services will essentially be engaging in discrimination by selling to some and refusing to sell to others.

Muslim cab drivers in Minneapolis attracted quite a bit of attention in 2006 after news reports emerged about many of them refusing fares if they involved transporting alcohol.[7]

The Messenger of Allah (ﷺ) said:

---

[6] Further details are available from Ibn Jibreen, "Selling things that may be used for haraam purposes," Islam-QA.com, accessed November 2, 2011, http://www.islam-qa.com/en/ref/21649.

[7] Lydersen, "Some Muslim Cabbies Refuse Fares Carrying Alcohol," *The Washington Post*, October 26, 2006, accessed October 23, 2011, http://www.washingtonpost.com/wp-dyn/content/article/2006/10/25/AR2006102501727.html.

«May Allah curse wine, the one who drinks it, the one who pours it, the one who sells it, the one who buys it, the one who squeezes (the grapes), the one for whom it is squeezed, the one who carries it, and the one to whom it is carried.» (Abu Dâwood; al-Albâni graded it as sound)

It is worthwhile to note that while discrimination without a valid reason is certainly reproachable, all business providers are required to engage in discrimination when valid reasons exist. For example, service providers in the U.S. reserve the right to refuse service under certain conditions. Turning a blind eye to criminal activity, and thus becoming complicit in it, must be avoided even if that essentially amounts to discrimination.

For example, if an employee in a hotel recognizes a fugitive whose face has been publicized, that employee should not simply rent him or her a suite without notifying the authorities. Similarly, Muslims should abstain from selling products or services to individuals if they know that they will use them in a haram manner.

The situation is not so clear when there is a possibility that an item can be used in haram ways but the seller is unaware of how the buyer will use it. Islam places tremendous importance on privacy.

$$ ﴿ ... ٱجۡتَنِبُواْ كَثِيرࣰا مِّنَ ٱلظَّنِّ إِنَّ بَعۡضَ ٱلظَّنِّ إِثۡمࣱ وَلَا تَجَسَّسُواْ ... ﴾ ۝ ﴿١٢﴾ $$

(سورة الحُجُرات: ١٢)

﴿...Avoid much suspicion; indeed some suspicions are sins. And spy not...﴾   *(Qur'an 49: 12)*

The Prophet (ﷺ) said:

«If you seek out people's faults, you will corrupt them or almost corrupt them.» (Abu Dâwood; al-Albâni graded it as sound)

In general, sinners are not to be exposed. Sins should be concealed as much as possible to avoid further corruption of the society. The Messenger of Allah (ﷺ) said:

«All of my Ummah will be fine except for those who commit sin openly. Part of committing sin openly is when a man does something at night and Allah conceals it; however, in the morning, he says: O So-and-so, last night I did such-and-such.

His Lord had covered his sin all night, but in the morning he removed the cover of Allah.» (Bukhari and Muslim)

Arguably, it is not usually necessary, or even valid, to probe and determine the intentions of a potential customer before deciding whether or not to make the sale. Even if sales agents are asked to use their judgement based on obvious clues, without probing, implementing such a program of individual assessment may prove difficult in light of today's mass marketing practices.

One simple approach is to inform potential customers about the gravity of sin. For example, every mp3 player box could have an informative 'warning' label that reminds the Muslim consumer to fear Allah and abstain from haram music. In cases where the sin is particularly grave, Muslims could even be asked to sign a form pledging not to use the item for haram purposes. Such a requirement provides the necessary da'wah while at the same time, inshallah, relieving the seller of any share of possible sin.

Finally, good businesses should monitor consumer behaviour at large and then tailor their policies accordingly. If it is found that a majority of the customers are using a product for haram purposes, the company could consider replacing it with something better: a substitute that does not offer haram options. If Internet Service Providers (ISPs) know that many members of the society are using the Internet to view pornography, they should block those kinds of sites, even at the risk of accidentally filtering out sites that are legal.

4. Businesses that sell only halal products but engage in haram practices

Whether because of ignorance or the vacuous aim of blindly following Western practices and ideals, many businesses sell halal products but engage in business administration tasks that are haram. We have already discussed that Islam is a complete religion that entails complete submission to Allah. Muslims cannot merely pick and choose certain Islamic requirements to follow, ignoring those that interfere with modern business administration methods. Some of the common practices that are haram are:

- Ribâ-based financing
- Prohibited intermingling between men and women at work
- Lewd advertisements or other applications of the idea that 'sex sells': for instance, placing female receptionists who are not dressed Islamically in the front office to attract more clients
- Misuse and waste of environmental resources
- Misleading marketing information
- Operating the business during Friday prayer time
- Adopting un-Islamic styles of clothing
- Sponsoring public relations events such as musical concerts

Some of these issues are more serious than others, and each has to be dealt with on an individual basis. We will discuss many of them in subsequent chapters, but in general, the haram must be avoided except in cases of true necessity. It is best to consult with scholars to determine whether or not a particular set of circumstances constitutes a necessity.

**5. Businesses that sell halal items and engage
in halal practices but implicitly support haram causes**

Some businesses sell only halal items and also implement halal business administration practices, yet their operations may implicitly be supporting haram causes. We can list a few examples:

- Selling food items under franchise agreements that ultimately help Israeli interests which are directly associated with such atrocities as the 2007-2008 genocide in Gaza.

- Buying products from countries that attack Muslim ideals. In 2005-2006, many Muslims around the world boycotted Danish products because of the Danish government's failure to address the offence caused to Muslim sentiments by the publication of tasteless caricatures in a Danish newspaper.

- Establishing a restaurant in a mall that is known to be a centre of indecent behaviour; for instance, where music is played loudly or throughout the mall.

- Marketing using online social networking sites such as Facebook, even after Facebook refused to ban the celebration of 'Draw Prophet Muhammad Day'.

Clearly, it is desirable to avoid any haram practices and to do what we can to reduce evil in the world and promote goodness, but we cannot necessarily conclude that participating in these types of business is entirely haram. It should be noted that the Prophet (ﷺ) conducted trade with his enemies, and at the time he died, his shield had been pawned to a Jewish man.[8] If the leader of the Muslim state deems it wise to implement a boycott, then clearly those in that state should observe the boycott; otherwise, it is at a person's own discretion, but that choice should not be imposed upon others.[9] When in doubt, it is best to consult a qualified Islamic scholar.

Other legal issues

When Muslims begin to set up businesses, they face the issue of complying with local regulations that may not be in accordance with the laws of Islam (and this may even be the case in Muslim countries). Registering the business, making tax arrangements, complying with

---

[8] Bukhari and Muslim.

[9] al-Fawzan, "Question about Boycotting Danish products," accessed October 23, 2011, *Salafitalk.net,* http://www.salafitalk.net/st/viewmessages.cfm?Forum=26&Topic=5198.

insurance requirements, formulating a charter, and many other activities may involve rules that directly contradict Islamic rulings. In many developing countries, where corruption is pervasive, the situation is often worse; often, new businesses can be set up only after bribing officials or engaging in other haram actions. Once again, the best approach is to obtain a fatwa from an Islamic scholar, particularly since laws differ across geographic locations.

There are many situations in which local laws contradict Islamic laws; this is not surprising because few modern nations actually implement Sharia. This is a serious offense in itself, as explained in this excerpt from the rulings of Shaykh Ibn Bâz:

> The one who rules according to something other than that which Allaah has revealed, knowing that it is obligatory to rule according to that which Allaah has revealed and that he is going against sharee'ah, but he thinks that this is permissible and that there is nothing wrong with it and that it is permissible for him to rule according to something other than the sharee'ah of Allaah, is a kaafir in the sense of major kufr, according to all scholars. This applies to ruling in accordance with man-made laws which have been invented by men, be they Christians or Jews or anyone else, if he claims that it is permissible to rule according to them, or that they are better than the rulings of Allaah, or that they are equal to the rulings of Allaah, and that man has the choice: if he wishes he may rule according to the Qur'aan and Sunnah, and if he wishes he may rule according to man-made laws. The one who believes that is a kaafir according to scholarly consensus, as stated above.

> But if a person rules according to something other than that which Allaah has revealed because of his whims and desires or because of some worldly interest he may achieve, knowing that he is disobeying Allaah and His Messenger, and that he is committing a great evil and that what he should do is rule according to the laws of Allaah, he is not guilty of major kufr because of that, but he

has committed a great evil, major sin and minor kufr, as stated by Ibn 'Abbaas, Mujaahid and other scholars, and he has committed thereby a lesser form of kufr, wrongdoing and evil, but it is not major kufr.[10]

He then quotes the following verses:

(سورة المائدة: ٤٩) ﴿ ٤٩ ... وَأَنِ احْكُم بَيْنَهُم بِمَآ أَنزَلَ اللَّهُ ﴾

《And so judge [you, O Muhammad] between them by what Allah has revealed…》
(Qur'an 5: 49)

(سورة المائدة: ٤٤) ﴿ ٤٤ وَمَن لَّمْ يَحْكُم بِمَآ أَنزَلَ اللَّهُ فَأُوْلَٰئِكَ هُمُ الْكَٰفِرُونَ ... ﴾

《…And whosoever does not judge by what Allah has revealed, such are the disbelievers.》
(Qur'an 5: 44)

(سورة المائدة: ٤٥) ﴿ ٤٥ وَمَن لَّمْ يَحْكُم بِمَآ أَنزَلَ اللَّهُ فَأُوْلَٰئِكَ هُمُ الظَّٰلِمُونَ ... ﴾

《…And whosoever does not judge by that which Allah has revealed, such are the wrongdoers.》
(Qur'an 5: 45)

(سورة المائدة: ٤٧) ﴿ ٤٧ وَمَن لَّمْ يَحْكُم بِمَآ أَنزَلَ اللَّهُ فَأُوْلَٰئِكَ هُمُ الْفَٰسِقُونَ ... ﴾

《…And whosoever does not judge by what Allah has revealed, such [people] are the rebellious to Allah.》
(Qur'an 5: 47)

﴿ فَلَا وَرَبِّكَ لَا يُؤْمِنُونَ حَتَّىٰ يُحَكِّمُوكَ فِيمَا شَجَرَ بَيْنَهُمْ ثُمَّ لَا يَجِدُواْ فِىٓ أَنفُسِهِمْ حَرَجًا مِّمَّا قَضَيْتَ وَيُسَلِّمُواْ تَسْلِيمًا ٦٥ ﴾ (سورة النساء: ٦٥)

《But no, by your Lord, they can have no faith until they make you [O Muhammad] judge in all disputes between them, and find in themselves no resistance against your decisions, and accept [them] with full submission.》
(Qur'an 4: 65)

﴿ أَفَحُكْمَ الْجَٰهِلِيَّةِ يَبْغُونَ وَمَنْ أَحْسَنُ مِنَ اللَّهِ حُكْمًا لِّقَوْمٍ يُوقِنُونَ ٥٠ ﴾ (سورة المائدة: ٥٠)

---

[10] "Ruling on taking lightly the matter of ruling in accordance with the sharee'ah of Allaah and not applying it," Islam-QA.com, accessed November 2, 2011, http://www.islam-qa.com/en/ref/111923.

❲Do they then seek the judgement of [the days of] ignorance? And who is better in judgement than Allah for a people who have firm faith?❳   *(Qur'an 5: 50)*

Clearly, a Muslim should be very concerned about following the Sharia. Allah has further mentioned:

﴿أَلَمْ تَرَ إِلَى ٱلَّذِينَ يَزْعُمُونَ أَنَّهُمْ ءَامَنُواْ بِمَآ أُنزِلَ إِلَيْكَ وَمَآ أُنزِلَ مِن قَبْلِكَ يُرِيدُونَ أَن يَتَحَاكَمُوٓاْ إِلَى ٱلطَّٰغُوتِ وَقَدْ أُمِرُوٓاْ أَن يَكْفُرُواْ بِهِۦ وَيُرِيدُ ٱلشَّيْطَٰنُ أَن يُضِلَّهُمْ ضَلَٰلًۢا بَعِيدًا ۝ وَإِذَا قِيلَ لَهُمْ تَعَالَوْاْ إِلَىٰ مَآ أَنزَلَ ٱللَّهُ وَإِلَى ٱلرَّسُولِ رَأَيْتَ ٱلْمُنَٰفِقِينَ يَصُدُّونَ عَنكَ صُدُودًا ۝﴾ (سورة النساء: ٦٠-٦١)

❲Have you not seen those [hypocrites] who claim that they believe in what has been sent down to you, and what was sent down before you, and they wish to go for judgement [in their disputes] to the *ṭâghoot* [false judges] while they have been ordered to reject them? But Satan wishes to lead them far astray. And when it is said to them: Come to what Allah has sent down and to the Messenger, you see the hypocrites turn away from you with aversion.❳   *(Qur'an 4: 60-61)*

The saddest fact is that Muslims today will often face this evil situation, where local laws contradict Islamic laws, even in Muslim countries! They should resist these laws as much as possible. As a first step, they can write to the concerned authorities to request exemptions on religious grounds. They can also inform the appropriate authorities of the gravity of the situation with respect to tawḥeed and so forth. In all these tasks, Muslims should carefully follow the Sunnah of the Prophet (ﷺ) so that they do not make rash mistakes or use unnecessary violence. Instead, they should be patient, persevere, educate their fellow Muslims, and sincerely ask Allah for help. In situations where they are completely helpless, they should remember that Allah has mentioned:

﴿يَٰٓأَيُّهَا ٱلَّذِينَ ءَامَنُواْ ٱتَّقُواْ ٱللَّهَ حَقَّ تُقَاتِهِۦ ... ۝﴾ (سورة آل عمران: ١٠٢)

❨O you who believe! Fear Allah as He should be feared...❩

(Qur'an 3: 102)

(سورة التغابن: ١٦)   ❨... فَٱتَّقُواْ ٱللَّهَ مَا ٱسْتَطَعْتُمْ ...❩ ﴿١٦﴾

❨So keep your duty to Allah and fear Him as much as you can...❩

(Qur'an 64: 16)

❨... وَمَن يَتَّقِ ٱللَّهَ يَجْعَل لَّهُۥ مَخْرَجًا ﴿٢﴾ وَيَرْزُقْهُ مِنْ حَيْثُ لَا يَحْتَسِبُ ...❩ ﴿٣﴾

(سورة الطلاق: ٢-٣)

❨...And whosoever fears Allah and keeps his duty to Him, He will make a way for him to get out [from every difficulty], and He will provide him from [sources] he never could imagine...❩ *(Qur'an 65: 2-3)*

(سورة الأنفال: ٢٩)   ❨... إِن تَتَّقُواْ ٱللَّهَ يَجْعَل لَّكُمْ فُرْقَانًا ...❩ ﴿٢٩﴾

❨...If you obey and fear Allah, He will grant you a criterion [by which to judge between truth and falsehood]...❩   *(Qur'an 8: 29)*

Let us revisit two inspirational cases where Muslims sacrificed their income due to fear of Allah, in the hope of making positive changes. May Allah accept their perseverance and sacrifices.

In 2005, many Muslims called for a global boycott of Danish products after a Danish newspaper with a large circulation invited cartoonists to draw caricatures of the Prophet (ﷺ). The offensive cartoons were condemned around the world. AFP reported on January 30, 2006 that former U.S. President Bill Clinton had denounced 'these totally outrageous cartoons against Islam' and added that he feared anti-Semitism was being replaced with anti-Islamic prejudice. Even after powerful global voices criticized the tasteless cartoons, the Danish government refused to intervene, citing 'freedom of speech'. The Muslims challenged this with their own action of 'freedom of trade'.

Abdullah al-Othaim, executive president of Al-Othaim Holding Company, reaffirmed yesterday his company's boycott of Danish products until that country's largest daily apologizes for publishing

12 cartoons that mocked the Prophet Muhammad (peace be upon him). Al-Othaim said that just as Denmark has freedom of the press, Muslims have freedom to buy or not to buy. The company is comprised of five subsidiaries... and owns around 60 branches across the Kingdom. Al-Othaim's decision, which he says includes a boycott of any supplier that includes Danish products, may help to impact SR1.3 billion worth of exports to Saudi Arabia. Danish food giant Arla Foods said in Copenhagen yesterday it was being targeted by the Saudi boycott because of the publication of the offensive cartoons. Arla Foods is Europe's second-largest dairy company and the leading Danish exporter to Saudi Arabia, where it sells an estimated two billion kroner ($328 million) worth of products every year.[11]

Our second inspirational example concerns the Muslim taxi drivers of Minnesota. In contrast to the first example, their individual sacrifice was far more important because it involved a choice between haram and halal. As mentioned earlier, several Muslim taxi drivers were in the limelight for refusing to transport passengers who were carrying alcohol. This was significant because approximately three-quarters of the 900 taxi drivers who served the Minneapolis–St. Paul area were Muslims. Subsequently, the airports commission began discussions with the Muslim American Society in order to find a solution; it proposed that coloured lights be displayed on top of taxis whose drivers were willing to transport alcohol.[12]

Many Muslims advocate change that is far more fundamental than these incremental advances. They argue that these efforts are superficial; they are not prescribed directly in the Sunnah and they

---

[11] Hasan and Tago, "Boycott of Danish Goods," *Arab News*, January 27, 2006.

[12] Lydersen, "Some Muslim Cabbies Refuse Fares Carrying Alcohol," *The Washington Post*, October 26, 2006, accessed October 23, 2011, http://www.washingtonpost.com/wp-dyn/content/article/2006/10/25/AR2006102501727.html.

only partially fulfil Islamic rules, thus they are not sustainable. Indeed, the boycott of products did not stop the publication of more cartoons attacking Islam and mocking the Prophet (ﷺ), nor did it prevent offensive Dutch films or genocide in Gaza. In Minnesota, the airport commission ended up withdrawing their proposal. Still, Muslims will be rewarded inshallah for their efforts to uphold the rules that Allah has enjoined, regardless of the outcome.

(سورة الزلزلة: ٧)   ﴿ فَمَن يَعْمَلْ مِثْقَالَ ذَرَّةٍ خَيْرًا يَرَهُ ۝ ﴾

﴾So whoever does good equal to the weight of an atom shall see it.﴿
(Qur'an 99: 7)

In many cases, Muslims who have firmly resolved to stay away from the haram face situations in which they see no other option. Giving bribes is a serious sin, yet in many situations, Muslims reach a stalemate where they cannot obtain their rights without bribing certain officials. 'Abdullâh ibn 'Amr (ﵟ) narrated:

«The Messenger of Allah (ﷺ) cursed the one who gives a bribe and the one who takes it.» (Aḥmad and Abu Dâwood; the grade for this hadith is acceptable)

If one can achieve the objective without paying a bribe, then he or she should do so. However, scholars have stated that it is permissible to give a bribe when one's rights cannot be obtained in any other way.[13]

The Messenger of Allah (ﷺ) said:

«One of them asks me for something and I give it to him, and he goes out with it, carrying it under his arm, and it is nothing but fire for him. 'Umar (ﵟ) asked: O Messenger of Allah, why do you give it to them?

He replied: They insist on asking me, and Allah insists that I should not be stingy.» (Aḥmad; al-Albâni graded it as sound)

---

[13] "Paying a bribe in order to get one's rights," Islam-QA.com, accessed November 2, 2011, http://www.islam-qa.com/en/ref/72268.

CHAPTER FIVE

FINANCE
AND ACCOUNTING

𝒥t has been estimated that the Islamic banking and finance industry manages over $800 billion in Sharia-compliant assets. It is a rapidly growing sector that has gained popularity in unexpected places; even large global conventional banks like HSBC now offer Islamic banking services. The Vatican has endorsed Islamic banking, suggesting that "the ethical principles on which Islamic finance is based may bring banks closer to their clients and to the true spirit which should mark every financial service."[1]

Sadly, Muslims themselves have not fully embraced Islamic banking and finance. This is surprising when one considers the severity of the warning against ribâ (upon which conventional banking is based):

﴿ يَـٰٓأَيُّهَا ٱلَّذِينَ ءَامَنُوا۟ ٱتَّقُوا۟ ٱللَّهَ وَذَرُوا۟ مَا بَقِىَ مِنَ ٱلرِّبَوٰٓا۟ إِن كُنتُم مُّؤْمِنِينَ ۝ فَإِن لَّمْ تَفْعَلُوا۟ فَأْذَنُوا۟ بِحَرْبٍ مِّنَ ٱللَّهِ وَرَسُولِهِۦ ۖ وَإِن تُبْتُمْ فَلَكُمْ رُءُوسُ أَمْوَٰلِكُمْ ... ۝ ﴾

(سورة البقرة: ٢٧٨-٢٧٩)

---

[1] Tataro, "Vatican Says Islamic Finance May Help Western Banks in Crisis," *Bloomberg.com*, March 4, 2009, accessed October 23, 2011, http://www.bloomberg.com/apps/news?pid=20601092&sid=aOsOLE8uiNOg&refer=italy.

❦O you who believe! Be afraid of Allah and give up what remains [due to you] from ribâ, if you are believers. If you do not do it, then take a notice of war from Allah and His Messenger; but if you repent, you shall have your capital sums...❧   *(Qur'an 2: 278-279)*

It can only be ignorance that prevents Muslims from choosing Islamic finance over conventional banking, for Islamic banking is a solution that both supports the practice of Islam and caters to modern banking needs.

The primary aspect of this ignorance concerns ribâ itself. In casual surveys, it is common to find Muslims who cannot define ribâ, not even in abstract terms or by means of examples. Some wrongly interpret ribâ to mean interest; others consider it to be usury, or excessive interest. This lack of knowledge about ribâ leads Muslims to casually draw dangerous conclusions about the permissibility of ribâ-based conventional banking. We shall see shortly what ribâ means in today's economic context, but to set the backdrop for that discussion, we first present an overview of the finance function of business administration.

Finance

If we return to the box model of a business that we introduced in Chapter Two, we are reminded that the core component of any business is the production engine (which was a bakery in our example). This engine requires input (in the form of raw materials and resources, including capital) to produce any output (products). Rarely does a business have all the necessary inputs on hand; most businesses will need to acquire them.

It is not surprising that one of the preliminary tasks of business administration is to gather financial resources to invest in the new company. Often this investment does not come directly from the owners; instead, they raise capital through such financing activities as taking out bank loans, offering bonds, or selling shares.

Financing is based on the simple concept of the time value of money. A dollar earned today is worth more than a dollar earned tomorrow. Even without a technical explanation of its causes, one can easily appreciate the time value of money since almost anyone living within an economy is aware of inflation.[2] Many refer to the time value of money as interest. The idea that finance is based on interest is actually quite simple: on the one hand, there are those (like business owners) who need financing; on the other hand, there are those who have money that they do not need immediately. A win-win solution is for those without an immediate need to offer their funds to those who need it, in return for compensation known as interest, which at the very least should cover the time value of the money.

Over time, specialized businesses, namely banks, have emerged to facilitate these transactions. Business owners no longer need to find investors; they can simply seek financing from the banks. To attract individuals who have funds to spare in the short term, banks provide interest-bearing opportunities such as savings accounts. Such arrangements are prohibited in the Sharia as they involve forbidden ribâ.

Islam does not prohibit those seeking investment and those seeking to invest from engaging in transactions, though. In fact, Islam encourages investment by discouraging hoarding.

﴿ ۞ يَـٰٓأَيُّهَا ٱلَّذِينَ ءَامَنُوٓاْ إِنَّ كَثِيرًا مِّنَ ٱلۡأَحۡبَارِ وَٱلرُّهۡبَانِ لَيَأۡكُلُونَ أَمۡوَٰلَ ٱلنَّاسِ بِٱلۡبَـٰطِلِ وَيَصُدُّونَ عَن سَبِيلِ ٱللَّهِۗ وَٱلَّذِينَ يَكۡنِزُونَ ٱلذَّهَبَ وَٱلۡفِضَّةَ وَلَا يُنفِقُونَهَا فِى سَبِيلِ ٱللَّهِ فَبَشِّرۡهُم بِعَذَابٍ أَلِيمٖ ۝ يَوۡمَ يُحۡمَىٰ

---

[2] One simple technical example is uncertainty about the future. A dollar collected today is worth more than a dollar collected tomorrow because we do not know what might happen tomorrow; we may not be able to collect the dollar tomorrow due to, say, bad weather. By the same token, we might prefer one immediate payment of $5,000 instead of a promised payment of even $6,000 after six months.

عَلَيْهَا فِي نَارِ جَهَنَّمَ فَتُكْوَىٰ بِهَا جِبَاهُهُمْ وَجُنُوبُهُمْ وَظُهُورُهُمْ ۖ هَٰذَا مَا

كَنَزْتُمْ لِأَنْفُسِكُمْ فَذُوقُوا مَا كُنتُمْ تَكْنِزُونَ ﴿٣٥﴾ ﴾   (سورة التوبة: ٣٤-٣٥)

《O you who believe! Verily, there are many of the rabbis and the monks who devour the wealth of humankind in falsehood, and hinder [them] from the way of Allah. And those who hoard gold and silver, and spend it not in the way of Allah, announce unto them a painful torment on the day when that will be heated in the fire of hell and with it will be branded their foreheads, their flanks, and their backs [and it will be said unto them]: This is the treasure which you hoarded for yourselves. Now taste of what you used to hoard.》

(Qur'an 9: 34-35)

﴿وَيْلٌ لِكُلِّ هُمَزَةٍ لُمَزَةٍ ﴿١﴾ ٱلَّذِى جَمَعَ مَالًا وَعَدَّدَهُ ﴿٢﴾ يَحْسَبُ أَنَّ مَالَهُۥٓ

أَخْلَدَهُۥ ﴿٣﴾ كَلَّا ۖ لَيُنۢبَذَنَّ فِى ٱلْحُطَمَةِ ﴿٤﴾ وَمَآ أَدْرَىٰكَ مَا ٱلْحُطَمَةُ ﴿٥﴾ نَارُ ٱللَّهِ

ٱلْمُوقَدَةُ ﴿٦﴾ ٱلَّتِى تَطَّلِعُ عَلَى ٱلْأَفْـِٔدَةِ ﴿٧﴾ إِنَّهَا عَلَيْهِم مُّؤْصَدَةٌ ﴿٨﴾ فِى عَمَدٍ مُّمَدَّدَةٍ

﴿٩﴾ ﴾   (سورة الهُمَزة: ١-٩)

《Woe to every slanderer and backbiter who has gathered wealth and counted it. He thinks that his wealth will make him last forever! Nay! Verily, he will be thrown into the crushing fire. And what will make you know what the crushing fire is? The fire of Allah, kindled, which leaps up over the hearts. Verily, it shall be closed in upon them, in pillars stretched forth.》   *(Qur'an 104: 1-9)*

There are no rulings in Islam that prohibit the establishment of banks or other businesses that facilitate these transactions. How, then, can we resolve the apparent contradiction that Islam encourages investment but discourages traditional banking? The answer is simple. By allowing the forbidden ribâ, traditional banking offers returns to investors without exposing them to any risk. Islamic banking, on the other hand, does not allow zero-risk arrangements such as interest-bearing accounts.[3]

Islamic banking results in equitable risk-sharing, since it leaves investment (with its associated risk) as the only option for individuals wishing to increase their wealth.

Islamic finance

Islamic banking (and finance) is a vast topic whose discussion requires an in-depth treatment that is beyond the scope of this book.[4] I encourage readers to research the topic, albeit with an important cautionary note: Today it is quite common to find financing activities that have received the blessings of shaykhs even though they somehow include ribâ. This should not be surprising, particularly if one realizes that the love of money and the fear of poverty can be a fatal combination for one's deen.

﴿ ٱلشَّيْطَٰنُ يَعِدُكُمُ ٱلْفَقْرَ وَيَأْمُرُكُم بِٱلْفَحْشَآءِ وَٱللَّهُ يَعِدُكُم مَّغْفِرَةً مِّنْهُ وَفَضْلًا وَٱللَّهُ وَٰسِعٌ عَلِيمٌ ﴿٢٦٨﴾ ﴾ (سورة البقرة: ٢٦٨)

❨Satan threatens you with poverty and orders you to immorality, whereas Allah promises you forgiveness from Himself and bounty, and Allah is All-Sufficient for His creatures' needs, the All-Knower.❩

(Qur'an 2: 268)

---

[3] Admittedly, interest-bearing accounts are not exactly zero-risk arrangements, as there is always some risk. A bank, for example, may go bankrupt or engage in fraud, thus introducing risks. Still, contractually at least, much risk is avoided in interest-bearing investments, particularly in comparison to profit-bearing investments that carry market risk.

[4] A contemporary book, written by the recognized expert Prof. Mahmoud El-Gamal of Rice University, is titled *Islamic Finance – Law, Economics and Practice*. His primer on Islamic finance, *A Basic Guide to Contemporary Islamic Banking and Finance,* is an excellent introduction for the novice reader.

﴿ٱلۡمَالُ وَٱلۡبَنُونَ زِينَةُ ٱلۡحَيَوٰةِ ٱلدُّنۡيَا ۖ وَٱلۡبَٰقِيَٰتُ ٱلصَّٰلِحَٰتُ خَيۡرٌ عِندَ رَبِّكَ ثَوَابٗا وَخَيۡرٌ أَمَلٗا ﴾ ٤٦

(سورة الكهف: ٤٦)

﴾Wealth and children are the adornment of the life of this world. But the good righteous deeds that last are better with your Lord for rewards and better in respect of hope.﴿   *(Qur'an 18: 46)*

﴿ قَالَ رَبِّ بِمَآ أَغۡوَيۡتَنِى لَأُزَيِّنَنَّ لَهُمۡ فِى ٱلۡأَرۡضِ وَلَأُغۡوِيَنَّهُمۡ أَجۡمَعِينَ ٣٩ إِلَّا عِبَادَكَ مِنۡهُمُ ٱلۡمُخۡلَصِينَ ٤٠ ﴾

(سورة الحجر: ٣٩-٤٠)

﴾[Satan] said: O my Lord! Because You misled me, I shall indeed adorn the path of error for them [humankind] on the earth, and I shall mislead them all except Your chosen [guided] slaves among them.﴿   *(Qur'an 15: 39-40)*

At the same time, it is true that Islamic finance is a highly relevant topic, and nearly every Muslim today will benefit by gaining knowledge about it. In this book, we will present some of the salient features of Islamic finance, with two objectives.

First, we hope, inshallah, that readers gain enough basic knowledge to be able to recognize ribâ as it appears in modern transactions and subsequently to perform their own assessment of Islamic finance when necessary. Secondly, we hope that they will be encouraged to continue learning about this important topic by studying the vast literature available, using a refined lens.

A question that frequently arises among both sincere Muslims and sceptics is whether there really are fundamental differences between Islamic and conventional banking, or whether the former is simply window dressing and a deceitful appeal to Muslim sentiments. They also ask a related question: Is Islamic banking (and finance) in itself halal?

To answer either question, we first need to understand what is meant by the ribâ that Allah has made strictly haram; with that understanding, we can then determine whether or not there are any fundamental differences between Islamic and conventional forms of banking.

I will borrow an example from Professor El-Gamal. A marriage is a marriage; it is the union of a man and a woman, which involves commitments, rights, and responsibilities. A Muslim marriage, however, has conditions that are different from those in Jewish or Christian marriages, and Islam recognizes the marriage only if those conditions are fulfilled. By the same token, Islamic and conventional banking may appear similar on the surface, but Islamic banking has certain conditions that make it fundamentally different.

What is ribâ?

Allah has strictly forbidden ribâ in the Qur'an:

(سورة البقرة: ٢٧٥) ﴿ ... وَأَحَلَّ ٱللَّهُ ٱلْبَيْعَ وَحَرَّمَ ٱلرِّبَوٰاْ ... ۝ ﴾

❨...Allah has permitted trading and forbidden ribâ...❩

(Qur'an 2: 275)

﴿ يَٰٓأَيُّهَا ٱلَّذِينَ ءَامَنُوٓاْ ٱتَّقُواْ ٱللَّهَ وَذَرُواْ مَا بَقِيَ مِنَ ٱلرِّبَوٰٓاْ إِن كُنتُم مُّؤْمِنِينَ ۝ فَإِن لَّمْ تَفْعَلُواْ فَأْذَنُواْ بِحَرْبٍ مِّنَ ٱللَّهِ وَرَسُولِهِۦ ۖ وَإِن تُبْتُمْ فَلَكُمْ رُءُوسُ أَمْوَٰلِكُمْ ... ۝ ﴾

(سورة البقرة: ٢٧٨-٢٧٩)

❨O you who believe! Be afraid of Allah and give up what remains [due to you] from ribâ, if you are believers. If you do not do it, then take a notice of war from Allah and His Messenger; but if you repent, you shall have your capital sums...❩ *(Qur'an 2: 278-279)*

What exactly is ribâ? Is it the same as the concept of interest in contemporary finance? To answer this question, we must look at the Sharia-based definition of ribâ, which is clear from the following hadiths.

Abu Sa'eed al-Khudri (⌘) reported that the Messenger of Allah (⌘) said:

«Gold for gold, silver for silver, wheat for wheat, barley for barley, dates for dates, and salt for salt, like for like, hand to hand, in equal amounts; any increase is ribâ.» (Muslim)

«Abu Sa'eed al-Khudri (⌘) also reported that Bilâl (⌘) visited the Messenger of Allah (⌘) with some high quality dates, and the Prophet (⌘) inquired about their source. Bilâl explained that he had traded two units of lower quality dates for one unit of higher quality.

The Messenger of Allah (⌘) said: This is precisely the forbidden ribâ! Do not do this. Instead, sell the first type of dates and use the proceeds to buy the other.» (Muslim)

From the hadiths above, we learn several important points regarding the definition of ribâ. Many Muslims argue that ribâ refers to medieval practices of excessive interest (or usury) that entrapped the poor in endless cycles of debt; they insist that the interest found in contemporary banking, with its lower rates, is not ribâ but is instead an innocuous tool for facilitating trade. Some also make the case that interest is a tool for abolishing poverty, as in the case of micro-credit, where the poor receive interest-based loans.

All these arguments are rendered baseless if one simply considers the second hadith above. If ribâ referred only to a demonic concept used to ensnare the poor, and it excluded such benevolent forms as the interest found in contemporary banking, then Bilâl (⌘) would not have made the mistake. Clearly, exchanging two bags of poorer quality dates for one bag of higher quality dates is not ethically questionable. It is an act that is apparently as harmless as the fixed nominal rate of return associated with a savings account, yet the Prophet (⌘) called it «precisely the forbidden ribâ».

The fact that the Prophet (⌘) had to help Bilâl, one of the most God-fearing men who ever lived, to recognize ribâ proves that its evil is not innately understood. Rather, it is an Islamic prescription from the Creator that has to be accepted unconditionally. Allah helps the believers to appreciate the evil of ribâ by mentioning it in terms that any human being can understand.

Abu Hurayrah (ﷺ) reported that the Messenger of Allah (ﷺ) said:

«Ribâ is of seventy different kinds, the least grave being equivalent to a man marrying (that is, having sexual intercourse with) his own mother.» (Ibn Mâjah; a sound hadith according to al-Albâni)

As we stated earlier, there is a common misconception that ribâ is identical to interest; another is that interest is not considered to be the haram ribâ. The correct concept is that ribâ is haram, whereas the time value of money is simply an element of a 'natural' phenomenon, to which the issue of legality is quite irrelevant. If interest refers to the time value of money, it is not haram in itself; however, if it refers to the surplus received for providing a loan – even if it is for the sake of the time value of money – it is clearly haram, whether that surplus is measured in pennies or in billions of dollars, and whether it is earned at a fixed or a floating rate.

To help explain this difference, suppose Ahmed wants to sell his car today for $4,000. Jamal would like to purchase this car, but he has only $1,000 now. Jamal is employed and can afford to save $300 a month; at that rate, he will need to wait almost a year before he can save enough to buy the car. If Ahmed agrees, Jamal can instead pay him $1,000 as a down payment and then follow it up with twelve monthly payments of $300 each, resulting in a total price of $4,600. Despite the increase of $600 in the price, Ahmed can agree to this arrangement because there is no ribâ involved.

But perhaps Ahmed is not willing to sell the item in instalments, despite the opportunity to charge $600 (or even more) for that privilege. Jamal needs the car, so in an alternative (and more common) arrangement, he goes to a bank, which provides him with $4,000 in cash after he pays them $1,000. Next, Jamal pays the bank $300 a month for twelve months (for a total of $3,600), so the total interest he pays to the bank is $600. This arrangement involves ribâ because Jamal and the bank exchanged money in different amounts; that difference is ribâ.

Despite their differences – with the most significant difference being that one form is halal and the other haram – many argue that the two transactions are the same. Indeed, in both cases, Jamal was charged the exact same amount for the time value of money: $600.

The main difference between the two arrangements is that in the former, the **price paid for the car** has changed to account for the time value of money, whereas in the latter, the **amount of money exchanged** between the parties has changed to account for that same time value of money.

With the halal arrangement, Ahmed (the seller) shares in the risk, whereas with the haram arrangement, Jamal (the buyer) bears all the risk himself. In the halal arrangement, Ahmed has to wait twelve months to receive the full payment for his car; this is risky for him due to the inherent uncertainty of the future. For example, Jamal might later be unable to make his payments after losing his job due to unforeseeable circumstances.

In contrast, with the haram arrangement, the risks associated with future uncertainty do not affect Ahmed because he receives the full payment from the bank upfront. Only Jamal suffers if he is unable to make the payments.

Some argue that Islamic financing is surreptitiously similar to conventional financing and merely introduces unnecessary impediments to trade. However, Allah has specified:

﴿ٱلَّذِينَ يَأْكُلُونَ ٱلرِّبَوٰا۟ لَا يَقُومُونَ إِلَّا كَمَا يَقُومُ ٱلَّذِى يَتَخَبَّطُهُ ٱلشَّيْطَـٰنُ مِنَ ٱلْمَسِّ ذَٰلِكَ بِأَنَّهُمْ قَالُوٓا۟ إِنَّمَا ٱلْبَيْعُ مِثْلُ ٱلرِّبَوٰا۟ وَأَحَلَّ ٱللَّهُ ٱلْبَيْعَ وَحَرَّمَ ٱلرِّبَوٰا۟ فَمَن جَآءَهُۥ

مَوْعِظَةٌ مِّن رَّبِّهِۦ فَٱنتَهَىٰ فَلَهُۥ مَا سَلَفَ وَأَمْرُهُۥٓ إِلَى ٱللَّهِ وَمَنْ عَادَ فَأُوْلَٰٓئِكَ أَصْحَٰبُ

ٱلنَّارِ هُمْ فِيهَا خَٰلِدُونَ ﴿٢٧٥﴾

❴Those who eat ribâ will not stand [on the Day of Resurrection] except like the standing of a person beaten by Satan leading him to insanity. That is because they say: Trading is only like ribâ, whereas Allah has permitted trading and forbidden ribâ. So whosoever receives an admonition from his Lord and stops eating ribâ shall not be punished for the past; his case is for Allah [to judge]; but whoever returns [to ribâ], such are the dwellers of the fire – they will abide therein forever.❵

(Qur'an 2: 275)

If we consider again the hadith about Bilâl and the dates, we can see that Islamic financing is not simply an artificial route to cater to the sentiments and needs of modern Muslims without actually differing from conventional banking. The Prophet (ﷺ) forbade us from exchanging dates of different qualities in different amounts because that involves ribâ. He asked us to sell one kind and then use the proceeds to purchase another kind.

The fact that Islam forbids ribâ means that many business practices, and some business models themselves, are haram. Conventional banking is based entirely on the exchange of money in different amounts in the form of interest, and this is ribâ. Thus, Muslims should abstain from founding, purchasing, or operating conventional banks.

Many jewellery stores are willing to exchange 'old' gold for 'new' gold in different weights, adjusting for the remainder in cash. In the halal system, the 'old' gold should first be sold and then the proceeds used to purchase 'new' gold.

An interesting example of ribâ appears under the guise of Islamic finance. Islamic banks nowadays offer credit cards, and for the convenience of using these credit cards, they charge a nominal, fixed annual fee and a per-service charge. The problem is that even though there is no interest charged, the service fee fits the definition of ribâ. That is because the banks are essentially giving loans to the customers, who are repaying a different (larger) amount. The most common arguments in favour of this are:

1. The amount of the service charge is small.
2. The amount of the service charge does not vary according to the transaction and thus is not interest.
3. The bank is not charging for the loan; it is simply charging for the convenience.
4. The bank does not profit from the service charge, which is used only to cover operating costs.

Based on our discussion thus far, we already know that points 1 and 2 are irrelevant. Regarding point 3, the argument is quite simple. It is not permissible to provide a convenience or a service that includes the haram, whether it is ribâ, adultery, or anything else.[5] It is established that the service includes something haram, so it is ironic that a bank would be interested in offering a haram service from which it does not profit. Thus, point 4 is not applicable.

Interestingly, there are arrangements under which the bank can charge for a service but avoid the haram ribâ. If the bank offers prepaid credit cards or debit cards, with which it does not provide a loan, then it can charge a service fee for them without fear of ribâ. This is analogous to paying the travel expenses of a messenger who delivers valuables to a client and then receives the payment and brings it back. The bank need not maintain a fixed rate for the service fee, and it can even profit from the transactions. (Indeed, trade and ribâ are distinct.)

---

[5] A reviewer pointed out that there may be an exception in the case of a fixed fee charged only for the (separate) service of convenient electronic payments. There may still be other reasons to avoid this: these fees may easily become a vehicle for ribâ, inadvertently or otherwise, and it may be difficult to make a distinction between the service of a loan and that of an electronic payment.

In cases where the bank would like to lend credit to the buyers, it can direct the operating expenses to the vendors (who do not want to lose the business of Muslim customers). In fact, it has long been a standard practice to charge vendors for the additional costs associated with a credit card sale.

Our credit card example is useful for highlighting an important point: Not all Islamic financing activities are actually halal, even though they may carry the label. In recent years, a huge demand for Islamic banking has emerged. While this is a good trend, alḥamdulillâh, it has unfortunately led to the development of Islamic banking practices that were the result of rushed Islamization of haram financial products, without due reflection on their permissibility. Even more sadly, many Islamic jurists have unwittingly provided religious rulings that validate these products. We will mention two such products.

The first comes under the label of 'Islamic bonds', or sukuk.[6] To provide some background, we will first explain what the term 'bond' means in conventional finance. Two of the options that businesses have for raising capital are issuing equity shares and issuing bonds. Equity shares offer ownership of shares in the business, whereas bonds are simply interest-based loans. Even without any detailed analysis, it is easy to recognize that equity shares are generally the more halal option, since interest-based loans are categorically haram. It should come as no surprise that many consider Islamic bonds to be controversial.

In the case of sukuk, the bond issuer sells some asset to a special purpose vehicle (SPV), which in turn sells share certificates. The SPV then leases the assets back to the issuer and passes on lease payments to the sukuk holders, who in turn are earning the 'rent'. At the end

---

[6] El-Gamal, "Incoherent pietism and Sharia arbitrage," *Financial Times*, May 23, 2007.

of the lease, the SPV sells the same property back to the bond issuer. Sukuk are thus based on ownership, making them clearly distinct from conventional bonds; as such, they are meant to offer the investment benefits of bonds while remaining within the framework of the Sharia.

Some forms of sukuk, however, are considered by many scholars to be a deception. The well-known Islamic finance scholar Mufti Taqi Usmani has noted that many forms of sukuk in the market do not confer true ownership but merely offer a right to returns. In that case, the transaction between sukuk holders and the firm will include ribâ. Also, if sukuk contracts take the form of a credit-based sale (*murâbahah*) instead of a lease (*ijârah*), then the controversial issue of the sale of credit arises whenever the sukuk certificates are bought and sold.[7]

Our second example of controversial Islamic finance products involves the haram forms of *tawarruq*.[8] In tawarruq, one buys an item from the bank in instalments and then delegates the bank to sell it for cash. The objective is to allow Muslims to attain cash loans from banks, but this transaction is haram if the borrowers do not actually possess the goods that they purchase from the bank. Many scholars have stated that, like sukuk, this is a form of deception.

It appears that in both of the examples given, there is a shameless attempt to circumvent Islamic rulings, leveraging loose morals to falsely identify loopholes. Islamic finance is not unique in being a

---

[7]   There are many other arguments that sukuk involves deception. Returns, for example, are frequently fixed-rate (based on the London Interbank Offered Rate, or LIBOR) and guaranteed. For further information, refer to "Mufti Taqi Usmani's critique of contemporary Sukuk issues," Islamic Finance Resource, May 11, 2008, accessed October 23, 2011, http://ifresource.com/2008/05/11/mufti-taqi-usmanis-critique-of-contemporary-sukuk-issues.

[8]   For further details, see Islam Q&A, "Tawarruq via the bank and differences in fatwas concerning it from fiqh councils and banks' scholars," Islam-QA.com, accessed November 2, 2011, http://www.islam-qa.com/en/ref/98124.

victim of this approach based on ill intentions. Some married couples, for example, choose to transfer all of their wealth from one spouse to the other every eleven lunar months, so as to evade the requirement of zakâh. Many of them even argue that the transaction costs they are charged are proof of their fear of Allah. However, Allah has commanded:

﴿يَٰٓأَيُّهَا ٱلَّذِينَ ءَامَنُوا۟ ٱتَّقُوا۟ ٱللَّهَ حَقَّ تُقَاتِهِۦ وَلَا تَمُوتُنَّ إِلَّا وَأَنتُم مُّسۡلِمُونَ ۝﴾

(سورة آل عمران: ١٠٢)

❴O you who believe! Fear Allah [by doing all that He has ordered and by abstaining from all that He has forbidden] **as** He should be feared, and die not except in a state of Islam.❵   *(Qur'an 3: 102)*

The search for loopholes is a method that Satan uses to deceive Muslims.

﴿ يَٰٓأَيُّهَا ٱلنَّاسُ ٱتَّقُوا۟ رَبَّكُمۡ وَٱخۡشَوۡا۟ يَوۡمًا لَّا يَجۡزِى وَالِدٌ عَن وَلَدِهِۦ وَلَا مَوۡلُودٌ هُوَ جَازٍ عَن وَالِدِهِۦ شَيۡـًٔا إِنَّ وَعۡدَ ٱللَّهِ حَقٌّ فَلَا تَغُرَّنَّكُمُ ٱلۡحَيَوٰةُ ٱلدُّنۡيَا وَلَا يَغُرَّنَّكُم بِٱللَّهِ ٱلۡغَرُورُ ۝ ﴾

(سورة لقمان: ٣٣)

❴O humankind! Be afraid of your Lord, and fear a day when no father can avail aught for his son, nor a son avail aught for his father. Verily, the promise of Allah is true, let not then this [worldly] present life deceive you, nor let the chief deceiver [Satan] deceive you about Allah.❵   *(Qur'an 31: 33)*

Muslims should be careful about their religion so that their faith will be free from hypocrisy. Otherwise they risk fooling themselves.

﴿ وَمِنَ ٱلنَّاسِ مَن يَقُولُ ءَامَنَّا بِٱللَّهِ وَبِٱلۡيَوۡمِ ٱلۡأٓخِرِ وَمَا هُم بِمُؤۡمِنِينَ ۝ يُخَٰدِعُونَ ٱللَّهَ وَٱلَّذِينَ ءَامَنُوا۟ وَمَا يَخۡدَعُونَ إِلَّآ أَنفُسَهُمۡ وَمَا يَشۡعُرُونَ ۝ فِى قُلُوبِهِم مَّرَضٌ فَزَادَهُمُ ٱللَّهُ مَرَضًا وَلَهُمۡ عَذَابٌ أَلِيمٌۢ بِمَا كَانُوا۟ يَكۡذِبُونَ ۝ وَإِذَا قِيلَ لَهُمۡ لَا تُفۡسِدُوا۟ فِى ٱلۡأَرۡضِ قَالُوٓا۟ إِنَّمَا نَحۡنُ مُصۡلِحُونَ ۝ أَلَآ إِنَّهُمۡ هُمُ ٱلۡمُفۡسِدُونَ وَلَٰكِن لَّا يَشۡعُرُونَ

وَإِذَا قِيلَ لَهُمْ ءَامِنُوا كَمَا ءَامَنَ ٱلنَّاسُ قَالُوٓا أَنُؤْمِنُ كَمَا ءَامَنَ ٱلسُّفَهَآءُ أَلَآ إِنَّهُمْ هُمُ ٱلسُّفَهَآءُ وَلَٰكِن لَّا يَعْلَمُونَ ﴿١٣﴾ وَإِذَا لَقُوا ٱلَّذِينَ ءَامَنُوا قَالُوٓا ءَامَنَّا وَإِذَا خَلَوْا إِلَىٰ شَيَٰطِينِهِمْ قَالُوٓا إِنَّا مَعَكُمْ إِنَّمَا نَحْنُ مُسْتَهْزِءُونَ ﴿١٤﴾ ٱللَّهُ يَسْتَهْزِئُ بِهِمْ وَيَمُدُّهُمْ فِي طُغْيَٰنِهِمْ يَعْمَهُونَ ﴿١٥﴾ أُوْلَٰٓئِكَ ٱلَّذِينَ ٱشْتَرَوُا ٱلضَّلَٰلَةَ بِٱلْهُدَىٰ فَمَا رَبِحَت تِّجَٰرَتُهُمْ وَمَا كَانُوا مُهْتَدِينَ ﴿١٦﴾

(سورة البقرة: ٨-١٦)

❮And of humankind, there are some [hypocrites] who say: We believe in Allah and the Last Day, while in fact they believe not. They [think to] deceive Allah and those who believe, while they only deceive themselves, and perceive [it] not! In their hearts is a disease [of doubt and hypocrisy], and Allah has increased their disease. A painful torment is theirs because they used to tell lies. And when it is said to them: Make not mischief on the earth, they say: We are only peacemakers. Verily! They are the ones who make mischief, but they perceive not. And when it is said to them [hypocrites]: Believe as the people have believed, they say: Shall we believe as the fools have believed? Verily, they are the fools, but they know not. And when they meet those who believe, they say: We believe, but when they are alone with their devils, they say: Truly, we are with you; verily, we were but mocking. Allah mocks them and gives them increase in their wrong-doings to wander blindly. These are they who have purchased error for guidance, so their commerce was profitless. And they were not guided.❯   *(Qur'an 2: 8-16)*

A few types of contracts have been studied by scholars and deemed to be halal, either through consensus or through analogy. These contracts are frequently referred to by their Arabic names.

- *Murâbaḥah*: adding a profit margin

A few people wrongly believe that adding profit margins, sometimes based on percentages, is haram. This is definitely not the case because the Prophet (ﷺ) allowed the sale of items at a premium (the cost plus a markup). Whether or not the margins are expressed in percentages is merely a matter of preference among equivalent options of mathematical expression.

• *Bay' al-âjil*: credit sales

It is allowed to sell items on credit so that the buyer can pay in instalments. The price must be fixed at the time of the agreement, and the buyer does not actually own the product until the full price is paid.

It was narrated that 'Â'ishah (ﷺ) said:

«The Messenger of Allah (ﷺ) bought some food on credit from a Jewish man, and he gave him a shield of his as collateral.» (Bukhari and Muslim)

Interestingly, sellers are allowed to raise the price for sales on credit;[9] this is the view of Shaykh al-Islâm Ibn Taymiyah and of Imam an-Nawawi. For example, an automobile seller can increase the price of a car from \$10,000 to \$12,000 if the buyer would like to pay in instalments, and that difference of \$2,000 is considered profit. It is not ribâ because there was no exchange of money (or any of the commodities mentioned in the relevant hadith) in unequal amounts; it was the price of the product that changed.

While some may argue that this practice is essentially equivalent to contemporary interest-based financing, it is in fact drastically different. For one thing, in bay' al-âjil, a greater share of the risk is borne by the seller than in the case of contemporary financing.

• *Ijârah*: leasing

One may sell the 'right to use a product' for a specified length of time. Unlike in conventional leasing, the lessor must own the product for the duration of the lease.

• *Mushârakah/mudârabah*: partnership

Partnerships can be used for financing a business. Mudârabah refers to a silent partnership, whereas mushârakah is a full partnership.

---

[9] This is simply because it is a direct application of *murâbahah*.

Criticism of Islamic finance

A major criticism of Islamic finance is that in essence, it only repli-cates conventional finance at (often ridiculously) higher rates. One can start with a simple argument: How is it possible for a Muslim to deposit money in a bank and then simply wait for more money? We have already offered one answer to that question: Muslims who deposit money in a Sharia-compliant bank cannot complain if they find less money after some time. Even if this looks the same, it is in fact different.

The problem is that many individuals assume from that answer that every financial transaction or contract **can** have a Muslim looka-like, although there is no basis for that assumption. Consequently, Muslims search for an Islamic lookalike for every conventional banking product, but a problem arises when they cannot one. Since (by definition) there is no wiggle room with respect to looks, they compromise on the 'Islamicity', resulting in the design of a para-doxical product, albeit with an Arabic name.

Our discussion above, concerning a few forms of un-Islamic prod-ucts or contracts that are offered under the label of Islamic finance, highlights a general problem associated with Islamic finance: that the 'Islamization' of conventional banking frequently defeats the purpose of prohibiting ribâ. Professor Mahmoud El-Gamal, Chair of Islamic Economics, Finance, and Management at Rice University, suggested that the essence of ribâ is the use of credit for profit-making.[10] He writes:

> Unfortunately, people's good intentions have been subverted in Islamic finance toward serving the interest of profit-maximizing multinational banks that have, de facto, rewritten modern Islamic

---

[10] El-Gamal, "Justification and the four-step vicious circle of 'Islamic finance'," *Islam and Economics*, January 23, 2010, http://elgamal.blog-spot.com/2010/01/justification-and-four-step-vicious.html.

jurisprudence to maximize their profitable arbitrage opportunities. Likewise... the very essence of micro finance has been subverted by rent seekers to enrich themselves at the expense of the poor debtors (who may benefit briefly, but will ultimately suffer when the bubble bursts).[11]

El-Gamal also discourages the entry of 'Utopians' (idealists) into Islamic finance. His rather straightforward (and convincing) argument is as follows:

The trend in Islamic finance is one of continued Islamization of conventional banking, with Sharia-compliancy advisors directly benefiting from their rulings as board members. Consequently, much of today's Islamic finance will disenchant 'Utopians' if they enter it. They are then either left to disengage or carry on. If they choose to carry on with a 'young industry fallacy' of eventually turning the industry back on course, they risk endeavouring for a lost cause. More sadly, many carry on because they find it too difficult to disentangle themselves from advanced careers in Islamic finance (that is not always entirely Islamic), from which they earn their livelihood.

Of course, there is also the question of whether or not Islamic financing is actually Islamic in spirit; many traditionalists argue that there was no banking system at the time of the Prophet (ﷺ). This difficult question is best left to qualified scholars who have the requisite knowledge, but we can humbly mention two small points.

1) To begin with, it may be better to engage in small entrepreneurial activities than to invest in growth funds with Islamic banks.

2) Many contemporary scholars argue that the field of Islamic banking and finance today emphasizes form over substance and is therefore targeting the 'wrong' (and perhaps less worthy) goal of designing halal options rather than trying to solve the economic problems in Muslim communities; as a result, in Islamic countries, the

---

[11] El-Gamal, "Microcredit and usury," *Islam and Economics*, August 13, 2009, http://elgamal.blogspot.com/2009/08/microcredit-and-usury.html.

poor still have no access to credit, while the very rich continue to get richer.[12]

Accounting

Although the field of accounting is generally based on 'harder' concepts, there are at least three points worth mentioning in the context of Islamic business administration.

1. The importance of following moral guidelines in practicing accounting cannot be overstated. (The ease with which the energy giant Enron collapsed is a good example of the ill fate of those who engage in fraudulent accounting practices.) Muslims should strive to record information truthfully and should follow the ethical guidelines that are found in Islam.

2. Accounting records must be witnessed by two male witnesses (or one male witness and two female witnesses).[13]

3. Accounting often facilitates ribâ-based transactions, but it is haram to record them because of the well-known hadith of Jâbir (رضي الله عنه), who said:

«The Messenger of Allah cursed the one who consumes ribâ, the one who gives it, the one who writes it down and the one who witnesses it. He said: All of them are equal in sin.» (Muslim)

---

[12] The counter-argument is that the objective of every individual is first and foremost to worship and obey Allah. Thus, designing halal options – whether or not they solve more macro problems like poverty in the Muslim economies – is the first priority. The questions of whether the rich become even richer and whether the poor become even poorer do not take precedence over a Muslim's personal objective to follow halal and avoid haram.

[13] For more information on this ruling, see al-Munajjid, "Why is the witness of two women considered to be equal to the testimony of one man?" Islam-QA.com, accessed November 2, 2011, http://www.islam-qa.com/en/ref/20051.

CHAPTER SIX

HUMAN RESOURCE
MANAGEMENT

﴿وَالتِّينِ وَالزَّيْتُونِ ۞ وَطُورِ سِينِينَ ۞ وَهَٰذَا الْبَلَدِ الْأَمِينِ ۞ لَقَدْ خَلَقْنَا الْإِنسَٰنَ فِي أَحْسَنِ تَقْوِيمٍ ۞ ثُمَّ رَدَدْنَٰهُ أَسْفَلَ سَٰفِلِينَ ۞ إِلَّا الَّذِينَ ءَامَنُوا وَعَمِلُوا الصَّٰلِحَٰتِ فَلَهُمْ أَجْرٌ غَيْرُ مَمْنُونٍ ۞ فَمَا يُكَذِّبُكَ بَعْدُ بِالدِّينِ ۞ أَلَيْسَ اللَّهُ بِأَحْكَمِ الْحَٰكِمِينَ ۞ ﴾

(سورة التين: ١-٨)

«By the fig, and the olive. By Mount Sinai, and by this city of security [Makkah]. Verily, We created humankind of the best stature. Then We reduced him to the lowest of the low. Except those who believe and do righteous deeds, then they shall have a reward without end [paradise]. Then what [or who] causes you to deny the recompense? Is not Allah the best of judges?» *(Qur'an 95: 1-8)*

Although it remains in essence a support function, HR management has become one of the most strategic sets of tasks for businesses today. This is hardly surprising when one considers the potential of human capital. Allah has mentioned:

﴿لَقَدْ خَلَقْنَا الْإِنسَٰنَ فِي أَحْسَنِ تَقْوِيمٍ ۞ ﴾ (سورة التين: ٤)

«Verily, We created humankind of the best stature.» *(Qur'an 95: 4)*

Today, the largest businesses in the world rely heavily on their knowledge workers. For example, software development is arguably the most critical component of Google's production engine, and those who are employed in that field are knowledge workers. Furthermore, given the increasing complexity of business landscapes and increasing levels of competition, effective strategic management is more crucial today than ever before, and this function can only be carried out by capable managers. Finally, economic forces have helped to globalize business models, resulting in a broad exchange of ideas, practices, and even workers. The HR requirements of the IT industry in the United States, for example, have brought about a significant influx of foreign workers to support the needs of businesses.

Just as HR management features significantly in modern businesses, Islam in turn features prominently in HR management. To highlight this, we will consider a recent example.

The infrastructure boom in the Arab Gulf countries is sustained using South Asian migrant workers for whom a few years of working in the Middle East appears to be the only way to ever afford to buy a house and educate their children. Unfortunately, many – if not most – of them arrive in the Gulf only to discover extremely harsh working and living conditions. After they have already taken out high-interest loans to cover their expenses, as well as having been cheated by intermediaries, their plight is thus made worse, with many of them relegated to the status of indentured servants. The situation is exacerbated when their dismal conditions promote further haram acts by encouraging these workers to be disloyal, to cheat and steal, and so on.

Most human rights experts have said that not only governments but also employers have a major role to play.[1] From a purely economic standpoint, profit-maximizing firms have no incentive to change their

---

[1]   Hendawi, "Plight of migrant workers blemishes Dubai's image," *USA Today*, May 25, 2008, accessed October 23, 2011, http://www.usatoday. com/news/world/2008-05-25-3622239990_x.htm.

behaviour, for they are faced with such significant challenges as short-ages of labour supervisors and land. As a result, government interven-tion is necessary. The Dubai government, for example, now requires contractors to deposit salaries electronically into workers' accounts so that they can be monitored more easily. Since direct intervention is often not feasible, authorities have resorted to trying to convince employers that happy, satisfied workers are more productive.

When economic rationale works against humanitarian needs, as in the case of the South Asian migrant workers, it becomes clear that the only solution is to practice Islam. Islam is based upon complete submission, and Muslim contractors should be reminded that their religion is not limited to dietary rules or acts of prayer; acts of oppres-sion can be grievous sins leading to serious negative consequences. Muslim contractors should fear Allah as He should be feared. Often it is only fear of the supreme authority that enables one to turn down profitable opportunities that depend on the exploitation of workers, particularly when the workers have little choice and the authorities cannot intervene.

Thus, the role of Islam in HR management is quite profound. In this chapter, we will consider the functional aspects of this role as well as its implicit influences on Muslim behaviour in general.

It is useful first to understand the function of HR management in business administration. HR management refers to the set of tasks related to the administration of employees, given the strategic objective of gaining a competitive advantage. These tasks include:

1. Setting employment policies

2. Planning for labour requirements

3. Implementing standardized (and fair) recruitment policies

4. Maintaining employment relationships

The strategic objective of HR management makes it distinct from the purely supportive administrative personnel function. The former involves a much more proactive approach than the latter, and it takes into account both short-term and long-term organizational needs. Major topics in HR management include compensation, appraisal, planning, recruitment, development, and legal issues.

Halal and haram careers

It was narrated from al-Miqdâm (ﷺ) that the Messenger of Allah (ﷺ) said:

«No one ever eats anything better than what he has earned with his own hands. The Prophet of Allah, David, used to eat what he had earned with his own hands.» (Bukhari)

Many students of business administration choose to pursue careers in management rather than starting their own businesses, so it is worthwhile to reflect on the issue of halal and haram in careers. As with businesses themselves, there are careers that are halal and careers that are haram.

A few careers are categorically haram. Working in ribâ-based banks, for example, is not halal under any circumstances; this even includes positions that are not directly related to the banking function (such as serving as a security guard).[2] The rationale for this is quite simple. As we saw in the previous chapter, the prohibition of ribâ is severe, as is evident in both the Qur'an and the Sunnah.

«Jâbir narrated: The Messenger of Allah (ﷺ) cursed the one who consumes ribâ, the one who gives it, the one who writes it down, and the one who witnesses it. He said: All of them are equal in sin.» (Muslim)

Commenting on this hadith, an-Nawawi (may Allah have mercy on him) states:

---

[2] al-Barraak, "Working in a riba-based (interest-based) bank," Islam-QA. com, accessed November 2, 2011, http://www.islam-qa.com/en/ref/866.

This is clearly a prohibition of the writing down or witnessing of a contract between the two parties involved in a riba-based deal. It also includes a prohibition of helping others to commit wrong acts. And Allaah knows best.[3]

Consequently, scholars have stated that Muslims are not allowed to work in ribâ-based banks because that would involve helping others in transgression.

Other careers have forbidden elements even though the profession in itself may not be haram. For example, teaching business courses at a university may be a halal career in general. However, a Muslim man should not teach in front of an audience that includes women, especially where hijab is not observed, nor should a woman teach in front of an audience that includes men.[4] A Muslim professor should not teach a topic like ribâ, which is taught in many financial derivatives courses, without explaining its true haram nature. Whether or not an individual is allowed to pursue such career paths is context-specific and must be determined on a case-by-case basis.[5]

Some of the jobs regarded by scholars as haram are:

- Working for an Internet Service Provider (ISP) that does not make any effort to block obscene content

- Working for a limousine service that caters to passengers who wish to visit bars

---

[3] an-Nawawi, *Sharḥ an-Nawawi 'alâ Muslim*, 468, quoted in "Working in a riba-based (interest-based) bank," Islam-QA.com, accessed November 2, 2011, http://www.islam-qa.com/en/ref/866.

[4] In the past, even during the time of the Prophet (ﷺ), male teachers taught female students (or mixed groups of males and females), and female teachers taught male students. However, their manners and decorum in such situations differed greatly from what we generally find today. Further, it should be noted that such lessons did not take place on every topic.

[5] Additional information is available from "Prohibited Jobs," Islam-QA.com, accessed November 2, 2011, http://www.islam-qa.com/en/cat/335.

- Working in a non-Muslim seminary[6]
- Working in a tobacco company
- Working in a financial institution that promotes haram financial dealings
- Working in a mixed environment where the etiquettes of proper male-female interaction are not observed

Compensation

Compensation is a critical function of HR management. Islam advocates fairness and justice, but unlike socialism or communism, it does not accommodate artificial methods of achieving perceived forms of justice. Islam does not set minimum or maximum wages; the Islamic philosophy is more likely to lean towards free-market principles,[7] as the following hadith suggests:

«When the prices became high in the Prophet's time and people asked him to fix prices for them, he replied: Allah is the one Who fixes prices, Who withholds, Who gives lavishly, and Who provides, and I hope that when I meet Him, none of you will have a claim against me for any injustice with regard to blood or property.» (Aḥmad and Abu Dâwood; a sound hadith according to al-Albâni)

---

[6] Please refer to "Ruling on teaching in a Christian school," Islam-QA.com, accessed November 2, 2011, http://www.islam-qa.com/en/ref/104002. The fatwa actually mentions the prohibition of teaching secular topics in such institutions; other jobs like cleaning are allowed.

[7] There are exceptions to this free-market approach; this should hardly be surprising given the balanced approach that Islam always advocates. Those exceptions include combating artificial increases in prices by hoarders in supply chains. As for wages, we are more interested in the micro perspective of HR management than in the macro perspective of labour economics and welfare. Clearly the requirement, if any, for price (or wage) control would be much more relaxed for HR managers than for labour policy makers.

Nonetheless, Muslims who set wages are reminded to foster positive relationships between employers and employees. The Prophet (ﷺ) said:

«None of you truly believes until he likes for his brother what he likes for himself.» (Bukhari and Muslim)

Islam emphasizes the importance of fulfilling contracts (by all the parties involved). The wages agreed upon, whether small or large, should be paid promptly and according to the employment contracts. Abu Hurayrah (ﷺ) narrated that the Prophet (ﷺ) said:

«Allah said: I will be an opponent of three types of people on the Day of Resurrection:

one who makes a covenant in My name but proves to be treacherous;

one who sells a free person (as a slave) and consumes his price; and

one who employs a labourer and takes full work from him but does not pay him for his labour.» (Bukhari)

As with other types of contracts in Islam (which we shall discuss in a later chapter), certain guidelines must be followed. The terms of employment should be outlined clearly in order to avoid confusion in the future. The employment contract cannot include excessive gharar, which would render it haram;[8] for example, it should not contain vague terms such as 'if your performance is extraordinary, we will reward you with a healthy bonus.' Finally, it is preferred that labour contracts be written down and agreed upon, preferably in front of witnesses.

Retirement funds are typically part of an employee compensation package, but it is well known that many retirement funds or programs involve ribâ. HR specialists should strive to offer halal options only, and employees should avoid ribâ-based growth funds.

---

[8] 'Gharar' may be translated as ambiguity; it is discussed in greater detail later in the book.

Performance assessment

A major role of HR management is performance assessment. Accurate performance assessment is essential for the long-term health of a business, for a variety of reasons.

– It improves productivity by matching incentives to work; consequently, employees are encouraged to work harder and more sincerely.

– It fosters greater loyalty by encouraging fair practices.

– It allows firms to better place their workers by matching talents and skills.

'Abdullâh ibn 'Amr (رضي الله عنهما) narrated:

«A Bedouin came to the Prophet (ﷺ) and asked: O Allah's Messenger, what are the biggest sins?

He replied: To join others in worship with Allah.

The Bedouin then asked: What is next?

The Prophet (ﷺ) answered: To be undutiful to one's parents.

He inquired again: What is next?

The Prophet (ﷺ) responded: To take an oath of *ghamoos*.

The Bedouin enquired: What is an oath of ghamoos?

The Prophet (ﷺ) explained: The false oath through which one (unjustly) deprives a Muslim of his property.» (Bukhari)

Assessment systems need to be designed to ensure that they offer a high likelihood of capturing the true performance qualities of employees. Those in charge of performance assessment must strive to provide honest evaluations;[9] they must fear Allah and ask Him to forgive any mistakes in their assessment. Assessment is essentially an act of judgement; in Islam, there are merits as well as pitfalls in

---

[9] Perfect assessment is likely to be impossible, unless Allah wishes. One's best effort is necessary so that it is sufficient inshallah – for Allah asks us to fear Him as much as we can. May Allah forgive our mistakes and accept our deeds.

judging.[10] There is a great deal of virtue in being able to judge fairly. It was narrated that 'Ali ibn Abi Ṭâlib (ﷺ) said:

> If the people knew what is involved in judging, they would not judge concerning the price of a piece of camel dung. But the people need judges and rulers, whether they are righteous or immoral.[11]

Allah has instructed:

$$ ﴿ يَـٰٓأَيُّهَا ٱلَّذِينَ ءَامَنُوا۟ لَا تَأْكُلُوٓا۟ أَمْوَٰلَكُم بَيْنَكُم بِٱلْبَٰطِلِ ... ۝ ﴾ $$

(سورة النساء: ٢٩)

﴿O you who believe! Do not eat up your property among yourselves unjustly...﴾
                                                            (Qur'an 4: 29)

It must be noted that while Islam does acknowledge the different ranks of individuals in terms of performance, it also encourages solidarity and brotherhood, as we shall find out shortly.

Nepotism and discrimination

Islam encourages good treatment of fellow Muslims and family members, but it precludes such negative practices as nepotism and discrimination. In many ways, nepotism and discrimination fall under the general definition of deception. Those who practice different forms of deception may actually make short-term gains, but they must realize that Allah is watching all our moves and is the fairest judge. When a candidate is advanced unfairly due to nepotism, deserving candidates are victimized and their rights violated.

Ibn 'Abbâs (ﷺ) narrated that when the Prophet (ﷺ) sent Mu'âdh to Yemen, he said to him:

---

[10] For more information see Islam Q&A, "Trying to avoid being appointed as a judge," Islam-QA.com, accessed November 2, 2011, http://www. islam-qa.com/en/ref/95366.

[11] al-Dabbi, *Akhbaar al-Qudaah.*

«You are going to a nation of the People of the Scripture. The first thing to which you should invite them is the oneness of Allah. If they learn that, tell them that Allah has enjoined on them five prayers to be offered in one day and one night. If they pray, tell them that Allah has enjoined on them the zakâh of their properties; it has to be taken from their rich and given to their poor. If they agree to that, take from them the zakâh, but avoid the best property of the people and safeguard yourself against the supplication of those who have suffered injustice, because there is no veil between their supplications and Allah.» (Bukhari)

This hadith indicates that even when taking properties for zakâh, those in positions of authority need to be wary of being unjust to people. Certainly then, nepotism and discrimination should be avoided if they lead to injustice.

Interestingly, not all forms of discrimination lead to injustice. A society discriminates against convicted criminals while they serve their jail terms and against known sexual predators when recruiting helpers for a daycare centre. Even affirmative action, practiced in many businesses to restore the rights of minorities, is a form of discrimination. Clearly, in some situations discrimination is necessary.

Likewise, Islamic measures to establish social justice may appear to be discriminatory at times, and these practices may be misunderstood by many. For example, Islam may appear to discriminate against women or non-Muslims in some instances. Before one challenges certain practices, it is important to remember that if they are the unquestionable dictates of the Sharia, then the source of wisdom is Allah, the Most Wise, the Most Generous.

Secondly, our Prophet Muhammad (ﷺ) was sent as the best example for us. Thus, his actions, however controversial they may seem in the context of current practices, can never be declared unacceptable. In that sense, Islam does require Muslims to discriminate for the sake of following Allah's commands, which in turn is a requisite for acknowledging tawḥeed al-uloohiyah.

Neglecting to follow these commands can result in the direct negation of one's beliefs. Allah has mentioned the following about the hypocrites who give preference to the disbelievers over the Muslims:[12]

$$ ﴿ ...وَيَقُولُونَ لِلَّذِينَ كَفَرُوا هَٰؤُلَاءِ أَهْدَىٰ مِنَ ٱلَّذِينَ ءَامَنُوا سَبِيلًا ۝ ﴾ $$

(سورة النساء: ٥١)

❨And they say to the disbelievers that they are better guided as regards the way than the believers [Muslims].❩   *(Qur'an 4: 51)*

$$ ﴿ ۝ يَٰأَيُّهَا ٱلَّذِينَ ءَامَنُوا لَا تَتَّخِذُوا ٱلْيَهُودَ وَٱلنَّصَٰرَىٰ أَوْلِيَآءَ بَعْضُهُمْ أَوْلِيَآءُ بَعْضٍ وَمَن يَتَوَلَّهُم مِّنكُمْ فَإِنَّهُۥ مِنْهُمْ... ۝ ﴾ $$

(سورة المائدة: ٥١)

❨O you who believe! Take not the Jews and the Christians as protectors or patrons; they are the protectors and patrons of one another. If any amongst you takes them as protectors and patrons, then surely he is one of them...❩   *(Qur'an 5: 51)*

$$ ﴿ وَدُّوا لَوْ تُدْهِنُ فَيُدْهِنُونَ ۝ ﴾ $$

(سورة القلم: ٩)

❨They wish that you should compromise [in religion out of courtesy] with them, so that they [too] would compromise with you.❩

(Qur'an 68: 9)

It is important to realize some of the benefits of these requirements. Allah's prescription of this perfect religion is part of His mercy to His creation, and he has defined the straight path so that it might lead us to success. Many of the mild forms of discrimination against non-Muslims may nudge them to think about this beautiful religion, which is the only way to succeed in this life and the eternal afterlife. This is

---

[12] "Clarification of the important rule: it is haraam to take kaafirs as close friends and protectors," Islam-QA.com, accessed November 2, 2011, http://www.islam-qa.com/en/ref/2179.

not unlike the situation of a parent engaging in reinforcement, even negative reinforcement, as part of responsible parenting. Those mild forms of discrimination should be combined with appropriate words of invitation to the religion as well as its privileges. For example, one may give gifts to the disbelievers with the aim of softening their hearts towards Islam.[13]

Admittedly, there are some stronger forms of prescribed discrimination in Islam. This is in the light of what Allah, the Most High, has revealed to us concerning the inner secrets of non-Muslims:

﴿ يَٰٓأَيُّهَا ٱلَّذِينَ ءَامَنُوا۟ لَا تَتَّخِذُوا۟ بِطَانَةً مِّن دُونِكُمْ لَا يَأْلُونَكُمْ خَبَالًا ... ﴿١١٨﴾ ﴾

(سورة آل عمران: ١١٨)

❨O you who believe! Take not as [your] advisors or consultants those outside your religion since they will not fail to do their best to corrupt you...❩   *(Qur'an 3: 118)*

Islam does not encourage discrimination against specific individuals; it simply recommends a general policy favouring the Muslims. Such policies are not uncommon in any setting. In the United States, for example, most employment opportunities are limited to those who possess the appropriate residency requirements; many positions preclude the hiring of non-U.S. citizens. Similarly, Islam may require that certain strategic administrative positions are reserved only for Muslims.

Imam Aḥmad reported that Abu Moosâ al-Ash'ari (ﷺ) said: I said to 'Umar: I have a Christian scribe.

He said: What is wrong with you, may Allah strike you dead? Have you not heard the words of Allah:

---

[13] "Accepting a gift from a kaafir on the day of his festival," Islam-QA.com, accessed November 2, 2011, http://islam-qa.com/en/ref/85108.

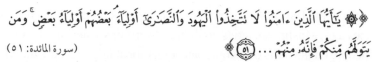

(سورة المائدة: ٥١)

◆O you who believe! Take not the Jews and the Christians as protectors or patrons; they are the protectors and patrons of one another. If any amongst you takes them as protectors and patrons, then surely he is one of them...◆ *(Qur'an 5: 51)*?

Why do you not employ a Muslim?

I explained: O Leader of the Believers, I benefit from his work, and he keeps his religion to himself.

He said: I will never honour them when Allah has humiliated them, and I will never bring them close to me when Allah has expelled them from His mercy.[14]

Another form of positive discrimination in Islam is the fact that women can demand other women when they need doctors, hair dressers, and teachers.

In light of this discussion, it is important to realize that statements that are common in contemporary HR practices may be too arbitrary to be accepted as the benchmark. A good example is the statement that frequently appears in publications by the HR departments of many U.S. firms: **"Company X does not discriminate with respect to race, colour, gender, religion, national origin, sexual orientation, or sexual preference."**

This statement is not appropriate in Islam because discrimination is required in some situations. Nevertheless, it is a profound realization that standards of non-discriminatory practices that were established

---

[14] al-Bayhaqi, *as-Sunan al-Kubrâ*, quoted in "Clarification of the important rule: it is haraam to take kaafirs as close friends and protectors," Islam-QA. com, accessed November 2, 2011, http://www.islam-qa.com/en/ref/2179. According to al-Albâni, its chain of narration is reliable.

only in the last century were part of Islam more than fourteen centuries ago. Muslim societies could not discriminate negatively against people on the basis of colour, race, or national origin. Allah, the Most High, has mentioned:

$$\text{﴿يَـٰٓأَيُّهَا ٱلنَّاسُ إِنَّا خَلَقْنَـٰكُم مِّن ذَكَرٍ وَأُنثَىٰ وَجَعَلْنَـٰكُمْ شُعُوبًا وَقَبَآئِلَ لِتَعَارَفُوٓاْ إِنَّ أَكْرَمَكُمْ عِندَ ٱللَّهِ أَتْقَىٰكُمْ إِنَّ ٱللَّهَ عَلِيمٌ خَبِيرٌ ١٣﴾}$$

(سورة الحُجُرات: ١٣)

❨O humankind! We created you from a male and female, and made you into nations and tribes that you may know one another. Verily, the most honourable of you in the sight of Allah is the most righteous of you. Verily, Allah is the All-Knowing, Well-Acquainted [with all things].❩   *(Qur'an 49: 13)*

The Prophet (ﷺ) said:

«Indeed, there is no excellence for an Arab over a non-Arab, or for a non-Arab over an Arab, or for a fair-skinned person over a dark-skinned one, or for a dark-skinned person over a fair-skinned one, except through piety.» (A sound hadith reported by Aḥmad)

Gender issues: Intermingling

The issue of intermingling between genders has become a hotbed of debate, even among Muslims. As we shall see later, unrestricted intermingling between genders is clearly haram; it is a serious sin that should be avoided. We will begin our discussion, however, by examining five common contemporary arguments against segregation:

1. **"While the hijab is obligatory, segregation is only a cultural practice. In fact, hijab eliminates the need for any kind of segregation."**

    There definitely are Islamic texts that deal with the issue of intermingling, so it is indeed more than just a cultural issue.

2. **There are many instances in the Sunnah where male and female Companions of the Prophet (ﷺ) communicated verbally; thus, intermingling is allowed.**

Islam is a comprehensive religion that commands a balanced approach. Men and women can communicate with each other when necessary, but it is important that they follow the etiquette of communication, which involves hijab, lowering the gaze, and speaking honourably. Allah has instructed:

﴿ يَٰنِسَآءَ ٱلنَّبِيِّ لَسْتُنَّ كَأَحَدٍ مِّنَ ٱلنِّسَآءِ إِنِ ٱتَّقَيْتُنَّ فَلَا تَخْضَعْنَ بِٱلْقَوْلِ فَيَطْمَعَ ٱلَّذِى فِى قَلْبِهِۦ مَرَضٌ وَقُلْنَ قَوْلًا مَّعْرُوفًا ﴿٣٢﴾ ﴾   (سورة الأحزاب: ٣٢)

﴿O wives of the Prophet! You are not like any other women. If you keep your duty [to Allah], then be not soft in speech, lest he in whose heart is a disease should be moved with desire, but speak in an honourable manner.﴾   *(Qur'an 33: 32)*

Some suggest that since this verse is clearly addressing only the wives of the Prophet (ﷺ), who ﴿are not like any other women﴾, that it is not applicable to other women. If one reflects on the verse, though, it is easy to recognize that the wives of the Prophet (ﷺ) are not being singled out with this command to the exclusion of other women. They are mentioned specifically because of their higher status in comparison to other women, but this does not suggest the permissibility of soft speech for other women, for Allah has mentioned that it has the negative effect of provoking evil desires. Communications research has established the concept that 'sex sells'; this is based on the same premise. Not surprisingly, there is not a single example of the Companions (ﷺ), men and women, engaging in casual intermingling. Clearly, intermingling is not compatible with the commands in the following verse:

﴿يَٰٓأَيُّهَا ٱلنَّبِيُّ قُل لِّأَزْوَٰجِكَ وَبَنَاتِكَ وَنِسَآءِ ٱلْمُؤْمِنِينَ يُدْنِينَ عَلَيْهِنَّ مِن جَلَٰبِيبِهِنَّ ذَٰلِكَ أَدْنَىٰٓ أَن يُعْرَفْنَ فَلَا يُؤْذَيْنَ وَكَانَ ٱللَّهُ غَفُورًا رَّحِيمًا ۝﴾

(سورة الأحزاب: ٥٩)

﴿O Prophet! Tell your wives and your daughters and the women of the believers to draw their cloaks [veils] all over their bodies. That will be better, that they should be known [as free, respectable women] so as not to be annoyed. And Allah is Ever Oft-Forgiving, Most Merciful.﴾

(Qur'an 33: 59)

Even though men and women are allowed to communicate honourably when necessary, efforts should be made to find alternatives and to design systems where this is not necessary.

3. **Muslims are not segregated by gender when they perform Hajj, so why should segregation be a requirement in the workplace?**

One must consider that the actions of pilgrims at the Hajj are not always correct and should not be taken as the standard for what is permissible. Also, there are distinct features of the rites of Hajj that may not be applicable at other times.

The Prophet's wife 'Â'ishah (رضي الله عنها) said:

«The riders used to pass by us when we were with the Messenger of Allah (ﷺ) in *ihrâm*[15] (at Hajj). When they came alongside us, we would lower our outer garments from our heads over our faces; when they had passed by, we would uncover them.» (Abu Dâwood; al-Albâni graded it as sound)

The hadith shows that there was no free intermingling of the sexes during Hajj; on the contrary, a great deal of modesty was practiced.

---

[15] *ihrâm:* the state of consecration for Hajj or *'umrah* (the minor pilgrimage); the special clothing worn by the pilgrim in such a state.

4. "Segregation is not practical and therefore is not a necessity in modern times."

To refute this argument, one need only understand the true nature of Islam as described in the earlier chapters. Islam is a complete religion, and it involves complete submission to Allah, the one true God. When Allah orders His creation to do something or refrain from something, they must comply. The Companions of the Prophet (ﷺ) were known for their readiness to accept Allah's commands.

Umm Salamah (ﷺ) said: When the following verse was revealed:

(سورة الأحزاب: ٥٩)   ﴿ ... يُدۡنِينَ عَلَيۡهِنَّ مِن جَلَٰبِيبِهِنَّ ... ٥٩ ﴾

﴿... to draw their cloaks [veils] all over their bodies...﴾

(Qur'an 33: 59)

– the women of the *Anṣâr*[16] came out looking as if there were crows on their heads because of their clothing. (Abu Dâwood; a sound narration according to al-Albâni)

If veiling were a part of medieval Arabian culture, there would have been no change in appearance among the women of the Anṣâr. In reality, they accepted the command of Allah without question, even if it involved adopting a new practice.

5. "Muslims are backwards and have lost their glory because half of their population – the female half – is prevented from being productive."

Any backwardness found among Muslims is due mostly to the fact that they have strayed from the full implementation of their religion. When Muslims believed and obeyed Allah, they constituted a great, leading civilization. This is why there are many

---

[16] *Anṣâr*: 'helpers': the Muslim citizens of Madinah who gave refuge to the Prophet (ﷺ) and the other Muslim emigrants from Makkah.

Muslim women who do not argue for the fall of Islam; rather, they simply want to have their rights under Islam fully returned to them.

There is no activity more meaningful or sublime than worshiping Allah, our Creator. The greatest achievements are rendered meaningless if their path requires deliberate defiance of Allah's orders. Allah has already mentioned worship as the purpose of human life, and a woman's soul is no less valuable than a man's. The means of worship is found in following His commands:

﴿ وَذَكِّرْ فَإِنَّ ٱلذِّكْرَىٰ تَنفَعُ ٱلْمُؤْمِنِينَ ۝ وَمَا خَلَقْتُ ٱلْجِنَّ وَٱلْإِنسَ إِلَّا لِيَعْبُدُونِ ۝ مَآ أُرِيدُ مِنْهُم مِّن رِّزْقٍ وَمَآ أُرِيدُ أَن يُطْعِمُونِ ۝ ﴾

(سورة الذاريات: ٥٥-٥٧)

❨And remind [by preaching the Qur'an, O Muhammad] for verily, the reminding profits the believers. And I [Allah] created not the jinn and humans except that they should worship Me [alone]. I seek not any provision from them, nor do I ask that they should feed Me.❩

(Qur'an 51: 55-57)

﴿ مَنْ عَمِلَ صَٰلِحًا مِّن ذَكَرٍ أَوْ أُنثَىٰ وَهُوَ مُؤْمِنٌ فَلَنُحْيِيَنَّهُۥ حَيَوٰةً طَيِّبَةً وَلَنَجْزِيَنَّهُمْ أَجْرَهُم بِأَحْسَنِ مَا كَانُوا۟ يَعْمَلُونَ ۝ ﴾   (سورة النحل: ٩٧)

❨Whoever works righteousness, whether male or female, while he [or she] is a true believer, verily to him [or her] We will give a good life, and We shall certainly pay them a reward in proportion to the best of what they used to do.❩   *(Qur'an 16: 97)*

﴿فَٱسْتَجَابَ لَهُمْ رَبُّهُمْ أَنِّى لَآ أُضِيعُ عَمَلَ عَٰمِلٍ مِّنكُم مِّن ذَكَرٍ أَوْ أُنثَىٰ بَعْضُكُم مِّنۢ بَعْضٍ ... ۝ ﴾

(سورة آل عمران: ١٩٥)

❨So their Lord accepted of them [their supplication and answered them]: Never will I allow to be lost the work of any of you, be he male or female. You are [members] one of another...❩

(Qur'an 3: 195)

Allah mentions Mary, the mother of Jesus (ﷺ), as a woman He has selected above all women:

﴿ وَإِذْ قَالَتِ ٱلْمَلَٰٓئِكَةُ يَٰمَرْيَمُ إِنَّ ٱللَّهَ ٱصْطَفَىٰكِ وَطَهَّرَكِ وَٱصْطَفَىٰكِ عَلَىٰ نِسَآءِ ٱلْعَٰلَمِينَ ۝ يَٰمَرْيَمُ ٱقْنُتِى لِرَبِّكِ وَٱسْجُدِى وَٱرْكَعِى مَعَ ٱلرَّٰكِعِينَ ۝ ﴾

(سورة آل عمران: ٤٢-٤٣)

﴾And [remember] when the angels said: O Mary! Verily, Allah has chosen you, purified you [from polytheism and disbelief], and chosen you above the women of the worlds. O Mary! Submit yourself with obedience to your Lord and prostrate yourself, and bow down along with those who bow down.﴿ *(Qur'an 3: 42-43)*

﴿ وَضَرَبَ ٱللَّهُ مَثَلًا لِّلَّذِينَ ءَامَنُوا۟ ٱمْرَأَتَ فِرْعَوْنَ إِذْ قَالَتْ رَبِّ ٱبْنِ لِى عِندَكَ بَيْتًا فِى ٱلْجَنَّةِ وَنَجِّنِى مِن فِرْعَوْنَ وَعَمَلِهِ وَنَجِّنِى مِنَ ٱلْقَوْمِ ٱلظَّٰلِمِينَ ۝ وَمَرْيَمَ ٱبْنَتَ عِمْرَٰنَ ٱلَّتِىٓ أَحْصَنَتْ فَرْجَهَا فَنَفَخْنَا فِيهِ مِن رُّوحِنَا وَصَدَّقَتْ بِكَلِمَٰتِ رَبِّهَا وَكُتُبِهِ وَكَانَتْ مِنَ ٱلْقَٰنِتِينَ ۝ ﴾

(سورة التحريم: ١١-١٢)

﴾And Allah has set forth an example for those who believe, the wife of Pharaoh, when she said: My Lord! Build for me a home with You in paradise, and save me from Pharaoh and his work, and save me from the people who are wrongdoers. And Mary, the daughter of 'Imrân who guarded her chastity; and We blew into [her garment] through Our angel [Gabriel], and she testified to the truth of the words of her Lord, and His scriptures, and she was of the devoutly obedient.﴿ *(Qur'an 66: 11-12)*

One can gauge the status of women in Islam from the following verses:

(سورة الذاريات: ٥٦) ﴿ وَمَا خَلَقْتُ ٱلْجِنَّ وَٱلْإِنسَ إِلَّا لِيَعْبُدُونِ ۝ ﴾

﴾And I [Allah] created not the jinn and humans except that they should worship Me [alone].﴿ *(Qur'an 51: 56)*

﴿ مَنْ عَمِلَ صَـٰلِحًا مِّن ذَكَرٍ أَوْ أُنثَىٰ وَهُوَ مُؤْمِنٌ فَلَنُحْيِيَنَّهُۥ حَيَوٰةً طَيِّبَةً وَلَنَجْزِيَنَّهُمْ أَجْرَهُم بِأَحْسَنِ مَا كَانُوا۟ يَعْمَلُونَ ﴿٩٧﴾ ﴾   (سورة النحل: ٩٧)

﴾Whoever works righteousness, whether male or female, while he [or she] is a true believer, verily to him [or her] We will give a good life [in this world with respect, contentment and lawful provision], and We shall certainly pay them a reward in proportion to the best of what they used to do.﴿   *(Qur'an 16: 97)*

﴿فَاسْتَجَابَ لَهُمْ رَبُّهُمْ أَنِّى لَا أُضِيعُ عَمَلَ عَٰمِلٍ مِّنكُم مِّن ذَكَرٍ أَوْ أُنثَىٰ بَعْضُكُم مِّنْ بَعْضٍ ... ﴿١٩٥﴾ ﴾   (سورة آل عمران: ١٩٥)

﴾So their Lord accepted of them [their supplication and answered them]: Never will I allow to be lost the work of any of you, be he male or female. You are [members] one of another...﴿
(Qur'an 3: 195)

Modern business environments, like all places, should be designed to avoid trouble and temptations. Those in authority should lay out policies to prevent their occurrence, and Muslims – both males and females – should stay away from events where flagrant intermingling between the genders occurs.

Segregation to prevent intermingling is a requirement in the mosques, where women's rows are completely separate from men's.

«Ibn 'Umar (رضي الله عنهما) said that Allah's Messenger (ﷺ) said: We should leave this door (of the mosque) for women.

Nâfi' said: Ibn 'Umar never again entered through that door as long as he lived.» (A sound hadith recorded by Abu Dâwood)

Abu Usayd al-Anṣâri (رضي الله عنه) narrated that Allah's Messenger (ﷺ) was leaving the mosque when he saw men and women mixing together on their way home. He said to the women:

«Give way. It is not appropriate for you to walk in the middle of the road.» (Abu Dâwood; a reliable hadith according to al-Albâni)

Scholars have stated that since segregation to prevent intermingling is necessary in the mosques, it must also be necessary elsewhere.[17] Muslim men and women are commanded to lower their gazes:

﴿قُل لِّلۡمُؤۡمِنِينَ يَغُضُّواْ مِنۡ أَبۡصَٰرِهِمۡ وَيَحۡفَظُواْ فُرُوجَهُمۡ ذَٰلِكَ أَزۡكَىٰ لَهُمۡ إِنَّ ٱللَّهَ خَبِيرُۢ بِمَا يَصۡنَعُونَ ۝ وَقُل لِّلۡمُؤۡمِنَٰتِ يَغۡضُضۡنَ مِنۡ أَبۡصَٰرِهِنَّ وَيَحۡفَظۡنَ فُرُوجَهُنَّ وَلَا يُبۡدِينَ زِينَتَهُنَّ إِلَّا مَا ظَهَرَ مِنۡهَا وَلۡيَضۡرِبۡنَ بِخُمُرِهِنَّ عَلَىٰ جُيُوبِهِنَّ وَلَا يُبۡدِينَ زِينَتَهُنَّ إِلَّا لِبُعُولَتِهِنَّ أَوۡ ءَابَآئِهِنَّ أَوۡ ءَابَآءِ بُعُولَتِهِنَّ أَوۡ أَبۡنَآئِهِنَّ أَوۡ أَبۡنَآءِ بُعُولَتِهِنَّ أَوۡ إِخۡوَٰنِهِنَّ أَوۡ بَنِىٓ إِخۡوَٰنِهِنَّ أَوۡ بَنِىٓ أَخَوَٰتِهِنَّ أَوۡ نِسَآئِهِنَّ أَوۡ مَا مَلَكَتۡ أَيۡمَٰنُهُنَّ أَوِ ٱلتَّٰبِعِينَ غَيۡرِ أُوْلِي ٱلۡإِرۡبَةِ مِنَ ٱلرِّجَالِ أَوِ ٱلطِّفۡلِ ٱلَّذِينَ لَمۡ يَظۡهَرُواْ عَلَىٰ عَوۡرَٰتِ ٱلنِّسَآءِ وَلَا يَضۡرِبۡنَ بِأَرۡجُلِهِنَّ لِيُعۡلَمَ مَا يُخۡفِينَ مِن زِينَتِهِنَّ وَتُوبُوٓاْ إِلَى ٱللَّهِ جَمِيعًا أَيُّهَ ٱلۡمُؤۡمِنُونَ لَعَلَّكُمۡ تُفۡلِحُونَ ۝﴾

(سورة النور: ٣٠-٣١)

﴿Tell the believing men to lower their gaze and protect their private parts. That is purer for them. Verily, Allah is All-Aware of what they do. And tell the believing women to lower their gaze, and protect their private parts, and not to show off their adornment except that which is apparent, and to draw their veils all over their bodies and not to reveal their adornment except to their husbands, their fathers, their husband's fathers, their sons, their husband's sons, their brothers or their brother's sons, their sister's sons, their [Muslim] women, or the [female] slaves whom their right hands possess, old male servants who lack vigour, or small children who have no sense of the shame of

---

[17] Please refer to al-Munajjid, "Evidence Prohibiting of Mixing of Men and Women," Islam-QA.com, accessed November 2, 2011, http://www. islam-qa.com/en/ref/1200.

sex. And let them not stamp their feet so as to reveal what they hide of their adornment. And beg Allah to forgive you all, O believers, that you may be successful.﴾   *(Qur'an 24: 30-31)*

It makes great sense, then, to segregate the genders so that this requirement can be easily fulfilled.

Dress codes

Nearly all businesses, Muslim and non-Muslim, have restrictions in place concerning what can and cannot be worn in the workplace. It is appropriate to expect that Muslim businesses will set up guidelines which conform to the Islamic teachings about clothing.

Dress codes should be designated for both men and women. In public areas, women should be required to wear loose outer garments and preferably a face veil.[18] Men should at all times keep their *'awrah*[19] covered and be dressed in dignified outfits that do not imitate non-Muslim styles.[20] In business environments where Muslims and

---

[18] An excellent book on the Muslim woman's dress in accordance with the Qur'an and the Sunnah is al-Albâni, *Jilbâb al-Mara'at al-Muslimah*. The full text is not yet available in English, but excerpts of it have been translated and are available on several trustworthy Islamic websites.
In addition, several reliable printed books and articles in English discuss the topic of the Muslim woman's dress in accordance with the Qur'an and the Sunnah. Please refer to the bibliography for details of the works of Dr. Jamal Badawi and Dr. Muhammad Ali al-Hashimi, for example.

[19] *'awrah:* the part of a person's body that must be screened from public view; for males it is the area between the navel and the knees, and for females it is everything except the hands and the face.

[20] For further information, see "Guidelines on the type of imitation of the mushrikeen that is haraam," Islam-QA.com, accessed November 2, 2011, http://www.islam-qa.com/en/ref/108996. See also "Ruling on imitating the kuffaar, and the meaning of the phrase, 'What the Muslims think is good is good before Allaah'," Islam-QA.com, accessed November 2, 2011, http://www.islam-qa.com/en/ref/45200.

non-Muslims meet, it is better for all involved to lean towards what is more modest.

It was narrated from Abu Sa'eed al-Khudri (ﷺ):

«The Prophet (ﷺ) said: You will certainly follow the ways of those who came before you, hand span by hand span, cubit by cubit, to the extent that if they enter the hole of a lizard, you will enter it too.

We asked: O Messenger of Allah, (do you mean) the Jews and the Christians?

He replied: Who else?» (Bukhari)

It was narrated that 'Abdullâh ibn 'Umar (ﷺ) reported that the Prophet (ﷺ) said:

«Whoever imitates a people is one of them.» (Abu Dâwood; al-Albâni graded it as sound)

Shaykh Ibn al-'Uthaymeen states:

With regard to the phrase "imitation of the [non-Muslims]", that does not mean that we should not use anything that they have manufactured. No one says such a thing. At the time of the Prophet (peace and blessings of Allaah be upon him) and afterwards the people used to wear clothes made by the [non-Muslims] and use vessels made by them.

Imitation of the [non-Muslims] means imitating their clothing and appearance, and the customs that are unique to them. It does not mean that we should not ride what they ride or wear what they wear. But if they ride in a specific way that is unique to them, then we should not ride in that way. If they tailor their clothes in a certain fashion that is unique to them, we should not do likewise. But if we have cars that are similar to theirs and fabric that is similar to theirs, there is nothing wrong with that.[21]

---

[21] Ibn al-'Uthaymeen, *Majmoo' Fatâwâ*, 12, question 177.

Although this is less true today than it was in the 1980s and 1990s, many women, in their efforts to shatter the corporate glass ceilings, dress in pant suits to give the impression of being no different from their male colleagues. In Islam, women should not imitate men and vice versa. On the other end of the spectrum, women must not wear outfits meant to provoke the desires of men.

Work design

A major concern in today's fast-paced business world is that the family lives of many Muslims are being negatively affected. An increasing number of Muslim brothers and sisters have very little time to dedicate to their families after working long hours at the office. Many marriages are ending in divorce because of this neglect of the family or because of the ill effects of working in mixed-gender settings, where spouses may become more attracted to their co-workers than they are to each other.

It is the responsibility of those in HR management to ensure that they are not aggravating such trends. They should create policies that encourage productivity at work but that also allow for sufficient time to be spent with families. Allah has instructed:

$$\text{﴿يَٰٓأَيُّهَا ٱلَّذِينَ ءَامَنُوا۟ قُوٓا۟ أَنفُسَكُمْ وَأَهْلِيكُمْ نَارًا وَقُودُهَا ٱلنَّاسُ وَٱلْحِجَارَةُ ... ٦﴾}$$

(سورة التحريم: ٦)

◆O you who believe! Ward off from yourselves and your families a fire [hell] whose fuel is men and stones...◆   *(Qur'an 66: 6)*

The Prophet (ﷺ) is reported to have said:

«Each of you is a shepherd, and each of you is responsible for his flock. The ruler of the people is a shepherd and is responsible for his flock. A man is the shepherd of his household and is responsible for his flock. A woman is the shepherd of her husband's house and children and is responsible for her flock...» (Bukhari)

Facilitating worship and avoiding evil

In general, HR practitioners should strive to help their fellow Muslims attain objectives in worship, which will in turn allow everyone to enjoy more productivity. Such efforts may include:

1. Daily e-mails reminding employees of Qur'an verses or of hadiths

2. Posters encouraging *dhikr Allâh* (remembering Allah by praising and supplicating got Him) and acts of worship

3. Handbooks and computer applications helping with zakâh calculations

4. Handbooks teaching supplications

5. Avoiding the imitation of cultural practices of the disbelievers such as birthday celebrations and happy hours

6. Arranging conferences and retreats to help employees learn more about their religion

7. Arranging meals to break the fast during Ramadan

The online repository of religious rulings in English, Islam-QA. com, provides a list of twenty-five things that an office worker can do in one minute to earn rewards. Such lists can be compiled for Muslim workers to use during free moments (for instance, while waiting for a meeting to start or when put on hold during a telephone call). Social media technologies like Facebook and Twitter can also be used to remind employees about these opportunities. Here are the first five ideas on the list; the rest are available at the Islam-QA.com website:

1. In one minute you can recite Soorat al-Faatihah 3 times, reciting rapidly and silently. Some scholars said that the reward for reading al-Faatihah is more than 600 hasanahs [rewards or blessings], so if you read it 3 times you will, by the permission of Allaah, gain more than 1800 hasanahs – all of that in one minute.

2. In one minute you can recite Soorat al-Ikhlaas (Qul Huwa Allaahu Ahad) 20 times, reciting rapidly and silently. Reciting it once is equivalent to one-third of the Qur'aan. If you read it 20 times it is equivalent to reading the Qur'aan 7 times. If you read it 20 times in one minute each day, you will have read it 600 times in one month, and 7200 times in one year, which will be equal in reward to reading the Qur'aan 2400 times.

3. You can read one page of the Book of Allaah in one minute.

4. You can memorize a short aayah of the Book of Allaah in one minute.

5. In one minute you can say Laa ilaaha ill-Allaah wahdahu laa shareeka lah, lahu'l-mulk wa lahu'l-hamd wa huwa 'ala kulli shay'in qadeer (There is no god except Allaah alone with no partner; to Him be dominion and praise, and He is Able to do all things) – 20 times. The reward for saying this is like freeing 8 slaves for the sake of Allaah from among the sons of Ismaa'eel.[22]

May Allah grant us the ability to worship Him in a perfect manner, stay away from sins, and make our lives meaningful.

---

[22] "What can you do in one minute?" Islam-QA.com, accessed November 2, 2011, http://www.islam-qa.com/en/ref/4156.

CHAPTER SEVEN

ORGANIZATIONAL BEHAVIOUR

﴿وَٱلْعَصْرِ ۝ إِنَّ ٱلْإِنسَٰنَ لَفِى خُسْرٍ ۝ إِلَّا ٱلَّذِينَ ءَامَنُواْ وَعَمِلُواْ ٱلصَّٰلِحَٰتِ
وَتَوَاصَوْاْ بِٱلْحَقِّ وَتَوَاصَوْاْ بِٱلصَّبْرِ ۝﴾ (سورة العصر: ١-٣)

﴿By time. Verily! Humankind is in loss, except those who have believed and done righteous good deeds, and recommend one another to the truth, and recommend one another to patience.﴾

(Qur'an 103: 1-3)

In the previous chapter, we considered the role of Islam in HR management. Despite its roots as a support function, HR management today plays a major strategic role in business administration. A primary reason for this development is that Allah has created human beings with immense potential, which needs to be tapped and utilized to achieve great outcomes.

The study of organizational behaviour in business administration considers how human beings behave in a setting more general and abstract than HR management. In a way, it is a superset of HR management, and its findings are useful for analyzing human behaviour in a variety of other organizational contexts. Conventionally, the field of organizational behaviour is seen as lying midway between psychology – the mother discipline – and areas that utilize its findings, such as consumer behaviour, HR management, and general management.

Those in the field of organizational behaviour have traditionally attempted to understand, predict, and control behaviour from a psychoanalytical perspective. Coursework in organizational behaviour includes lessons on identifiable personality traits and their effects on management styles, and on topics such as motivation, affect (expression of emotions), group dynamics, and psychological contracts.

It is easy to appreciate the strong influence that Islam has on organizational behaviour because it affects both the psyche and behaviour. It has been prescribed by the One Who creates human beings; He knows what is in our hearts and minds, and He has taught us how to conduct ourselves:

﴿فَأَمَّا ٱلْإِنسَٰنُ إِذَا مَا ٱبْتَلَىٰهُ رَبُّهُۥ فَأَكْرَمَهُۥ وَنَعَّمَهُۥ فَيَقُولُ رَبِّيٓ أَكْرَمَنِ ۝ وَأَمَّآ إِذَا مَا ٱبْتَلَىٰهُ فَقَدَرَ عَلَيْهِ رِزْقَهُۥ فَيَقُولُ رَبِّيٓ أَهَٰنَنِ ۝ كَلَّا ۖ بَل لَّا تُكْرِمُونَ ٱلْيَتِيمَ ۝ وَلَا تَحَٰٓضُّونَ عَلَىٰ طَعَامِ ٱلْمِسْكِينِ ۝ وَتَأْكُلُونَ ٱلتُّرَاثَ أَكْلًا لَّمًّا ۝ وَتُحِبُّونَ ٱلْمَالَ حُبًّا جَمًّا ۝﴾ (سورة الفجر: ١٥-٢٠)

❝As for humankind, when his Lord tries him by giving him honour and gifts, then he says: My Lord has honoured me. But when He tries him by straitening his means of life, he says: My Lord has humiliated me! Nay! But you do not treat the orphans with kindness and generosity, and you do not urge the feeding of the poor! You devour inheritance – all with greed, and you love wealth with much love!❞

(Qur'an 89: 15-20)

﴿وَلَقَدْ صَرَّفْنَا فِي هَٰذَا ٱلْقُرْءَانِ لِلنَّاسِ مِن كُلِّ مَثَلٍ ۚ وَكَانَ ٱلْإِنسَٰنُ أَكْثَرَ شَيْءٍ جَدَلًا ۝﴾ (سورة الكهف: ٥٤)

❝And indeed We have put forth every kind of example in this Qur'an, for humankind. But humankind is ever more quarrelsome than anything.❞

(Qur'an 18: 54)

﴿ كَانَ ٱلنَّاسُ أُمَّةً وَٰحِدَةً فَبَعَثَ ٱللَّهُ ٱلنَّبِيِّـۧنَ مُبَشِّـرِينَ وَمُنذِرِينَ وَأَنزَلَ مَعَهُمُ ٱلۡكِتَٰبَ بِٱلۡحَقِّ لِيَحۡكُمَ بَيۡنَ ٱلنَّاسِ فِيمَا ٱخۡتَلَفُوا۟ فِيهِۚ وَمَا ٱخۡتَلَفَ فِيهِ إِلَّا ٱلَّذِينَ أُوتُوهُ مِنۢ بَعۡدِ مَا جَآءَتۡهُمُ ٱلۡبَيِّنَٰتُ بَغۡيًۢا بَيۡنَهُمۡۖ فَهَدَى ٱللَّهُ ٱلَّذِينَ ءَامَنُوا۟ لِمَا ٱخۡتَلَفُوا۟ فِيهِ مِنَ ٱلۡحَقِّ بِإِذۡنِهِۦۗ وَٱللَّهُ يَهۡدِى مَن يَشَآءُ إِلَىٰ صِرَٰطٍ مُّسۡتَقِيمٍ ﴿٢١٣﴾ ﴾   (سورة البقرة: ٢١٣)

﴾Humankind was one community, and Allah sent prophets with glad tidings and warnings, and with them He sent the scripture in truth to judge between people in matters wherein they differed. And only those to whom [the scripture] was given differed concerning it after clear proofs had come to them through hatred, one to another. Then Allah by His leave guided those who believed, to the truth of that wherein they differed. And Allah guides whom He wills to the straight path.﴿

(Qur'an 2: 213)

The Prophet (ﷺ) said:

«The worst things that can be in a man are greedy impatience and unrestrained cowardice.» (Recorded by Ibn Ḥibbân with a sound chain of narration)

When we remember that Allah is our Creator, it is humbling to realize the extent of His control over us as well as our dependency upon Him. Allah has mentioned:

﴿ قُلۡ إِن تُخۡفُوا۟ مَا فِى صُدُورِكُمۡ أَوۡ تُبۡدُوهُ يَعۡلَمۡهُ ٱللَّهُۗ وَيَعۡلَمُ مَا فِى ٱلسَّمَٰوَٰتِ وَمَا فِى ٱلۡأَرۡضِۗ وَٱللَّهُ عَلَىٰ كُلِّ شَىۡءٍ قَدِيرٌ ﴿٢٩﴾ ﴾   (سورة آل عمران: ٢٩)

﴾Say [O Muhammad]: Whether you hide what is in your breasts or reveal it, Allah knows it, and He knows what is in the heavens and what is in the earth. And Allah is able to do all things.﴿

(Qur'an 3: 29)

﴿ وَلَا تَقُولَنَّ لِشَاْىۡءٍ إِنِّى فَاعِلٌ ذَٰلِكَ غَدًا ﴿٢٣﴾ إِلَّآ أَن يَشَآءَ ٱللَّهُۚ وَٱذۡكُر رَّبَّكَ إِذَا نَسِيتَ وَقُلۡ عَسَىٰٓ أَن يَهۡدِيَنِ رَبِّى لِأَقۡرَبَ مِنۡ هَٰذَا رَشَدًا ﴿٢٤﴾ ﴾   (سورة الكهف: ٢٣-٢٤)

❲And never say of anything: I shall do such and such thing tomorrow. Except [with the saying]: If Allah wills! And remember your Lord when you forget, and say: It may be that my Lord guides me unto a nearer way of truth than this.❳   *(Qur'an 18: 23-24)*

﴿ لَا يُكَلِّفُ ٱللَّهُ نَفْسًا إِلَّا وُسْعَهَا ... ﴾ (٢٨٦)   (سورة البقرة: ٢٨٦)

❲Allah burdens not a person beyond his scope...❳   *(Qur'an 2: 286)*

Guidance from Allah is the greatest blessing for human beings because it delivers them out of darkness. Without the light of guidance from Allah, human beings are aimless and merely biological creatures. No goal is meaningful if its intention is not to please the Creator.

﴿ٱللَّهُ وَلِيُّ ٱلَّذِينَ ءَامَنُواْ يُخْرِجُهُم مِّنَ ٱلظُّلُمَٰتِ إِلَى ٱلنُّورِ وَٱلَّذِينَ كَفَرُوٓاْ أَوْلِيَآؤُهُمُ ٱلطَّٰغُوتُ يُخْرِجُونَهُم مِّنَ ٱلنُّورِ إِلَى ٱلظُّلُمَٰتِ أُوْلَٰٓئِكَ أَصْحَٰبُ ٱلنَّارِ هُمْ فِيهَا خَٰلِدُونَ﴾ (٢٥٧)   (سورة البقرة: ٢٥٧)

❲Allah is the guardian of those who believe. He brings them out from darkness into light. But as for those who disbelieve, their guardians are the ṭâghoot; they bring them out from light into darkness. Those are the dwellers of the fire, and they will abide therein forever.❳

(Qur'an 2: 257)

The behavioural prescriptions in Islam are thus part of the abundant blessings we receive from Allah. When the early Muslims followed those prescriptions, they were able to emerge from being unknown to becoming the leaders of the world.

﴿ مَنْ عَمِلَ صَٰلِحًا مِّن ذَكَرٍ أَوْ أُنثَىٰ وَهُوَ مُؤْمِنٌ فَلَنُحْيِيَنَّهُ حَيَوٰةً طَيِّبَةً وَلَنَجْزِيَنَّهُمْ أَجْرَهُم بِأَحْسَنِ مَا كَانُواْ يَعْمَلُونَ ﴾ (٩٧)   (سورة النحل: ٩٧)

❲Whoever works righteousness — whether male or female — while he [or she] is a true believer, verily to him [or her] We will give a good life, and We shall certainly pay them a reward in proportion to the best of what they used to do.❳   *(Qur'an 16: 97)*

Today, Muslims have forgotten their beautiful, perfect religion.
Amidst their busy lives, they have forgotten the excellent example
they have in the last Prophet, Muhammad (ﷺ). They even justify their
perfunctory approach to religion, claiming that earning a livelihood
consumes much of their available time. After nearly forsaking their
religion, they have started learning religion from others, as Western
thoughts and values have eventually trickled down to handbooks and
textbooks on management and other functions. In addition to the great
loss that human beings face from being ignorant about their religion,
they risk angering Allah by blindly accepting prescriptions that are
contradictory to Islam.

﴿ ٱلشَّيْطَٰنُ يَعِدُكُمُ ٱلْفَقْرَ وَيَأْمُرُكُم بِٱلْفَحْشَآءِ ۖ وَٱللَّهُ يَعِدُكُم مَّغْفِرَةً مِّنْهُ
وَفَضْلًا ۗ وَٱللَّهُ وَٰسِعٌ عَلِيمٌ ۝ يُؤْتِى ٱلْحِكْمَةَ مَن يَشَآءُ ۚ وَمَن يُؤْتَ ٱلْحِكْمَةَ
فَقَدْ أُوتِىَ خَيْرًا كَثِيرًا ۗ وَمَا يَذَّكَّرُ إِلَّا أُوْلُواْ ٱلْأَلْبَٰبِ ۝ ﴾

(سورة البقرة: ٢٦٨-٢٦٩)

❨Satan threatens you with poverty and orders you to commit immorality; whereas Allah promises you forgiveness from Himself and bounty,
and Allah is All-Sufficient for His creatures' needs, All-Knower. He
grants wisdom to whom He pleases, and he to whom wisdom is
granted is indeed granted abundant good. But none remember except
people of understanding.❩   *(Qur'an 2: 268-269)*

Example in our Prophet (ﷺ)

In the following hadith, Anas (ﷺ) describes the noble character of
the Prophet (ﷺ):

«I served the Messenger of Allah (ﷺ) for ten years and he never
said to me: *Uff*![1] If I did something, he never said: Why did you do

---

[1] *Uff*: an expression of impatience and disrespect.

that? If I did not do something, he never said: Why did you not do that?» (Muslim)

Anas (ﷺ) also said:

«The Prophet (ﷺ) never used obscene language or uttered curses and insults. If he wanted to rebuke someone, he would say: What is the matter with him? May his forehead be covered with dust![2]» (Bukhari)

In learning about behaviour, we find the best example in our Prophet Muhammad (ﷺ). Allah has praised him by saying:

$$ ﴿ وَإِنَّكَ لَعَلَىٰ خُلُقٍ عَظِيمٍ ۝ ﴾ $$

(سورة القلم: ٤)

﴾And verily you [O Muhammad] are on an exalted standard of character.﴿
(Qur'an 68: 4)

$$ ﴿ لَّقَدْ كَانَ لَكُمْ فِى رَسُولِ ٱللَّهِ أُسْوَةٌ حَسَنَةٌ لِّمَن كَانَ يَرْجُوا۟ ٱللَّهَ وَٱلْيَوْمَ ٱلْءَاخِرَ وَذَكَرَ ٱللَّهَ كَثِيرًا ۝ ﴾ $$

(سورة الأحزاب: ٢١)

﴾Indeed in the Messenger of Allah you have a good example to follow for him who hopes for [the meeting with] Allah and the Last Day, and remembers Allah much.﴿
(Qur'an 33: 21)

«Sa'd ibn Hishâm once asked 'Â'ishah (ﷺ): Tell me about the character of the Prophet (ﷺ).

She replied: His character was the Qur'an.» (Abu Dâwood: a sound hadith according to al-Albâni)

His life demonstrated for us how best to implement our deen.

- He was an exemplary leader; he worked at the front lines, even while leading the entire Muslim nation.
- He planned strategically, using foresight, yet he placed all his trust in Allah.
- He was wise and eloquent, yet humble and gentle.
- He was strict, with firm resolve and strong will, yet merciful and forgiving.

---

[2] Possibly so he spends longer times in prostration for increased guidance.

- He was a successful businessman and business manager, yet he was known throughout his life for his honesty.

- He did not neglect any aspect of the deen, including kindness to his family.

In order to succeed, we must learn about his Sunnah and implement it to the highest degree in our lives.[3]

Enjoining what is right and forbidding what is wrong

Allah has instructed:

$$﴿ وَلْتَكُن مِّنكُمْ أُمَّةٌ يَدْعُونَ إِلَى الْخَيْرِ وَيَأْمُرُونَ بِالْمَعْرُوفِ وَيَنْهَوْنَ عَنِ الْمُنكَرِ وَأُوْلَئِكَ هُمُ الْمُفْلِحُونَ ﴾$$

(سورة آل عمران: ١٠٤)

《Let there rise out of you a nation inviting to what is good, enjoining what is right and forbidding what is wrong. And it is they who are the successful.》 *(Qur'an 3: 104)*

Abu Sa'eed al-Khudri (ﷺ) reported that he heard the Prophet (ﷺ) say:

«Among you, he who sees something wrong should correct it with his hand. If he is unable to do that, he should condemn it with his tongue. If he is unable to do that, he should at least resent it in his heart, and this is the lowest degree of faith.» (Muslim)

Based on this hadith, we must attempt to remind each other of the elements in the Sharia that our brothers and sisters forget. For example, we should remind our brothers to lower their gaze when we see it wandering, as Allah has mentioned:

$$﴿ قُل لِّلْمُؤْمِنِينَ يَغُضُّوا مِنْ أَبْصَارِهِمْ ... ﴾$$

(سورة النور: ٣٠)

---

[3] A good book on the life of the Prophet (ﷺ) is al-Mubarakpuri, *The Sealed Nectar*.

《Tell the believing men to lower their gaze...》   *(Qur'an 24: 30)*

Mutual respect

There should be mutual respect in an Islamic business culture. 'Abdullâh ibn 'Amr (ﷺ) narrated that the Prophet (ﷺ) said:

«A Muslim is the one who avoids harming (other) Muslims with his tongue and hands.» (Bukhari)

Allah has mentioned:

$$ ﴿ وَأَمَّا مَن جَآءَكَ يَسْعَىٰ ۞ وَهُوَ يَخْشَىٰ ۞ فَأَنتَ عَنْهُ تَلَهَّىٰ ۞ كَلَّآ إِنَّهَا تَذْكِرَةٌ ۞ ﴾ $$

(سورة عبس: ٨-١١)

《But as to him who came to you running and is afraid [of Allah and His punishment] – of him you are neglectful and divert your attention to another. Nay [do not do like this]; indeed it [this Qur'an] is an admonition.》   *(Qur'an 80: 8-11)*

The Prophet (ﷺ) said:

«Do not envy one another, do not outbid one another (in order to inflate prices), do not hate one another, do not run away from one another, and do not enter into a transaction when others have already entered into it. O servants of Allah, be brothers. A Muslim is the brother of a Muslim. He does not oppress him, humiliate him, or look down upon him. Taqwâ is here – and while saying this, he pointed to his chest three times. It is evil enough for a man to look down upon his Muslim brother. The whole of a Muslim's being is sacred to another Muslim – his blood, his wealth, and his honour are inviolable.»[4] (Muslim)

Finally, Islamic business environments should encourage kindness among Muslims. Allah has specified:

---

[4] It is interesting that kindness and business transactions are both mentioned in this one hadith. Too many Muslims today are kind when it comes to their leisure activities but aggressive in business transactions.

﴿... وَٱلْكَـٰظِمِينَ ٱلْغَيْظَ وَٱلْعَافِينَ عَنِ ٱلنَّاسِ ۗ وَٱللَّهُ يُحِبُّ ٱلْمُحْسِنِينَ

(سورة آل عمران: ١٣٤)   ﴾ ⟨١٣٤⟩

﴾...[those] who repress anger and pardon [all] people – for Allah loves the good-doers.﴿   *(Qur'an 3: 134)*

The Prophet (ﷺ) said:

«Smiling at your brother is an act of charity.» (at-Tirmidhi; a sound hadith according to al-Albâni)

'Abdullâh ibn 'Amr narrated:

«A man asked the Prophet (ﷺ): What sort of deeds or (what qualities of) Islam are good?

The Prophet (ﷺ) replied: To feed (the poor) and to greet those whom you know and those whom you do not know.» (Bukhari)

Dignity and honesty

The Prophet (ﷺ) said:

«You will find among the worst people in the sight of Allah on the Day of Judgement the one who is two-faced, who approaches some people in one way and some in another.» (Bukhari)

He also said:

«Do not argue with your brother, do not joke excessively with him, and do not make a promise to him and then break it.» (Bukhari)

Resisting haram cultural imports

A great deal of management research is taking place in non-Muslim circles, but Muslims are responsible for filtering out the ideas that contradict Islamic principles. Unfortunately, this is often not done, and as a result, many of the imported corporate cultures go against the Sharia.

One example is the definition of professional attire; many Muslim men shave their beards and wear silk ties to appear professional.

Another example is men and women shaking hands with each other, even though the Prophet (ﷺ) said:

«If one of you were to be stabbed in the head with a piece of iron, it would be better for him than if he were to touch a woman whom it is not permissible for him to touch.» (A sound hadith recorded by aṭ-Ṭabarâni)

Leadership

Our foremost example is the Prophet (ﷺ), who was a great leader. He strove to defeat such huge challenges as the deep-rooted ignorance that was prevalent among his people. He was also a strategic thinker and planner.

Different leadership styles exist within Islam. At the time of the Prophet (ﷺ), he chose different Companions to lead different expeditions. Each of the four Rightly-Guided Caliphs who succeeded the Prophet (ﷺ) had his own individual style of leadership. One lesson we learn is that we need to educate ourselves about the various kinds of leadership shown by the Prophet (ﷺ), his Companions (رضي الله عنهم), and the righteous predecessors.

Another, perhaps more important, lesson for us is that all the different leadership styles arose from the efforts of individuals to lead their people while at the same time remaining righteous Muslims, with a fear of Allah and a common goal of obeying Him – while acknowledging their own advantages and shortcomings. Therefore, we may benefit most from our knowledge of the Sharia, which is developed from the Qur'an and the Sunnah.

Muslims should not always try to attain leadership positions in groups of fellow Muslims or to monopolize discussions at meetings. Leaders should not show off or be arrogant.[5] The Prophet (ﷺ) said:

---

[5] For more information, see "Ridding oneself of arrogance," Islam-QA.com, accessed November 2, 2011, http://www.islam-qa.com/en/ref/9229.

«Whoever shows off, Allah will expose him.» (Bukhari)

Muslim leadership is inclusive and involves consultation. Even the Prophet (ﷺ) used to seek the opinions of his Companions. The Companions (ﷺ) responded to this call and were supportive[6] yet humbled by their regard for the Prophet (ﷺ).[7] The practice of shoorâ was continued by the Rightly-Guided Caliphs.[8]

In the Qur'an we find other examples of leadership. Prophet Joseph (ﷺ), who became Egypt's chief minister, knew when it was the right time for a leader to forgive the faults of others:

$$ قَالَ لَا تَثْرِيبَ عَلَيْكُمُ ٱلْيَوْمَ يَغْفِرُ ٱللَّهُ لَكُمْ وَهُوَ أَرْحَمُ ٱلرَّٰحِمِينَ $$

(سورة يوسف: ٩٢)

{He [Joseph] said: No reproach on you this day. May Allah forgive you, and He is the Most Merciful of those who show mercy!}

(Qur'an 12: 92)

Allah gave Dhul-Qarnayn great authority in his time, and Dhul-Qarnayn chose to reward and punish his subjects according to the laws of Allah and the status of their belief in Him:

$$ إِنَّا مَكَّنَّا لَهُۥ فِي ٱلْأَرْضِ وَءَاتَيْنَٰهُ مِن كُلِّ شَيْءٍ سَبَبًا فَأَتْبَعَ سَبَبًا $$

(سورة الكهف: ٨٤-٨٥)

{Verily, We established him [Dhul-Qarnayn] in the earth, and We gave him the means of everything. So he followed a way.}

(Qur'an 18: 84-85)

---

6 Salmân al-Fârisi, for example, recommended the digging of the trench.

7 The Companions would often ask the Prophet (ﷺ) whether his opinions were based on divine inspiration or whether suggestions were welcome.

8 Before he died, the Rightly-Guided Caliph 'Umar ibn al-Khaṭṭâb appointed a shoorâ council, made up of six senior Companions, to choose his successor.

﴾ قَالَ أَمَّا مَن ظَلَمَ فَسَوْفَ نُعَذِّبُهُ ... ﴿٨٧﴾ ﴾

(سورة الكهف: ٨٧)

﴾He [Dhul-Qarnayn] said: As for him who does wrong, we shall punish him...﴿

(Qur'an 18: 87)

﴾ وَأَمَّا مَنْ ءَامَنَ وَعَمِلَ صَالِحًا فَلَهُۥ جَزَآءً ٱلْحُسْنَىٰ وَسَنَقُولُ لَهُۥ مِنْ أَمْرِنَا يُسْرًا ﴿٨٨﴾ ﴾

(سورة الكهف: ٨٨)

﴾[Dhul-Qarnayn said:] But as for him who believes and works righteousness, he shall have the best reward, and we shall speak unto him mild words.﴿

(Qur'an 18: 88)

﴾ قَالَ مَا مَكَّنِّى فِيهِ رَبِّى خَيْرٌ فَأَعِينُونِي بِقُوَّةٍ أَجْعَلْ بَيْنَكُمْ وَبَيْنَهُمْ رَدْمًا ﴿٩٥﴾ ﴾

(سورة الكهف: ٩٥)

﴾He [Dhul-Qarnayn] said: The [wealth, authority and power] in which My Lord had established me is better. So help me with strength, and I will erect between you and them a barrier.﴿

(Qur'an 18: 95)

Motivation

In many cases, motivation can significantly improve the quality and/or quantity of a person's output; thus, it can be an excellent managerial tool for improving productivity. Marketers also use motivation to encourage potential customers to make purchases. Motivation is particularly useful when individuals either harbour distaste for a task or feel shy about participating in it. People can be motivated by soft methods, such as words of encouragement, which invoke positive emotions, or by harder methods like the promise of financial bonuses or other extrinsic rewards.

Allah has motivated the believers through promises in the Qur'an:

﴾ إِنَّ ٱلْأَبْرَارَ لَفِى نَعِيمٍ ﴿٢٢﴾ عَلَى ٱلْأَرَآئِكِ يَنظُرُونَ ﴿٢٣﴾ تَعْرِفُ فِى وُجُوهِهِمْ نَضْرَةَ ٱلنَّعِيمِ ﴿٢٤﴾ يُسْقَوْنَ مِن رَّحِيقٍ مَّخْتُومٍ ﴿٢٥﴾ خِتَٰمُهُۥ مِسْكٌ وَفِى ذَٰلِكَ فَلْيَتَنَافَسِ ٱلْمُتَنَٰفِسُونَ

وَمِزَاجُهُ مِن تَسْنِيمٍ ۝ عَيْنًا يَشْرَبُ بِهَا ٱلْمُقَرَّبُونَ ۝ إِنَّ ٱلَّذِينَ أَجْرَمُواْ
كَانُواْ مِنَ ٱلَّذِينَ ءَامَنُواْ يَضْحَكُونَ ۝ وَإِذَا مَرُّواْ بِهِمْ يَتَغَامَزُونَ ۝ وَإِذَا ٱنقَلَبُوٓاْ إِلَىٰ
أَهْلِهِمُ ٱنقَلَبُواْ فَكِهِينَ ۝ وَإِذَا رَأَوْهُمْ قَالُوٓاْ إِنَّ هَٰٓؤُلَآءِ لَضَآلُّونَ ۝ وَمَآ أُرْسِلُواْ
عَلَيْهِمْ حَٰفِظِينَ ۝ فَٱلْيَوْمَ ٱلَّذِينَ ءَامَنُواْ مِنَ ٱلْكُفَّارِ يَضْحَكُونَ ۝ عَلَى ٱلْأَرَآئِكِ يَنظُرُونَ
۝ هَلْ ثُوِّبَ ٱلْكُفَّارُ مَا كَانُواْ يَفْعَلُونَ ۝ ❁ (سورة المطفّفين: ٢٢-٣٦)

❲Verily, the pious who fear Allah and avoid evil will be in delight. On
thrones, looking [at all things]. You will recognize in their faces the
brightness of delight. They will be given to drink pure sealed wine.
The last thereof [that wine] will be the smell of musk, and for this
let [all] those strive who want to strive. It [that wine] will be mixed
with the highest spring in paradise, a spring whereof those nearest
to Allah drink. Verily, those who committed crimes used to laugh at
those who believed. Whenever they passed by them, [they] used to
wink one to another; when they returned to their own people, they
would return jesting, and when they saw them, they said: Verily, these
have indeed gone astray! But they had not been sent as watchers over
them [the believers]. But this day [the Day of Resurrection], those
who believe will laugh at the disbelievers. On [high] thrones, looking
[at all things]. Are not the disbelievers paid [fully] for what they used
to do?❳   *(Qur'an 83: 22-36)*

While Muslim managers can motivate employees and others
through good words and actions, three cautionary notes need to be
made in that regard:

1. <u>The motivation should be genuine and balanced</u>: It is extremely
   important to be honest when attempting to motivate others.
   Many individuals get carried away by their emotions or their
   blind fervour in trying to achieve their goals, and they try to
   motivate others without a sincere assessment. Muslims should

not lie, even if it is to joke or achieve a good purpose.[9] Muslims also should not make promises they cannot keep, because breaking promises is a characteristic of a hypocrite. In keeping with their honesty and fear of Allah, Muslims should balance any motivational tools by clearly explaining any significant consequences. They should want for their brothers and sisters what they want for themselves, as we learned from a hadith in the previous chapter.

2. It should not encourage excessive work: In today's competitive work environments, Muslim practitioners of business administration find themselves on roller coasters, requiring tremendous levels of output; thus the Muslim managers naturally tend to require their subordinates to adopt similar, fast-paced work lifestyles.

This has clear negative effects. Due to high workloads, Muslims often miss valuable opportunities for performing acts of worship. Ironically, the high workloads are not even opportunities for earning extraordinary returns; they are only the means for supporting a basic livelihood. In these situations, Muslim managers are faced with a dilemma. If they motivate their workers to work extra hard, they may prevent those workers from engaging in righteous deeds, but if the managers do not encourage their team members, their own careers or even the entire firm's position may be jeopardized. The Muslim managers should at least inform team members from the beginning about the level of work expected of them. When they have the opportunity to sacrifice individual or corporate profits in order to improve the lifestyles of employees, they should certainly do so.

---

[9]   The exceptions to this rule are well known from the authentic hadith, mentioned previously, regarding the permissibility of lying in a few specific situations.

﴿ٱلْمَالُ وَٱلْبَنُونَ زِينَةُ ٱلْحَيَوٰةِ ٱلدُّنْيَا ۖ وَٱلْبَٰقِيَٰتُ ٱلصَّٰلِحَٰتُ خَيْرٌ عِندَ رَبِّكَ ثَوَابًا وَخَيْرٌ أَمَلًا ﴾ ٤٦

(سورة الكهف: ٤٦)

﴿Wealth and children are the adornment of the life of this world. But the good righteous deeds that last are better with your Lord for rewards and better in respect of hope.﴾   *(Qur'an 18: 46)*

﴿... وَقَالَ لَأَتَّخِذَنَّ مِنْ عِبَادِكَ نَصِيبًا مَّفْرُوضًا ۝ وَلَأُضِلَّنَّهُمْ وَلَأُمَنِّيَنَّهُمْ وَلَآمُرَنَّهُمْ فَلَيُبَتِّكُنَّ ءَاذَانَ ٱلْأَنْعَٰمِ وَلَآمُرَنَّهُمْ فَلَيُغَيِّرُنَّ خَلْقَ ٱللَّهِ ۚ وَمَن يَتَّخِذِ ٱلشَّيْطَٰنَ وَلِيًّا مِّن دُونِ ٱللَّهِ فَقَدْ خَسِرَ خُسْرَانًا مُّبِينًا ۝ يَعِدُهُمْ وَيُمَنِّيهِمْ ۖ وَمَا يَعِدُهُمُ ٱلشَّيْطَٰنُ إِلَّا غُرُورًا ﴾ ۝

(سورة النساء: ١١٨-١٢٠)

﴿...And he [Satan] said: I will take an appointed portion of your slaves; verily, I will mislead them. Surely, I will arouse in them false desires, and certainly, I will order them to slit the ears of cattle, and indeed I will order them to change the nature created by Allah. Whoever takes Satan as a guardian instead of Allah has surely suffered a manifest loss. He [Satan] makes promises to them, and arouses in them false desires, and Satan's promises are nothing but deceptions.﴾   *(Qur'an 4: 118-120)*

3. <u>Muslims motivate themselves and their brothers and sisters by using reminders from the Qur'an and the Sunnah</u>: Muslim managers should not motivate others in their organization to engage only in worldly tasks. We have already discussed that Muslims should be actively engaged in da'wah.

Collaborative effort

Over the past few decades, there has been considerable interest in the efficacy, advantages, and challenges of team-based and other group activities in organizations. While competition among individuals can bring about work of superior quality, group work may result in synergistic effects.[10] Recent research into collaborative activities recommends competition among different groups for even better output from employees in terms of both quality and quantity. Like management literature itself, the studies on collaborative effort are recent developments, whereas Islam enjoined solidarity amongst the Muslims over fourteen hundred years ago. Moreover, the Islamic models of collaboration are based on taqwâ and do not involve the ills that are traditionally associated with group work, such as free-riding and leadership struggles.

(سورة الحُجُرات: ١٠)　　　 ﴾إِنَّمَا ٱلْمُؤْمِنُونَ إِخْوَةٌ ... ﴿①﴾

﴾The believers are nothing but brothers [to each other]...﴿

(Qur'an 49: 10)

The Prophet (ﷺ) said:

«Believers are like a structure, parts of which support the other parts.» (Bukhari and Muslim)

The Prophet (ﷺ) also said:

«The believers – in their mutual friendship, mercy, and affection – are like one body; if any part of it complains, the rest of the body will also stay awake in pain.» (Bukhari and Muslim)

The Prophet (ﷺ) said:

«The believer is the mirror of his brother. The believer is the brother of a believer; he protects him from ruin and guards his back.» (Bukhari)

«Once a man prayed out loud: O Allah, forgive me and Muhammad only!

The Prophet (ﷺ) said: You have denied it to many people.» (Bukhari)

---

[10] Spence, "Job Market Signaling;" Lazear and Rosen, "Rank-Order Tournaments as Optimum Labor Contracts."

Avoiding backbiting, gossiping, and spying

Backbiting, gossiping, and spying can all be grievous sins, and organizations benefit if their members abstain from those practices. Evil and vain speech is often the conduit for office politics that result in sins, the departure of righteous people, and eventually the hindrance of healthy organizational growth and performance.

﴿يَٰٓأَيُّهَا ٱلَّذِينَ ءَامَنُوا ٱجۡتَنِبُوا كَثِيرًا مِّنَ ٱلظَّنِّ إِنَّ بَعۡضَ ٱلظَّنِّ إِثۡمٌ وَلَا تَجَسَّسُوا وَلَا يَغۡتَب بَّعۡضُكُم بَعۡضًا أَيُحِبُّ أَحَدُكُمۡ أَن يَأۡكُلَ لَحۡمَ أَخِيهِ مَيۡتًا فَكَرِهۡتُمُوهُ وَٱتَّقُوا ٱللَّهَ إِنَّ ٱللَّهَ تَوَّابٌ رَّحِيمٌ ۝﴾   (سورة الحُجُرات: ١٢)

﴿O you who believe! Avoid much suspicion; indeed some suspicions are sins. Spy not, nor backbite one another. Would one of you like to eat the flesh of his dead brother? You would hate it [so hate backbiting]. And fear Allah. Verily, Allah is the One Who forgives and accepts repentance, the Most Merciful.﴾   *(Qur'an 49: 12)*

The Prophet (ﷺ) said:

«Beware of suspicion, for speaking on the basis of suspicion is the worst kind of lie. Do not seek out one another's faults, do not spy on one another, do not compete with one another, do not envy one another, do not hate one another, and do not turn away from one another. O servants of Allah, be brothers.» (Muslim)

CHAPTER EIGHT

OPERATIONS MANAGEMENT

$\mathcal{I}$n business administration, operations management attempts to streamline the processes of the core production engine. It comprises the set of tasks that make production activities lean enough to be commercially viable; these include planning, forecasting, eliminating inefficiencies, managing quality, and procuring necessary resources. The overall objective of operations management is to minimize mismatches between supply and demand.[1] The production engine of a business generates the supply, and its products are sold in response to demand; effective operations management helps to ensure that the right product is available at the right place, time, and price.

The set of tasks that constitute operations management will differ significantly in various contexts, since operations themselves vary from firm to firm. For example, the management of operations in a hospital is very different from that in a software firm. At the same time, one can easily appreciate that many aspects of their management will be quite similar, not least because organizations of either type are heavily dependent upon highly-skilled workers. The discipline of operations management has thus identified a set of topics that are pervasive in most organizations; their emphasis is upon improving both efficiency and responsiveness. Many of these topics offer rigorous techniques with quantitative foundations.

---

[1] Cachon and Terwiesch, *Matching Supply and Demand: An Introduction to Operations Management.*

Similar to the way issues are discussed in the general field of operations management, we will attempt to address a few topics that we consider relevant for most organizations. Clearly, the general topic of Islam in operations management is much larger than this presentation, but a more comprehensive treatment is beyond the scope of this book.

Work design

Although work design is often considered part of the HR management function, it also affects operations management, and often in a more enduring way.[2] Let us consider an example that demonstrates this fact.

In a newly-constructed university campus in a Muslim country, it was discovered that the prayer room was too small to accommodate a sizable congregation. Apparently, no more space could be found; the campus had been constructed with space constraints in an urban setting. Since the prayer rooms were situated inside the lounge, Muslim students and faculty members had to go through the lounge to reach the prayer rooms.

The problem was that the atmosphere in the lounge was extremely un-Islamic, with music blaring from audio speakers and television programming displaying scantily-clad women dancing in music videos. Muslims who wanted to pray were not able to make the lounge quiet, even temporarily, let alone convince everyone to join in the prayers. Sadly, the Muslims had to continue entering the prayer rooms through the un-Islamic lounge area and praying in a zone where lewd music was clearly audible. This situation arose because the operations management team did not consider Islam when designing the facilities.

We have categorized some aspects of work design into the following sections: gender issues, work hours, worship issues, and safety.

---

[2] It can actually be argued that HR management is a subset of operations management.

Gender issues

In the chapter on HR management, we discussed important gender issues in Islam: the prohibition of unrestricted intermingling, the practice of lowering the gaze, and issues of clothing. Regarding the first two issues, operations management can play a significant role. Cubicles, workstations, and work processes should be designed so that there is no room for any kind of intermingling between the genders. Even in public areas, there should be separate queues and spaces for brothers and sisters. This helps to build an organizational culture based on dignity and taqwâ.

There are many creative approaches to achieving these objectives. Architecture students in their final year at an American university were given the task of designing a mosque, and they were told that there should be no intermingling. After finishing their designs, they verified that intermingling would not take place by overlaying transparencies having blue and red flow lines representing the two genders; when all the lines were completely visible, this meant that the pathways for men and women were completely separate.

Work hours

Increased competition has placed intense pressure on most businesses. One effect has been an increase in the number of work hours for everyone, from line workers all the way up to CEOs. This takes a negative toll upon the workers as their family and personal lives are affected. Competition among the workers, as they eye senior positions, has even led some to voluntarily increase their work hours. Under the topic of motivation (in the chapter on organizational behaviour), we described how Muslim workers should not be excessive in their pursuit of wealth, authority, or other worldly gains. Operations managers should strive to promote a healthful work-life balance by implementing procedures that improve overall productivity and efficiency.

If necessary, they should enforce regulations limiting the number of work hours.

Worship issues

Effective operations management needs to accommodate, facilitate, and encourage worship in the workplace. The call to prayer should be audible, prayer facilities should be accessible, and measures should be taken to minimize un-Islamic tendencies in the work environment.

Since operations comprise, among other things, the day-to-day activities of a business, it is essential for the operations managers to ensure that Muslims in their organizations can easily perform the day-to-day acts of worship. Some of the following steps can be taken in this regard:

- Having an accessible and spacious prayer room
- Having facilities for performing ablution
- Ensuring that all Muslim employees suspend work-related activities (including meetings) during prayer times and go for prayer
- Ensuring that the cafeteria is not serving food during the day in the holy month of Ramadan
- Removing distractions (for example, elevator music or televisions) that can interfere with employees' efforts to practice their religion
- Encouraging congregational prayer and other acts of worship
- Having a proper system in place to handle grievances, disciplinary issues, and so on

Safety

There are often numerous hazards in the workplace. Workers on the manufacturing line are frequently victims of occupational accidents, as are construction workers on site. Operations managers should recognize their responsibilities to be aware of these hazards, to assess the dangers, and to protect others from harm. The Prophet (ﷺ) said: «The believers – in their mutual friendship, mercy, and affection – are like one body; if any part of it complains, the rest of the body will also stay awake in pain.» (Bukhari and Muslim)

Contracts

Effective operations management is often achieved through contract formulation. Contracts are important because they can serve as strategic tools for achieving desirable outcomes. For example, supplier commitments are often enforced through the appropriate clauses in contracts. To be valid in Islam, contracts must fulfil certain conditions. In general, contracts that involve uncertainty are not valid because the Prophet (ﷺ) forbade ambiguous transactions (as was narrated by Imam Muslim in his *Ṣaḥeeḥ*). The following types of contracts, which are common in business today, are actually haram:

Bartering certain commodities

Bartering refers to the direct exchange of goods, like firewood for rice, for example. This was probably a typical transaction before the establishment of currency or a monetary system. Despite its prehistoric look, in many situations, bartering is seen as a convenient win-win alternative. This is largely because of the transaction costs associated with purchases and sales, including those that arise due to the volatile nature of spot prices.

Many manufacturers use surplus, unsold inventory to make 'payments'. As an example of commercial bartering, unsold parkas or other garments are often used by apparel manufacturers to pre-purchase travel services for their employees.

In certain cases, though, bartering becomes illegal in Islam. 'Old gold' in the form of jewellery of a certain weight, for instance, cannot be exchanged for 'new gold' of another weight because the difference is considered ribâ. The old gold should be sold first, and then the funds should be used to purchase the new gold.

Bartering can also be haram if there is uncertainty in the product. Returning to our example of unsold parkas, let us suppose that the manufacturer barters stock lots of surplus inventory, a considerable portion of which may be defective. If these stock lots are sold 'as is', without giving the buyer any opportunity to inspect them, this transaction may be haram due to the considerable level of uncertainty.

Consignment or 'buy-back' clauses

A consignment, or 'buy-back', clause is used when demand is uncertain. It requires one party to bear the cost (partial or full) of items not sold by the other party. For example, a supplier of fashion retail items may offer to buy back all unsold inventory from the retailer at a salvage price at the end of the season, or a manufacturer of beverages may buy back unsold crates of beverages from the distributor. The purpose is to encourage the buyer to place larger orders. Despite the increased risk (and costs) to the manufacturers, they often prefer this arrangement because their overall sales and profits increase when buyers place larger orders.

From an Islamic perspective, since the 'unsold inventory' is not well-defined in terms of its quantity, there is a large degree of uncertainty, or gharar, which renders the contract illegal.

Futures and options

Futures are commonplace in commodity trading around the world, and they are becoming increasingly popular in business administration, along with other financial derivative products like real options. These are haram because they are, in essence, gambling. Allah has mentioned:

﴿يَـٰٓأَيُّهَا ٱلَّذِينَ ءَامَنُوٓا۟ إِنَّمَا ٱلْخَمْرُ وَٱلْمَيْسِرُ وَٱلْأَنصَابُ وَٱلْأَزْلَـٰمُ رِجْسٌ مِّنْ عَمَلِ ٱلشَّيْطَـٰنِ
فَٱجْتَنِبُوهُ لَعَلَّكُمْ تُفْلِحُونَ ۝ ﴾   (سورة المائدة: ٩٠)

﴿O you who believe! Intoxicants, gambling, animals that are sacrificed on stone altars for idols, and arrows for seeking luck or decision are abominations of Satan's handiwork. So avoid that in order that you may be successful.﴾   *(Qur'an 5: 90)*

All of these forms of contracts appear to be good for business, but in reality they have many negative consequences; in their indulgence, naïve and impetuous human beings fail to realize this. Speculative 'good for business' practices and haram financial derivative products, combined with ribâ, were some of the main contributors to the global economic crises of 2008 – 2009. There is always much wisdom and benefit in following Allah's commands.

Following Allah's commands need not make Muslims uncompetitive. With a little ingenuity and creativity, alternative and halal forms of contracts can achieve many or all of the desired objectives.

Instead of a 'buy-back' arrangement, a company can use revenue sharing. Consider the case of a manufacturer selling items to a retailer who, in turn, sells those items to consumers. In order to increase its overall sales volume, the manufacturer wants to encourage the retailer to order more. Through revenue sharing, the manufacturer offers the retailer a discount on each item in return for a share of the retailer's future revenue from sales of that item. The element of gharar is removed, but the objective – a larger order – is still achieved. Moreover, this eliminates a disadvantage associated with buy-back, which is that retailers might promote competing products because (with no option to sell them back) they carry higher risks.

In many situations, it appears that gharar cannot be avoided. Consider supply chain management, where early commitments are critical, yet production may not physically be possible so far in advance. Another example is the sale of fruits before trees flower. According to scholarly consensus, it is not permissible to sell fruits before their condition is known because:[3]

«It was narrated from Ibn 'Umar (ﷺ) that the Prophet (ﷺ) forbade selling fruits before their condition is known, and he forbade both the seller and the buyer.» (Bukhari and Muslim)

There are exceptions to that rule in a few situations, though. The fruits can be sold along with the trees, or the fruits can be cut and taken at the time of purchase.

The six major books of Hadith report on the authority of Ibn 'Abbâs (ﷺ) that:

«The Messenger of Allah (ﷺ) came to Madinah and found its inhabitants entering *salam* contracts (with the price paid in advance) in fruits for one, two, and three years.

He said: If someone enters into a salam contract, let him (or her) specify a known volume or weight and a known term of deferment.» (Bukhari and al-Bayhaqi)

Salam contracts reduce the uncertainty since the product, amount, and time are specified. However, since there are other regulations associated with salam contracts, those considering their use should consult an appropriate scholar from ahl as-Sunnah wal-jamâ'ah.

Finally, there are numerous other guidelines associated with contracts. The Prophet (ﷺ) said:

«Do not envy one another, do not outbid one another (in order to inflate prices), do not hate one another, do not run away from one another, and do not enter into a transaction when others have already entered into it. O servants of Allah, be brothers. A Muslim is the brother of a Muslim. He does not oppress him, humiliate him, or look down upon him. Taqwâ is here – and while saying this, he pointed to his chest

---

[3] See "Ruling on buying apricot orchards before they become ripe," Islam-QA.com, accessed November 2, 2011, http://www.islam-qa.com/en/ref/72505.

three times. It is evil enough for a man to look down upon his Muslim brother. The whole of a Muslim's being is sacred to another Muslim – his blood, his wealth, and his honour are inviolable.» (Muslim)

Readers are requested to refer to the chapter on transactions (*Kitâb al-Buyoo '*) in *Ṣaḥeeḥ Muslim* for a comprehensive overview of contracts in Islam. Before concluding this section, we list a few examples of transaction rules in Islam:

- Ibn 'Umar (رضي الله عنه) reported that Allah's Messenger (ﷺ) said:

  «Do not go out to meet merchandise on the way; (wait) until it is brought into the market.»[4] (Recorded by Aḥmad with a sound chain of narration)

- Ibn 'Umar (رضي الله عنه) reported that Allah's Messenger (ﷺ) said:

  «None of you should enter into a transaction when another is bargaining.» (Recorded by Aḥmad with a sound chain of narration)

- Abu Hurayrah (رضي الله عنه) reported directly from Allah's Messenger (ﷺ) that he said:

  «The townsman should not sell for a man from the desert (with the intention of taking advantage of his ignorance of the market conditions in the city).» (Bukhari)

  «Zuhayr reported from the Prophet (ﷺ) that he forbade the townsman from selling on behalf of the man from the desert.» (Bukhari)

- Ibn 'Abbâs (رضي الله عنه) reported that Allah's Messenger (ﷺ) said:

  «He who buys (food) grain should not sell it until he has taken possession of it.» (Bukhari)

- Ibn 'Umar (رضي الله عنه) reported that Allah's Messenger (ﷺ) said:

  «Both parties in a business transaction have the right to annul it as long as they have not separated, except in transactions which

---

[4] This hadith has been reported on the authority of Ibn Numayr, but with a slightly different wording.

have been made subject to the right of parties to annul them.»
(Bukhari and Abu Dâwood)

• Râfi' ibn Khadeej (ﷺ) reported:

«We used to rent out land during the lifetime of Allah's Messenger (ﷺ). We rented it for a one-third or one-fourth share of
the (produce) along with a definite quantity of corn.

One day, one of my uncles came to us and said: Allah's Messenger (ﷺ) has forbidden this act, which was a source of benefit for
us, but obedience to Allah and to His Messenger (ﷺ) is more
beneficial for us. He has forbidden that we should rent land in
return for one-third or one-fourth (of the produce) and a measure
of corn; he ordered the owner of the land to cultivate it or let it
be cultivated by other (persons), but he disapproved of renting
it or anything besides it.» (Muslim and an-Nasâ'i)

• «Ḥandhalah ibn Qays reported that he asked Râfi' ibn Khadeej
(ﷺ) about the renting of land, and he replied: Allah's Messenger
(ﷺ) forbade the renting of the land. I asked: Is it forbidden (even
if it is paid) in gold (dinars) and silver (dirhams)? He replied:
If it is paid in gold and silver, there is no harm in it.» (Muslim)

Risk mitigation

Insurance

Issues dealing with insurance come up very frequently in business
settings. Businesses often purchase insurance to minimize their operational risks, even if that reduces the expected profits. When businesses operate in various countries, they may purchase insurance, for
example, that covers losses they may incur in the event of natural
disasters. Sometimes they are required to purchase insurance to protect
the interests of others; for example, many businesses are required to
provide health insurance to employees or to purchase occupational
safety hazard insurance.

All kinds of commercial insurance are haram, for two reasons. Firstly, they involve ribâ because money is exchanged, always in unequal amounts and with a delay in one of the payments. Furthermore, the insurance companies almost always take the money they receive as premiums and invest it in ribâ-bearing securities. Secondly, the business itself has enough gharar to be labelled as pure gambling.

There are many claims that so-called 'Islamic insurance' models are halal. Scholars have stated that there is a lot of deception in these models and that most, if not all, are indeed haram.

Risk reduction is not haram

Proponents of insurance argue that insurance is necessary for reducing risks to acceptable levels. While Islam promotes reliance on Allah foremost, it does not discourage risk reduction. What Islam forbids is the **sale** of risk.

An example of a halal method of risk reduction is risk pooling. Here, demand is aggregated across some dimension (such as time or geography) so that there is less overall variation. For instance, inventory can be kept in fewer locations, each of which serves a greater number of retail points. Subsequently, the same safety stock levels will provide greater cushioning against variations in demand.

Rigour or *tawakkul*?

Operations management utilizes rigorous tools. In fact, one of the distinct features of operations management is its quantitative approach. Students in an operations management course learn how to measure and improve forecast accuracy, how to balance inventory holding costs against setup costs, how to optimize process flows, how to efficiently allocate resources, and many other quantitative methods. Although the rigour in operations management increases the steepness of learning curves, it has proven useful in the long run for its contribution to making operations more cost-effective, efficient, profitable, and hence competitive. Not surprisingly, industries provide considerable impetus for continued development of the field.

There has been a lot of criticism regarding the over-reliance of operations management on rigour. As business management has become increasingly complicated, academics appear to obsess over crafting ever more complicated mathematical models and utilizing even fancier techniques for deriving solutions – to the extent that the end results are frequently too complicated for the average manager to interpret. Meanwhile, advocates of rigorous approaches are often dogmatic about the superiority of rigorous techniques over other, softer approaches.

Islam does not advocate one approach over another. There is nothing inherently haram about adding rigour, of any level, to a management approach. Islam, however, requires that managers avoid arrogance or pride and that they practice full tawakkul. We will use forecasting as an example to highlight this.

Suppose that a marketing manager needs to estimate sales in the next few selling seasons. He can utilize one or more of many forecasting options, like ARIMA modelling.[5] This form of forecasting is the polar opposite of consulting a fortune teller or a mystic; it is based on rational, mathematical analysis, whereas fortune telling is based on superstition and is contradictory to tawheed. In fact, at the very foundation of mathematical forecasting is the idea that forecasts are always wrong and are merely guesswork.

At the same time, a marketing manager can never believe that a mathematical model is the determinant of events, even if past data has consistently conformed to such models. Many wrongly assume

---

[5] An ARIMA (autoregressive integrated moving average) model is fitted to time series data either to predict (forecast) future points in the series or to better understand the data. (Editor)

that events happen only due to chance. For example, they may believe that the traits children inherit from their parents are the result of a probabilistic combination of genes. Allah has specified:

﴿ هُوَ ٱلَّذِى يُصَوِّرُكُمْ فِى ٱلْأَرْحَامِ كَيْفَ يَشَآءُ ... ۝ ﴾   (سورة آل عمران: ٦)

﴾He it is Who shapes you in the wombs as He pleases...﴿

(Qur'an 3: 6)

Muslim managers understand that the conformance of aggregate data to trends is simply another beautiful creation by the Creator, Allah; they do not confuse the concept by considering it to be a creative force in itself. The fact that patterns in data and events can be observed is a gift from Allah, and it is one that facilitates our reasoning and planning. Thus, even when a mathematical model has been adopted and tested empirically, one should never assume that it is a determinant.

At the same time, one should not attribute events to luck or fortune. In Islam, there is no such thing as chance or luck; a Muslim acknowledges that everything happens by the will of Allah. The falling of leaves can be modelled as random both in the popular and technical sense of the word,[6] yet not a leaf falls without Allah's knowledge:

﴿ وَعِندَهُۥ مَفَاتِحُ ٱلْغَيْبِ لَا يَعْلَمُهَآ إِلَّا هُوَ وَيَعْلَمُ مَا فِى ٱلْبَرِّ وَٱلْبَحْرِ وَمَا تَسْقُطُ مِن وَرَقَةٍ إِلَّا يَعْلَمُهَا وَلَا حَبَّةٍ فِى ظُلُمَٰتِ ٱلْأَرْضِ وَلَا رَطْبٍ وَلَا يَابِسٍ إِلَّا فِى كِتَٰبٍ مُّبِينٍ ۝ ﴾   (سورة الأنعام: ٥٩)

﴾And with Him are the keys of all that is hidden; none knows them but He. And He knows whatever there is in [or on] the earth and in

---

[6] The falling of leaves can be modelled quite easily as a Poisson process. (The Poisson process is one of the important random processes in probability theory, used to model random points in time and space, such as arrival times of customers at a service centre or the positions of flaws in a piece of material. [Editor])

the sea; not a leaf falls, but He knows it. There is not a grain in the darkness of the earth or anything fresh or dry, but is written in a clear record.❱   *(Qur'an 6: 59)*

CHAPTER NINE

MARKETING

$\mathscr{M}$arketing is one of the most critical functions in business administration. Much to the chagrin of marketing executives and academics, it is often confused with sales. While marketing does have its roots in sales, sales today are considered to be only one part of marketing. To understand the development of the more exhaustive paradigm adopted by marketing academics and executives, we can analyze how its role arises in a business.

It is easy to appreciate the importance of the selling function because the only way a business earns revenues is through sales. Unless it manufactures a miraculous product – say, a flying car – it needs to engage in some activity that will boost sales. The company needs to find the right time and place to inform potential customers about its products. It gathers information about their willingness to pay and their product preferences, and then it can use such information to fine tune the designs and prices of the products. Businesses should also work to build long-lasting relationships with customers in order to gain their loyalty and eventually benefit from repeated sales.

The American Marketing Association website defines marketing as:

> ...the activity, set of institutions, and processes for creating, communicating, delivering, and exchanging offerings that have value for customers, clients, partners, and society at large.

Given the mission-critical role of marketing, and the wide range of activities it covers, recent trends in marketing are actually not surprising. Organizations have been spending more and more resources in marketing, as reflected in the increases in salaries of marketing executives and in marketing budgets, and in the adoption of such sophisticated marketing tools as customer relations management (CRM), which uses technology to help businesses manage their relationships with customers. In 2007, advertising was estimated to be a $150 billion industry in the United States alone.

Unfortunately, the fervour of businesses in blindly adopting so-called 'best-marketing practices' that have been shown to raise revenues has resulted in a passive stance with respect to Islamic violations. The situation is exacerbated by the growth of marketing's tentacles, which can now reach every domain within a business and its environment.

At a certain level, the dilemma faced by businesses may appear to be quite genuine. A classic marketing example that highlights this fact is that when a government bans the advertisement of tobacco products, it actually helps the tobacco companies. Without the ban, the tobacco companies find themselves in a prisoners' dilemma because no single company can afford not to advertise. Similarly, when all the other companies are willing to violate Islamic rules in marketing practices, Muslim managers feel afraid to take risks by being the only ones to shun un-Islamic practices. For those familiar with the simple (managerial applications of) game theory, a game in the normal form is presented in Figure 9.1.

PERSON 1 \ PERSON 2	Follow Islamic Principles	Disregard Islamic Principles
Follow Islamic Principles	30, 30	15, 45
Disregard Islamic Principles	45, 15	30, 30

Figure 9.1 A game in normal
form showing the prisoners' dilemma

In this payoff matrix, the first number in each pair is Person 1's payoff, while the second number is Person 2's payoff. When they both take the same approach (both either following or disregarding Islamic principles), they are in the state called 'Nash equilibrium'.[1] When only one of them disregards Islamic principles, his or her payoff appears to be higher. Ultimately, though, one can expect higher payoffs from following Islamic principles, because the 'accounting' that really matters is done by Allah. One can also reasonably expect that when both parties follow Islamic principles, the payoffs are higher than they would be if both parties were violating them. For example, a society that does not allow lewd marketing is obviously a better society in which to raise children.

Once again, Muslims need only remember that Allah is the controller of all affairs and the source of all strength. He commands us to fear Him as He should be feared. Thus, Muslim managers who honestly follow their Islamic convictions and who act with integrity should not fear losing out to the competition. Instead, they should strive to strengthen their eemân by acquiring greater knowledge.

It is extremely difficult to even imagine anything other than detrimental results from choosing such a strategy; one can refer again to

---

[1] Nash equilibrium: a state in which neither player has anything to gain by unilaterally changing his or her own strategy. (Editor)

Figure 9.1 to understand that clearly. The problem with this mindset is that we forget the important lesson in the following verses:

﴿ ... وَمَن يَتَّقِ ٱللَّهَ يَجْعَل لَّهُۥ مَخْرَجًا ۝ وَيَرْزُقْهُ مِنْ حَيْثُ لَا يَحْتَسِبُ وَمَن يَتَوَكَّلْ عَلَى ٱللَّهِ فَهُوَ حَسْبُهُۥٓ إِنَّ ٱللَّهَ بَٰلِغُ أَمْرِهِۦ قَدْ جَعَلَ ٱللَّهُ لِكُلِّ شَىْءٍ قَدْرًا ۝ ﴾

(سورة الطلاق: ٢-٣)

﴿...And whosoever fears Allah and keeps his duty to Him, He will make a way for him to get out [from every difficulty], **and He will provide him from [sources] he never could imagine.** And whosoever puts his trust in Allah, then He will suffice him. Verily, Allah will accomplish his purpose. Indeed Allah has set a measure for all things.﴾

(Qur'an 65: 2-3)

Muslims view this game from a different perspective, even though the empirical 'evidence' may not seem to support their view. This is because Muslims trust Allah; they realize that they need not rely upon 'evidence' in this instance.

Perhaps the greatest challenge concerns the differences between the principals (the owners) and the agents (the Muslim marketing managers). Too often, the principals are unwilling or unable to foresee the true results of their actions. They ignore the reality that Allah controls all affairs, so they fail to understand the actions of marketing managers who follow Allah's rulings; in fact, they may even consider their behaviour irrational. These marketing managers need not worry, though. They should steadfastly continue to follow the guidance of Allah, knowing that even if they were forced to leave their positions, Allah would provide something better.

In the remainder of this chapter, we shall attempt to highlight some of the topics most relevant for Muslims in the marketing field. Because of the dynamic nature of marketing, the focus will be on general issues rather than specific activities.

Prohibition of music, certain drawings, and photography

Music can be associated with many marketing activities today:

- advertisements
- ring-back tones on customer service lines
- the music industry
- music as a supplementary product (for example, music down-loads by ISPs, mobile operators, YouTube)
- sponsorship of concerts

As a result of marketing strategies, music is more entrenched in the lives of individuals today than ever before. The issue of whether or not music is haram has attracted a lot of attention. Critics of Islam are quick to use this prohibition as evidence of the radical nature of Islam; they wonder what can be so harmful about music that requires its prohibition. Many modern Muslims refuse to acknowledge that it is haram and insist upon a modern interpretation of this ruling. We must first understand whether music is indeed haram; then we can use this ruling as a guide for marketing and other activities. Allah has mentioned:

$$﴿ وَمِنَ ٱلنَّاسِ مَن يَشۡتَرِي لَهۡوَ ٱلۡحَدِيثِ لِيُضِلَّ عَن سَبِيلِ ٱللَّهِ ... ۝ ﴾$$

(سورة لقمان: ٦)

❨And of humankind is he who purchases idle talks [a phrase inter-preted to mean music and singing] to mislead [people] from the path of Allah...❩
(Qur'an 31: 6)

A number of prominent Companions of the Prophet (ﷺ) and their successors commented on the meaning of this verse. Ibn 'Abbâs (ﷺ) said it refers to singing. Mujâhid said that it refers to playing the drum.[2] Al-Ḥasan al-Baṣri said that the verse concerns singing

---

[2] aṭ-Ṭabari, *Tafseer aṭ-Ṭabari*, 21:40.

and musical instruments (literally, woodwind instruments).[3] Allah has also mentioned:

$$\left\{ \text{(٦٤)} ... \text{وَٱسۡتَفۡزِزۡ مَنِ ٱسۡتَطَعۡتَ مِنۡهُم بِصَوۡتِكَ} \right\}$$ (سورة الإسراء: ٦٤)

《[Allah said to Iblees:] And befool them gradually, those whom you can among them with your voice [interpreted as songs, music, and any other call for disobedience to Allah]...》   *(Qur'an 17: 64)*

$$\left\{ \text{أَفَمِنۡ هَٰذَا ٱلۡحَدِيثِ تَعۡجَبُونَ (٥٩) وَتَضۡحَكُونَ وَلَا تَبۡكُونَ (٦٠) وَأَنتُمۡ سَٰمِدُونَ (٦١)} \right\}$$

(سورة النجم: ٥٩–٦١)

《Do you then wonder at this recitation [the Qur'an]? And you laugh at it and weep not, wasting your [precious] lifetime in pastime and amusements [singing].》   *(Qur'an 53: 59-61)*

Sufyân ath-Thawri narrated from his father from Ibn 'Abbâs (ﷺ) that "(this means) singing."[4]

The Messenger of Allah (ﷺ) said:

«Among my Ummah, there will certainly be people who permit adultery, silk, alcohol, and musical instruments...» (Bukhari)

From these explanations, it should be categorically understood that in the majority of cases today, music is indeed haram. An exception is made, for example, for Islamic-oriented songs consisting of positive prose[5] that is read or sung melodiously without musical instruments.

Most marketing communications utilize artwork; we rarely find a poster, television advertisement, banner advertisement, or pamphlet that does not contain artistic expressions. Some forms of art,

---

[3] Ibn Katheer, *Tafseer Ibn Kathir.*

[4] Ibn Katheer, *Tafseer Ibn Kathir*, 9:342.

[5] For example, to praise Allah or to motivate children to obey their parents, and so on.

particularly the drawing of animate beings, are forbidden in Islam.[6] A number of prominent Companions of the Prophet (ﷺ) commented on this.

«Ibn ʿAbbâs (ﷺ) reported that the Prophet (ﷺ) said: Every image maker will be in the fire, and for every image that he made, a soul will be created for him which will be punished in the fire.

Ibn ʿAbbâs (ﷺ) said: If you must do that, make pictures of trees and other inanimate objects.» (Muslim)

The Prophet (ﷺ) also said:

«The makers of these images will be punished on the Day of Resurrection. They will be told: Give life to what you have created.» (Recorded by Aḥmad with a sound chain of narration)

ʿAbdullâh ibn Masʿood (ﷺ) reported that the Prophet (ﷺ) said:

«Those who will be most severely punished by Allah on the Day of Resurrection will be the image makers.» (Bukhari)

Abu Hurayrah (ﷺ) reported that the Prophet (ﷺ) said:

«Allah, may He be exalted, says: Who does more wrong than the one who tries to create something like My creation? Let him create a grain of wheat or a kernel of corn.» (Bukhari)

Artists should eschew photographs and drawings of animate beings such as people and animals. They may express their artistic talent by drawing or using photographs of inanimate objects like flowers or cars.

In many ways, art has become exceptionally important in advertising. The absence of illegal forms of attention-grabbers in a Muslim's marketing communications simply means that Muslim marketers need to be more resourceful and imaginative. Tasteful, quality art can

---

6 See Ibn Bâz, "Ruling on drawing animate beings," Islam-QA.com, accessed October 23, 2011, http://www.islam-qa.com/en/ref/39806.

replace tasteless, un-Islamic practices. We can see many excellent and creative halal marketing practices by Muslims.

For example, a global fast food franchise outlet in Bangladesh refrains from using music or photographs. They rely instead on an advertising campaign that is aesthetically designed and that features exceptionally witty comments, which draw the attention of consumers and also entertain them.

Product design

A common practice in marketing is to define or design products after an assessment of customer needs. Generally, the superior products are those that best meet the customers' needs, but Muslim marketing professionals also need to assess each product to determine whether or not it is halal to produce and sell it. As a simple example, the fact that customers enjoy entertainment on their mobile devices does not mean that the operator is allowed to provide all forms of entertainment. Glory be to Allah! In today's world, even pornography has become an accepted, legal form of entertainment in many countries, protected under the banner of free speech. Other, more subtle forms of entertainment that are haram include music and horoscope services.

In addition, customer needs cannot be met in haram ways, even if the need itself is halal. For example, farming businesses should not use pesticides that are known to be harmful to their employees or their consumers, even though the produce itself is halal and farming is also halal.

Much of the discussion in earlier chapters is relevant here. The setting up of a business depends upon the definition of the product to be sold. For instance, it is not halal to design and offer some financial products like bonds.

Communication, advertising, and promotions

Communication is a critical aspect of marketing. Marketing students in business administration spend a considerable amount of time studying the fields of consumer psychology and behaviour, so that they can understand the efficacy of marketing communication. Even the tone of communications can affect the attitudes of potential buyers, which in turn can impact sales.

Marketing communication is deemed to be effective if it generates sales. In general, the quality of marketing is often judged by the likelihood that a specific communication will result in a purchase by the consumer. Thus, marketing communication tends to shun negative or even neutral comments about one's own products while belittling those of competitors. Governments play an important role in protecting the interests of consumers who may be misled by marketing communications.

In the United States, the Federal Communications Commission (FCC) offers guidelines for acceptable advertising practices. For instance, TV and radio advertisements for drugs must mention any known side effects (even if they are listed in a ridiculously fast manner).

For a Muslim manager, there are at least five guidelines relevant to contemporary advertising:

1. Do not exaggerate the qualities of the products or praise them excessively.

2. Reveal the faults of the products before selling them.

3. Try to avoid belittling competitors' products.

4. Do not waste money on advertising (for example, through wasteful branding activities).

5. Do not encourage extravagance.

We will explain the rationale behind those guidelines below.

Islam prohibits trading in gharar, or uncertainty, so this should be eliminated or minimized. Before a product is sold, the buyers need to inspect it so that they have a clear idea about its true nature. The seller should not disguise its faults or embellish its appearance, either by describing it inaccurately or by using photographic alterations, for this is a kind of deception. The guideline is that the vendor should refrain from saying anything that could later result in regret on the part of the purchaser.

Abu Dharr (﷽) reported that the Prophet (ﷺ) said:

«There are three (kinds of) people towards whom Allah will not look (with mercy) on the Day of Resurrection, nor will He make them pure, and for them is a painful punishment.

Abu Dharr (﷽) asked: Who are they, O Messenger of Allah? Indeed they are the unsuccessful and the losers.

He replied: The one who brags about his favours, the one who drags his lower garment (wearing it below his ankles), and the one who swears falsely when selling his wares.» (Muslim)

The seller should reveal any shortcomings in the items. Ḥakeem ibn Ḥizâm (﷽) reported that the Messenger of Allah (ﷺ) said:

«The two parties to a transaction have the option (of cancelling it) until they part. If they are honest and disclose any defects, their transaction will be blessed, but if they lie and conceal any defects, the blessing will be erased.» (Bukhari and Muslim)

The seller should not belittle others' services and should not try to harm others unjustly. The Prophet (ﷺ) said:

«There should be no harm and no reciprocation of harm.» (A reliable hadith recorded by Aḥmad and al-Bayhaqi)

When advertising, the seller should neither exercise nor encourage extravagance, for Allah has commanded:

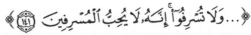

(سورة الأنعام: ١٤١)

⁅...and waste not by extravagance. Verily, He [Allah] likes not those who waste by extravagance.⁆ *(Qur'an 6: 141)*

Why Islamic advertising is better

Many of the guidelines mentioned above may seem overly restrictive; this should not be surprising because most contemporary advertising practices contradict those guidelines. Advertisers use so many deceptive tricks to improve the appearances of their products that consumers have learned to expect such deception! In the midst of such uncontrolled advertising, studies on the 'economics of attention' have investigated how products can attract consumers' attention without overwhelming them. One practice is branding. Huge sums of money are spent nowadays to promote brands whose actual production costs may be negligible.

Not long ago, however, these Islamic guidelines were the norm in advertising. It used to be considered impolite – and still is in many countries – to belittle competitors' products, even implicitly. Islamic guidelines in advertising and other marketing activities can bring about greater benefits. When sellers do not engage so much in praising their products or hiding their products' faults, they will need to allocate more resources for actually improving their products. The consumers' surplus (the difference between what consumers are willing to pay versus what they actually pay) will improve because products will be better. Consumers will also be happier since they will be faced with less 'noise' in the market.

In addition, the producer surplus (the difference between the minimum price they are willing to accept and the price they actually get) will also improve when they no longer need to spend on wasteful branding exercises. Sales will improve, along with the quality of their products.

Of course, it may appear difficult for marketers to unilaterally follow Islamic guidelines while their competitors violate them. Once again, they should rely upon Allah and realize that following the Sharia is more important than anything else, and that all success and honour comes from Allah. It is also important that governments, or at least communication regulatory bodies, implement legal measures to protect the welfare of both consumers and sellers.

Electronic commerce

Online sales have become a common phenomenon today, and they offer many advantages. They allow easier matching between supply and demand by reducing the need for physical proximity. They also reduce the startup and operating costs of retailers, which in turn can increase competition and lower prices. Finally, they can offer such conveniences as the option to request more information online. There are at least two issues of concern, though:

- Gharar

It is sometimes very difficult to judge the true quality of a product when viewing it online. Marketing communication policy should establish policies that promote satisfactory standards for describing the items. If necessary, the marketing policy should offer the option of returning a product to reduce the ill effects of unavoidable gharar.

- The sale of gold, silver or money

From the hadiths on ribâ, we know that gold and silver – and according to scholars, money – cannot be exchanged if it is not hand-to-hand. Hence, the online sale of gold is haram since the gold is not received immediately.

CHAPTER TEN

MANAGEMENT

$\mathcal{T}$he term 'management' is very broad and is often erroneously used interchangeably with business administration. Although the two terms are not equivalent, their definitions reveal the reason behind this practice. Management refers to the activities involved in utilizing allocated resources to achieve certain objectives. Business administration constitutes the set of tasks that support the operation of a business. Much of business administration involves management.

We have already looked at two specific classes of management in business administration: HR management and operations management. We have also implicitly discussed management in other areas of business administration such as finance and marketing.

The broad scope of management makes it a challenging task to determine the exact normative management guidelines that are relevant across functional boundaries in organizations. Business administration research in management most frequently appears under specific classes, but a few general topics have been identified. The basic set of tasks common to all management sub-disciplines includes planning, setting goals, implementation, and feedback.

Naceur Jabnoun presents a detailed analysis of Islam and management in his book of the same title,[1] which sheds light on the Islamic approach to major management functions such as planning, organizing, leading, and motivating. It includes useful case studies and a

---

[1] Jabnoun, *Islam and Management.*

special chapter on the outstanding leadership of 'Umar ibn al-Khaṭṭâb, the second caliph of Islam. There is also a detailed 'value-based management model that can be a useful guide to Muslim managers.'[2] We certainly cannot outdo Jabnoun's excellent presentation (may Allah reward him for his efforts) and thus we refer our readers directly to his book to gain important relevant knowledge. In the remainder of this chapter, we shall present some highlights from the book.

The Muslim organization, Jabnoun explains, is based on a strong foundation: the principle of maintaining unity while calling people to what is good and forbidding what is evil. Jabnoun explains that the presence of Muslim managers should result in an exceptional organizational culture that reflects the faith of Muslims. To understand the practical aspects of this ideal culture, one needs to consider the culture of the Prophet's Companions (ﷺ). All their deeds, including worldly ones, revolved around tawḥeed: the oneness of Allah. This reflected their deep belief in the hereafter, with full acknowledgment of the prospects of reward and punishment. The Muslim organizational culture is empowering, with Muslims liberated by their faith. It encourages participation, justice, dignity, and respect; it commands privacy and promotes trust, dialogue, and efficiency.

Planning

Muslims have a clear mission. Jabnoun writes:

> The mission of Muslims in this world is to worship Allah (ﷻ) and be His vicegerents by submitting to His will, as is evident in the following verses of the Qur'an:

$$﴿ قُلْ إِنَّ صَلَاتِي وَنُسُكِي وَمَحْيَايَ وَمَمَاتِي لِلَّهِ رَبِّ ٱلْعَٰلَمِينَ ۝ لَا شَرِيكَ لَهُۥ ۖ وَبِذَٰلِكَ أُمِرْتُ وَأَنَا۠ أَوَّلُ ٱلْمُسْلِمِينَ ۝ ﴾$$

(سورة الأنعام: ١٦٢–١٦٣)

---

[2] Jabnoun, *Islam and Management*, 311ff.

❨Say: Indeed, my prayer, my rites of sacrifice, my living and my dying are for Allah, Lord of the worlds. No partner has He. This I have been commanded, and I am the first [among you] of the Muslims.❩
(Qur'an 6: 162-163)[3]

Thus, all the goals and activities of an organization should be components of the Muslims' overall mission. In practice, all organizational missions should begin with 'the worship of Allah through...' An important guideline for Muslims is that although the ends may count much more than any transient or temporary results, they do not justify the means.

In planning, Muslims should not overburden themselves or lose hope.

﴿ لَا يُكَلِّفُ ٱللَّهُ نَفْسًا إِلَّا وُسْعَهَا ... ﴿٢٨٦﴾ ﴾ (سورة البقرة: ٢٨٦)

❨Allah burdens not a person beyond his scope...❩   *(Qur'an 2: 286)*

﴿ فَٱتَّقُوا۟ ٱللَّهَ مَا ٱسْتَطَعْتُمْ ... ﴿١٦﴾ ﴾ (سورة التغابن: ١٦)

❨So keep your duty to Allah and fear Him as much as you can...❩
(Qur'an 64: 16)

In managing their affairs, Muslims should put into practice the participatory methods that involve investigation, discussion, and consultation.

﴿ وَٱلَّذِينَ ٱسْتَجَابُوا۟ لِرَبِّهِمْ وَأَقَامُوا۟ ٱلصَّلَوٰةَ وَأَمْرُهُمْ شُورَىٰ بَيْنَهُمْ وَمِمَّا رَزَقْنَٰهُمْ يُنفِقُونَ ﴿٣٨﴾ ﴾ (سورة الشورىٰ: ٣٨)

❨And those who answer the call of their Lord, and perform the prayer, **and who [conduct] their affairs by mutual consultation**, and who spend of what We have bestowed on them.❩   *(Qur'an 42: 38)*

---

3 Jabnoun, *Islam and Management,* 68.

﴿ فَبِمَا رَحْمَةٍ مِّنَ ٱللَّهِ لِنتَ لَهُمْ وَلَوْ كُنتَ فَظًّا غَلِيظَ ٱلْقَلْبِ لَٱنفَضُّوا۟ مِنْ حَوْلِكَ فَٱعْفُ عَنْهُمْ وَٱسْتَغْفِرْ لَهُمْ وَشَاوِرْهُمْ فِى ٱلْأَمْرِ فَإِذَا عَزَمْتَ فَتَوَكَّلْ عَلَى ٱللَّهِ إِنَّ ٱللَّهَ يُحِبُّ ٱلْمُتَوَكِّلِينَ ﴿١٥٩﴾ ﴾

(سورة آل عمران: ١٥٩)

﴾And by the mercy of Allah, you [Muhammad] dealt with them gently. Had you been severe and harsh-hearted, they would have broken away from about you; so pass over [their faults], and ask [Allah's] forgiveness for them, **and consult them in the affairs**. Then when you have taken a decision, put your trust in Allah; certainly Allah loves those who put their trust [in Him].﴾

(Qur'an 3: 159)

Implementation

In implementation, Muslim managers are unique because of their practice of patience and tawakkul.

﴿ فَٱصْبِرْ إِنَّ وَعْدَ ٱللَّهِ حَقٌّ وَٱسْتَغْفِرْ لِذَنۢبِكَ وَسَبِّحْ بِحَمْدِ رَبِّكَ بِٱلْعَشِىِّ وَٱلْإِبْكَـٰرِ ﴿٥٥﴾ ﴾

(سورة غافر: ٥٥)

﴾So be patient [O Muhammad]. Verily, the promise of Allah is true, and ask forgiveness for your faults, and glorify the praises of your Lord in the evening and the morning.﴾

(Qur'an 40: 55)

﴿ فَٱصْبِرْ إِنَّ وَعْدَ ٱللَّهِ حَقٌّ فَإِمَّا نُرِيَنَّكَ بَعْضَ ٱلَّذِى نَعِدُهُمْ أَوْ نَتَوَفَّيَنَّكَ فَإِلَيْنَا يُرْجَعُونَ ﴿٧٧﴾ ﴾

(سورة غافر: ٧٧)

﴾So be patient [O Muhammad]. Verily, the promise of Allah is true, and whether We show you [O Muhammad in this world] some part of what We have promised them, or We cause you to die, then it is to Us they all shall be returned.﴾

(Qur'an 40: 77)

﴿ وَقَالَ ٱلَّذِينَ أُوتُوا۟ ٱلْعِلْمَ وَيْلَكُمْ ثَوَابُ ٱللَّهِ خَيْرٌ لِّمَنْ ءَامَنَ وَعَمِلَ صَـٰلِحًا وَلَا يُلَقَّىٰهَآ إِلَّا ٱلصَّـٰبِرُونَ ﴿٨٠﴾ ﴾

(سورة القصص: ٨٠)

❨But those who had been given [religious] knowledge said: Woe to you! The reward of Allah is better for those who believe and do righteous good deeds, and this none shall attain except those who are patient.❩   *(Qur'an 28: 80)*

Jabnoun points out an interesting lesson: having patience may require us to gain knowledge, experience, or understanding.[4] This is demonstrated in the story of Khiḍr:

$$ ❨ قَالَ إِنَّكَ لَن تَسْتَطِيعَ مَعِيَ صَبْرًا ۝ وَكَيْفَ تَصْبِرُ عَلَىٰ مَا لَمْ تُحِطْ بِهِۦ خُبْرًا ۝ ❩ $$

(سورة الكهف: ٦٧-٦٨)

❨He [Khiḍr] said: Verily! You will not be able to have patience with me! And how can you have patience about a thing which you know not?❩   *(Qur'an 18: 67-68)*

Muslim managers also try to adopt positive leadership traits, which include strength, listening skills, forgiveness, consultation, knowledge and wisdom, fairness, forbearance, vision, and awareness of limitations. Jabnoun writes:

Conventional management has undeniably contributed to the efficiency and effectiveness of organisations the world over. We should, however, pay attention to the danger of the cut-and-paste approach. We cannot just practice any management approach we learn from conventional management without asserting its validity in our environment and its consistency with our values.[5]

An Islamic management model for Muslims therefore incorporates all of the following:

• Seeking the pleasure of Allah

• Learning from the inexhaustible source of knowledge – that is, the Qur'an

---

4 Jabnoun, *Islam and Management,* 133.

5 Jabnoun, *Islam and Management,* 313.

- Having ethical guidelines with absolute scales
- Achieving unity of purpose by resolving any conflicts between worldly aims and success on the Day of Judgement
- Improving organizational performance and competitiveness
- Developing our Ummah
- Developing a knowledge bank of case studies and contemporary role models
- Contributing to the field of management

The model itself is distinct from all other management models in that its core identity is based on tawḥeed and freedom from tyranny. This creates a values-oriented foundation for all managerial activities. Practices of different managerial classes are selected based on the degree to which they uphold these Islamic values. In a profound statement, Jabnoun writes:

> Unlike many quality models, this model is not divided into enablers and results. This is because Islam focuses on the process and not on results.[6]

Jabnoun recommends that the model be calibrated using a 'joint system' by which each of the following factors is given a weight based on its prominence: Islamic values, leadership, planning, decision-making, HR management, and systems and structure.

---

[6] Jabnoun, *Islam and Management*, 316.

PART THREE

PART THREE

CHAPTER ELEVEN

BUSINESS ETHICS

Over the last several years, the term 'ethics' has become pervasive within business administration. Indeed, 'business ethics' has emerged as an entire sub-field alongside such traditional areas as accounting or HR management. Firms are recruiting ethics specialists and adopting ethical business practices. Nearly every major business school in the world sponsors research related to business ethics. Meanwhile, business news worldwide regularly includes reports of sensational cases involving 'ethical violations', which the public are often quick to judge as being criminal. As this chapter was being written, the top news outlets were all covering 2010's British Petroleum (BP) oil spill in the Gulf of Mexico.

Casual observation prompts a compelling question: What is driving this newfound emphasis, among academics and practitioners alike, on ethics?

One answer is that industry players are realizing that an organization achieves higher returns when it adopts business practices that conform to ethical standards. Generally known as the 'doing well by doing good' principle, firms sacrifice short term profits for better business habits that eventually lead to stakeholder contentment in the long term. For example, a firm that is 'greener' (more environmentally conscious) will be appreciated by its customers and patrons over its competitors, resulting in deeper customer loyalty. Likewise, a firm that treats its employees fairly, even when that means sacrificing profits, will be preferred by talented members of the labour population.

If firms indeed are interested in 'doing well by doing good' rather than 'doing good for the sake of doing good', then the adoption of ethical business practices is merely another business requirement in some ways, like having to pay government taxes. Unlike taxes, though, it is planned and enforced through a soft regulatory framework based upon 'punishment' and 'reward' by consumers and other stakeholders. As such, one can question whether ethical practices involve ethics at all; can benevolence be imposed without its being reduced to just another tax or fine? Often the lack of true goodwill is quite blatant, as in the case of anti-smoking campaigns sponsored by tobacco companies.

Research efforts in business ethics are frequently aimed at defining true ethical standards. This is a difficult task, since one can claim that ethical standards are not clear to begin with, for a variety of reasons. For one thing, individuals can blame ethical violations on ignorance, because malicious intent is not always apparent. Also, ethical standards may not be universally applicable or uniformly accepted; due to cultural differences,[1] a practice that is termed unethical in one particular nation may be considered to be quite ethical in another nation. Furthermore, standards of ethics may change over time, making it difficult to determine whether or not firms should be punished for past actions.

Let us consider an example. Many Western companies invest in developing nations and often engage in illegal but common business practices like giving bribes, or unfair practices such as providing working conditions that do not meet the safety standards established in their home nations. Should these companies be punished, or should their practices be overlooked in light of the much-needed foreign direct investment (FDI)? Is a company guilty of ethical violations even if its safety standards are far higher than those required by the host nation?

---

[1] A more technically sound term is 'cultural relativism'.

In addition to the inherent lack of clarity in identifying whether ethical violations exist, a major challenge associated with promoting ethical standards is the cost of pursuing ethical violations. Laws are usually written in a deliberately vague manner, thus making litigation difficult, if not impossible, in the case of ethical violations.

Consider, for example, the warnings that the FCC requires pharmaceutical companies to provide. Even if the warnings are obviously written in too small a print, it may be far too expensive to prove illegality in the firm's conduct on a fair platform based on due process.

Despite the challenges, the trend is positive as more and more firms are embracing ethical practices. They seem to care more about their citizens, communities, and environments than ever before, and businesses with Muslim workers are no exception. Corporate social responsibility (CSR) is the buzzword, even among firms based in developing countries.

While this is praiseworthy, it is ironic that many Muslim managers learn about ethical practices and standards as if they were established only recently and in secular circles; they are unaware of the higher ethical standards that were prescribed centuries ago as part of their own religion.

The relationship between ethics and Islam

To understand the relationship between ethics and Islam, we must first define the term 'ethics'. In general, ethics is a branch of philosophy that addresses moral issues regarding what is good and bad; right and wrong; noble and virtuous; praiseworthy or blameworthy. In particular, normative ethics is the study of pragmatic approaches to arriving at moral guidelines.

Although most people do not consider ethics to be a religion – at least not in the original, spiritual sense of the word, it essentially overlaps with many religions in various aspects. As we have already discussed, Islam is characterized by its completeness. Islam is a religion of submission, requiring Muslims to accept what is halal and shun what is haram.

﴿...ٱلۡيَوۡمَ أَكۡمَلۡتُ لَكُمۡ دِينَكُمۡ وَأَتۡمَمۡتُ عَلَيۡكُمۡ نِعۡمَتِي وَرَضِيتُ لَكُمُ ٱلۡإِسۡلَٰمَ دِينًا... ۝﴾ (سورة المائدة: ٣)

﴿...This day, I have perfected your religion for you, completed My favour upon you, and chosen for you Islam as your religion...﴾

(Qur'an 5: 3)

For example, with regard to food and drink, Allah has specified in the Qur'an:

﴿...قُلۡ أُحِلَّ لَكُمُ ٱلطَّيِّبَٰتُ... ۝﴾ (سورة المائدة: ٤)

﴿...Say: Lawful unto you are all kinds of halal food...﴾ *(Qur'an 5: 4)*

﴿ ۞ يَسۡـَٔلُونَكَ عَنِ ٱلۡخَمۡرِ وَٱلۡمَيۡسِرِ قُلۡ فِيهِمَآ إِثۡمٌ كَبِيرٌ وَمَنَٰفِعُ لِلنَّاسِ وَإِثۡمُهُمَآ أَكۡبَرُ مِن نَّفۡعِهِمَا... ۝﴾ (سورة البقرة: ٢١٩)

﴿They ask you [O Muhammad] concerning alcoholic drink and gambling. Say: In them is a great sin, and [some] benefit for people, but the sin of them is greater than their benefit...﴾ *(Qur'an 2: 219)*

In Islam, Allah has prescribed justice and good and forbidden evil.

﴿ ۞ إِنَّ ٱللَّهَ يَأۡمُرُ بِٱلۡعَدۡلِ وَٱلۡإِحۡسَٰنِ وَإِيتَآيِٕ ذِي ٱلۡقُرۡبَىٰ وَيَنۡهَىٰ عَنِ ٱلۡفَحۡشَآءِ وَٱلۡمُنكَرِ وَٱلۡبَغۡيِ يَعِظُكُمۡ لَعَلَّكُمۡ تَذَكَّرُونَ ۝﴾ (سورة النحل: ٩٠)

﴿Indeed Allah orders justice and good conduct and giving to relatives and forbids immorality and bad conduct and oppression.﴾

(Qur'an 16: 90)[2]

---

[2] Saheeh International, *The Qur'an: Arabic Text with Corresponding English Meanings.*

For a Muslim, the question of morality – of good and bad – is not left to arbitrary human standards. It is replaced by the nobler, more meaningful, and more just issue of obedience to the Creator with respect to what He has declared to be halal and haram. This elevates the status of Muslims but does not preclude ethics; in fact, it defines the ethical standards for them.

We argue that Islam is more noble, meaningful and just than secular ethics because it begins with a clear objective for doing good: to worship Allah, which is the very purpose for which humans were created. Allah has mentioned:

﴿ وَذَكِّرْ فَإِنَّ ٱلذِّكْرَىٰ تَنفَعُ ٱلْمُؤْمِنِينَ ۞ وَمَا خَلَقْتُ ٱلْجِنَّ وَٱلْإِنسَ إِلَّا لِيَعْبُدُونِ ۞ مَآ أُرِيدُ مِنْهُم مِّن رِّزْقٍ وَمَآ أُرِيدُ أَن يُطْعِمُونِ ۞ ﴾   (سورة الذاريات: ٥٥-٥٧)

❨And remind [by preaching the Qur'an, O Muhammad], for verily, the reminding profits the believers. And I [Allah] created not the jinn and humans except they should worship Me [Alone]. I seek not any provision from them, nor do I ask that they should feed Me.❩

(Qur'an 51: 55-57)

In contrast, the field of secular ethics can at best advocate 'doing good for the sake of doing good'. Allah has warned us about such vacuous tasks, in particular the futility of doing good to seek anything other than His pleasure:

﴿ قُلْ هَلْ نُنَبِّئُكُم بِٱلْأَخْسَرِينَ أَعْمَٰلًا ۞ ٱلَّذِينَ ضَلَّ سَعْيُهُمْ فِى ٱلْحَيَوٰةِ ٱلدُّنْيَا وَهُمْ يَحْسَبُونَ أَنَّهُمْ يُحْسِنُونَ صُنْعًا ۞ أُوْلَٰٓئِكَ ٱلَّذِينَ كَفَرُواْ بِـَٔايَٰتِ رَبِّهِمْ وَلِقَآئِهِۦ فَحَبِطَتْ أَعْمَٰلُهُمْ فَلَا نُقِيمُ لَهُمْ يَوْمَ ٱلْقِيَٰمَةِ وَزْنًا ۞ ذَٰلِكَ جَزَآؤُهُمْ جَهَنَّمُ بِمَا كَفَرُواْ وَٱتَّخَذُوٓاْ ءَايَٰتِى وَرُسُلِى هُزُوًا ۞ ﴾

(سورة الكهف: ١٠٣-١٠٦)

❨Say [O Muhammad]: Shall We tell you the greatest losers in respect of [their] deeds? Those whose efforts have been wasted in this life while they thought that they were acquiring good by their deeds. They are those who deny the signs of their Lord and the meeting with

Him. So their works are in vain, and on the Day of Resurrection, We shall assign no weight for them. That shall be their recompense: hell, because they disbelieved and took My signs and My messengers by way of jest and mockery.»   *(Qur'an 18: 103-106)*

Islam also warns about doing good deeds merely for the sake of warm feelings or showing off. The Prophet (ﷺ) said:

«What I fear for you the most is the minor shirk: showing off in worship. Allah will say on the Day of Judgement, when He is rewarding the people for their actions: Go to those for whom you were showing off in the world, and see if you find the reward with them.» (Recorded by Aḥmad with an authentic chain of narration)

This showing off means to do something with the intention of pleasing someone other than Allah. An example is improving the quality of one's prayer when others are watching. Since one's prayer should be performed only to please Allah, it should be performed perfectly at all times; its quality should not change when others are present.

The superiority of Islam over secular business ethics

From our discussion above, it is clear that Islam and secular ethics are not merely interchangeable approaches to the same result of reaching higher moral ground. Islam provides a purpose for ethical conduct, whereas secular ethics interfere with the purpose of life. Islam specifies legal rulings, whereas secular ethics are plagued in their attempt to develop a universal moral code. Thus, Islam is clearly superior to secular ethics.

Specifically in the context of business ethics, Islam arguably provides better epistemological stances. To prove this, we will utilize the example of CSR (corporate social responsibility).

What is CSR? It is easier to explain by example than to provide a technical definition. When a hospital sponsors a free clinic in an inner-city location, a large mobile phone company engages in a city cleanup program, or a bank offers scholarships to needy students, it is engaging in CSR activities. In general, CSR refers to corporations doing something positive for the public welfare. Firms are coming under growing pressure – from everyone from consumers to lawmakers – to enhance their CSR. In the absence of any analysis, it seems that CSR, which involves firm-level ethical behaviour, is nothing but good.

However, when CSR was first emerging almost forty years ago, Milton Friedman (an American recipient of the Nobel Prize for Economics) strongly opposed it. He even recommended that legal measures be taken to prevent managers from engaging in CSR activities. His rationale was quite simple; he argued that managers should not interfere with the firms' profit-maximization objectives by imposing CSR, because both firms and societies are better off with successful firms. Although Friedman's stance endures today among his staunch supporters, most managers and other members of society have embraced CSR. Surprisingly, researchers of ethics have not been able to accurately explain why that is.

It is obvious that there are many missing parts in the CSR theory, beginning with the lack of an accurate definition of CSR. In particular, is a firm really doing any good if it is motivated by profits? Should a firm engage in CSR if it is not profitable? If so, how much profit should it sacrifice, and what level of support should it give to CSR? Does a positive outcome from CSR outweigh the inefficiency it introduces, since some of the firm's resources are being used on activities that are not suitable for optimizing the firm's production of goods or services?

While studies in secular business ethics have yet to generate a complete CSR theory that addresses these questions, Islam provides all the answers, as well as perfect normative guidelines. The Islamic approach is superior to the secular approach for two reasons.

First of all, Islam properly maintains the distinctions in levels between firms and managers. Islam imposes restrictions explicitly on individuals and only implicitly on firms (since firms are an aggregation of people and their activities). Thus, Islam does not impose firm-level ethical behaviour.

CSR is not explicitly encouraged or discouraged in Islam. Consequently, the Islamic approach is not even subject to the question that cripples the secular approach to business ethics, namely: why should firms engage in CSR activities that do not lead to profits, particularly when it cannot even 'feel' any warm glow?

Secondly, Islam challenges any seemingly ethical behaviour on the part of individuals (creations) that is not motivated by the worship of Allah (their Creator) because actions are judged by intentions. In sharp contrast, the secular business ethics approach encourages managers (and, oddly, firms, which are not human) to engage in ethical behaviour by suggesting such rewards as profits or pride. The issues of validating profit-driven CSR or the morality of firm-level trickery do not arise at all in Islam.

Despite the fact that Islam prescribes social responsibility for individuals, and not at an organizational level, companies led by Muslim managers and owners will practice what are arguably the most socially-responsible business practices – and it is easy to see why. Islam advocates charity, and the exemplary Companions of Prophet Muhammad (ﷺ) set incredibly high standards in their practice of charity. Thus, Muslim owners who fear Allah and seek His blessings will sacrifice dividends for morals. These forgone profits, untainted by marketing or other profit motives, can be managed efficiently, leading to the highest levels of CSR. Moreover, Muslim managers who fear Allah will ensure that the firm's activities are not unfair or dishonest.

Narrated Ibn 'Abbâs:

People were afflicted by drought during the time of Abu Bakr.

They went to him and said: The sky has not rained, and the earth has not grown. People are going through severe hardship.

Abu Bakr said: Go, and have patience, for the night will not fall until Allah, the Beneficent, has brought you relief. Before long, 'Uthmân's merchants returned from the Levant with one hundred camels carrying wheat — or food. People went to his house and knocked upon his door.

'Uthmân came out to the group of people and asked: What are you here for?

They replied: We are going through times of drought; the sky has not rained and the earth has not grown. People are going through severe hardship, but we have heard that you have food. Sell us some

so we may distribute it to the Muslims who are poor and needy.

'Uthmân said: By all means, welcome! Come in and buy!

They entered and found the food waiting there.

He said: O merchants, How much will I profit by selling you my merchandise from the Levant?

They offered: We give you twelve for ten.

'Uthmân responded: They offered me more.

They said: Fifteen for ten.

'Uthmân replied: They offered me more.

Now the merchants said: Abu 'Amr, there are no merchants left in Madinah but us! Who offered you more?

He answered: Allah, the Exalted and the Sublime, offered me ten for every dirham. Do you have more?

They stated: By God, no.

He declared: Then I bear witness that I have given this food as charity to the poor and needy Muslims.[3]

Due to the superiority of the Islamic approach, many of its features have crept into the secular approach. Far from producing a comprehensive theory of CSR with a solid foundation, a decade-long formal study of CSR from a secular approach has reported empirical results that show positive, neutral, and even negative effects on profits. Former Academy of Management president Dave Whetten found evidence in his research that firms having ethical owners and/or senior executives were more likely to practice CSR.[4] This is hardly surprising when viewed through an Islamic lens because Islam requires ethical behaviour from individuals, which results in ethical business practices among firms.

The superiority of the Islamic approach can be seen readily in the case of advertising, where contemporary practices have been criticized for their questionable ethical standards.[5] The numerous criticisms include:

1. Hyper-commercialism

2. Wasteful practices and extravagance

3. Hyper-sexualization

4. Introduction of biases into media

---

[3] Sallabi, Dr. Ali Muhammad. *'Uthmân ibn Affân: His Life and Times.* (This means that Allah had promised to reward him ten times over for his charity. Editor)

[4] From a seminar presented by Dave Whetten, Ph.D. at the University of Kansas School of Business.

[5] A good summary has been provided by Wikipedia contributors, "Criticism of Advertising," *Wikipedia, The Free Encyclopedia,* accessed October 23, 2011, http://en.wikipedia.org/wiki/Criticism_of_advertising.

5. Negative consequences from the commercialization of public space[6]

6. Stereotyping

7. Targeting children and adolescents

If Islamic rules were applied, each and every one of these ills could be prevented. We have already seen that Islam forbids extravagance and such shameful practices as sexualization, and that Muslims are required to speak the truth, even when joking. In selling products, Muslims are required to point out any defects, not just the good points. With such high ethical standards in practice, there is little fear that adolescents, children, and other impressionable groups can be targeted for commercial exploitation through hyper-consumerism.

Today, well-known tobacco companies run advertisements that discourage smoking in their countries, while at the same time they continue to make tobacco products. Even worse, these same companies hypocritically run advertisements promoting smoking in poorer nations. Many Muslims today, instead of following the Islamic guideline that the sale of tobacco products is haram, are running anti-smoking advertisements while manufacturing and selling cigarettes to fellow Muslims!

Normative guidelines in ethical management

While we have casually highlighted the superiority of the Islamic approach to ethics over the secular approach, the actual differences

---

[6] An example is the erection of billboards along a highway. While billboards provide some value in the form of information, there are many negative externalities; they can ruin natural beauty, pose a threat in inclement weather, distract drivers and thus cause accidents, or feature advertisements that some may consider offensive or ugly.

between them are far more profound than we have explained. As a prescription from Allah, Islam provides the solution to every ethical crisis, so Muslims have no need to resort to sources external to Islam to learn about morality or its philosophy. It is quite surprising that Muslims today have forgotten this and are striving to learn morality from secular approaches. Why would they choose an inferior approach over a superior one?

One reason might be the newfound emphasis upon ethics in non-Muslim circles. Rather than assuming the role of leaders in this field, many Muslims in modern times have shown a tendency to merely imitate and follow the research and theories of others. The recent emphasis upon ethics does not seem to reflect an increase in unethical behaviour. Perhaps it is an attempt to develop a universal moral code that crosses geographic borders and religions. Practices that in the past would have been challenged as being 'un-Christian' or 'un-Islamic' can now be labelled simply 'unethical'. Of course, labels are inconsequential as long as a Muslim's actions and intentions are satisfactory. The problem is that a universal code of ethics drafted in secular circles may contradict Islam. For this reason, we recommend this standard response for Muslims regarding business ethics: If it conforms to Islam, embrace it; if it contradicts Islam, reject it.

The following are a few specific guidelines for implementing this general principle:

• Gain knowledge of Islam

Muslims today are highly ignorant about the beautiful religion that Allah has prescribed. Their actions, done out of ignorance, pave the way for continued violation of ethical standards. Sadly, this has allowed many with anti-Islamic opinions to argue that Islamic guidelines are insufficient for maintaining ethical standards, thus paving the way for secular ethics. In reality, secular ethics are artificial and selfish, whereas the act of pleasing Allah is a most noble deed. As part of ethics, Muslims should first gain knowledge of Islam. True tawakkul then is to have taqwâ, give up the haram, practice the halal, trust Allah, and be content with what Allah decides.

- Promote ethics through Islam

Muslims should not oppose morality; on the contrary, they should promote it. They should also remember their duty to call others to Islam. Thus, the issue of ethics can be used by knowledgeable Muslims to highlight the truth of Islam by demonstrating the perfect code of conduct advocated in this religion, as prescribed by Allah, and by encouraging others to ponder the greatness of Allah's religion.

- Design CSR projects that reflect Islamic ethics

Today there are many social problems that firms can tackle through CSR. Managers should use their wisdom, acknowledge their duty to Allah, and select the best projects. As an example, firms could sponsor micro-credit initiatives to replace the ribâ on which existing projects depend for funding. This can be a meaningful CSR effort that helps to defeat ribâ.

- Strive to increase taqwâ

Muslims should be vigilant about being conscious of Allah at all times, fearing Him and remembering that He is always watching and aware. Allah has mentioned:

$$ \text{﴿ وَلَقَدْ هَمَّتْ بِهِۦ وَهَمَّ بِهَا لَوْلَآ أَن رَّءَا بُرْهَٰنَ رَبِّهِۦ ۚ كَذَٰلِكَ لِنَصْرِفَ عَنْهُ السُّوٓءَ وَٱلْفَحْشَآءَ ۚ إِنَّهُۥ مِنْ عِبَادِنَا ٱلْمُخْلَصِينَ ﴾} $$

(سورة يوسف: ٢٤)

{And indeed she did desire him, and he would have inclined to her desire had he not seen the evidence of his Lord. Thus it was, that We might turn away from him evil and illegal sexual intercourse. Surely, he was one of Our chosen [guided] slaves.} *(Qur'an 12: 24)*

«An-Nu'mân ibn Basheer (﷽) narrated: I heard the Messenger of Allah (﷽) say – and an-Nu'mân pointed to his ears: whatever is lawful is plain and whatever is unlawful is plain; between the two of them are doubtful matters, about which not many people know. Thus, he who avoids doubtful matters clears himself with regard to his religion and his honour, but he who falls into doubtful matters falls into what is unlawful; he becomes like the shepherd who herds his sheep around a sanctuary, all but grazing in it. Truly every king has a sanctuary, and truly Allah's sanctuary is His prohibitions. Truly in the body there is a morsel of flesh; if it is sound, all the body is sound, and if it is corrupt, all of it will be corrupt. Truly it is the heart.» (Muslim)

Sustainability and waste management

Allah has instructed:

(سورة الأنعام: ١٤١)   ﴿... وَلَا تُسْرِفُوٓا۟ إِنَّهُۥ لَا يُحِبُّ ٱلْمُسْرِفِينَ ۝﴾

﴿...and waste not by extravagance. Verily, He likes not those who waste by extravagance.﴾   *(Qur'an 6: 141)*

Extravagance means spending too much money on permissible things; waste means to spend money on things that are inappropriate. We should not waste the resources at our disposal.

Currently, developed nations like the United States are placing a great deal of emphasis upon sustainability, but in many ways, there is a great deal of hypocrisy in it. They are spending money to design 'green buildings', whereas the problems are far more fundamental. In other words, the United States, which produces more waste than any other country, is simply replacing waste with extravagance. If the average human being consumed the same amount of resources as the average American, the world could only sustain two billion people. On the other hand, if the average human being lived like an average citizen of a developing nation, the world could potentially sustain forty billion people.[7]

In Bangladesh, recycling is not practiced as much as it is in the U.S., yet there is a great deal of reuse of items, and this can be superior to recycling. Since plastic sandwich bags are not readily available, disposable food items such as noodle packets are reused instead. Rarely are bottles (even plastic ones) used only once. Organic materials are used in construction, such as bamboo for scaffolding and jute for rope.

Unfortunately, with blind imports of foreign technology and management, many of the sustainable practices found in poorer countries are being lost. In Bangladesh in the 1980s, electricity consumption was very low; unfortunately, with the rapid growth of businesses, the use of air conditioning spread rapidly. Despite manifold increases in capacity, the country continues to face a crisis, with insufficient power being generated. One reason is that very little insulation is used, and this renders the air conditioning needlessly inefficient.[8]

Compensation for work injuries

With respect to occupational safety, there are roles to be played at both the policy-making and the operational levels. Policy makers should outline procedures that ensure the safety of workers, and they should fully inform the workers about any risks. In the case of an accidental death or injury, they should consult a qualified scholar from ahl

---

[7] Layton, "Has the Earth reached its carrying capacity?" *HowStuffWorks. com,* accessed October 23, 2011, http://science.howstuffworks.com/environmental/green-science/earth-carrying-capacity1.htm.

[8] One may argue that insulation entails extravagance, and that is likely to be correct. The solution is not using air conditioning in every room while ignoring insulation completely; rather, a few rooms should be air conditioned, but only after installing the appropriate insulation.

as-Sunnah wal-jamâ'ah to determine whether or not blood money is due. Allah has mentioned:

﴿وَمَا كَانَ لِمُؤْمِنٍ أَن يَقْتُلَ مُؤْمِنًا إِلَّا خَطَأً وَمَن قَتَلَ مُؤْمِنًا خَطَأً فَتَحْرِيرُ رَقَبَةٍ مُّؤْمِنَةٍ وَدِيَةٌ مُّسَلَّمَةٌ إِلَىٰ أَهْلِهِ إِلَّا أَن يَصَّدَّقُوا ... ٩٢﴾

(سورة النساء: ٩٢)

❲It is not for a believer to kill a believer except [that it be] by mistake; and whosoever kills a believer by mistake, [it is ordained that] he must set free a believing slave and a compensation [blood money] be given to the deceased's family unless they remit it...❳

(Qur'an 4: 92)

CONCLUSION

Islam was delivered as the final message from God through His last messenger. Since the advent of Islam, societies, economies, political systems, and cultures have undergone enormous changes. Especially over the last century, there has been an incredible growth in the generation, implementation, and exchange of ideas. While this exchange has highlighted differences, it has also shown that people across the globe have many similar goals. Despite differences in cultures and religions, the growth in the populations of hard working, talented individuals in every part of the world has fuelled the rise of today's knowledge-based economies.

Islam has endured for fourteen centuries, with its form intact, because it is the perfect religion for humankind. It is our Creator's greatest gift to us. Islam leads a person from darkness into light, giving direction and purpose to human life. Islam is the blessed way to the peace that we all seek. It is a religion for all walks of life, equally applicable to medieval agrarian economies and modern knowledge-based economies.

Anas ibn Mâlik (ﷺ) narrated that Allah's Messenger (ﷺ) said: «If the son of Adam had a valley full of gold, he would like to have two valleys, for nothing fills his mouth except dust. And Allah forgives the one who repents to Him.» (Bukhari)

Human desire leads to improved performance, which increases competition, which in turn augments desires... and the cycle continues ad infinitum. Therefore, it is not surprising that prosperous, knowledge-based economies seem to be all the rage today. Still, people need guidance from the Creator, and He provides it. Even what seems like success will have its perils if it goes unchecked, as the global economic crisis of the twenty-first century demonstrated.

Ḥakeem ibn Ḥizâm narrated:

«I asked the Prophet (ﷺ) (for some money) and he gave to me; then again I asked him and he gave to me; then again I asked him and he gave to me. Then he said: This wealth is (like) green and sweet (fruit). Allah will bless it for the one who takes it without greed, but Allah will not bless it for the one who takes it with greed; he will be like the one who eats but is never satisfied. And the upper (giving) hand is better than the lower (taking) hand.» (Bukhari)

Had the principles of Islamic finance been followed, the catastrophic economic meltdown of 2008-2010 would most likely have been averted. It is not surprising to hear that even non-Muslims (like the Pope) have praised and recommended the Islamic financial system.[1]

The teachings of Islam form a complete code of life, offering both spiritual and practical guidance. Clearly, we must first learn about this code before we can implement it. The aim of this book has been to highlight elements of this code in one of the most pervasive contexts of modern life.

Far from making any significant knowledge-based contribution, this book merely reflects the dearth of quality research in the particular area of Islam in financial management and business administration. In our conclusion then, we appeal to business researchers around the globe to conduct more research in this area. This can be a worthwhile endeavour for both Muslim and non-Muslim practitioners as well as

---

[1] Tiberge, "Vatican Paper Supports Islamic Finance. France Wants Its Share of Sharia Banking," *Brussels Journal,* March 12, 2009, accessed April 27, 2012, http://www.brusselsjournal.com/node/3819.

researchers of financial topics. Muslims can learn more about their beautiful religion, transform mundane tasks into acts of worship, and perform the noble task of da'wah. Non-Muslims can gain insights regarding the role of Islam in a most common context, which can prove useful in today's multicultural business landscapes.

Finally, remember that a career in business has the potential to bring success in this life as well as in the hereafter. One only needs to follow the two rules that apply to all aspects of life: do everything with the intention to please Allah, and do it in accordance with the way Allah has prescribed. May Allah bless you with success in all your ventures.

We ask Allah to guide us as He guided the Rightly-Guided Caliphs.

Wa âkhir da'wânâ an il-ḥamdu lillâhi rabbil-'âlameen.

And our final declaration is: all praise is for Allah, Lord of the worlds.

The following is an excerpt from a hadith about three persons who were walking when it began to rain. After they entered a cave to take shelter:

«...A big rock rolled over and blocked the mouth of the cave. They said to each other: Invoke Allah with the best deed you have performed (so Allah might remove the rock)...

(The first two made their invocations, and the rock moved a little each time...)

Then the third man said: O Allah, I employed a few labourers and paid them their wages, with the exception of one man who did not take his wages and went away. I invested his wages, and I got much property from that.

(After some time,) the man came and requested: O Allah's slave! Pay me my wages.

I responded: All the camels, cows, sheep, and slaves you see are yours.

He implored: O Allah's slave! Do not mock me.

I emphasized: I am not mocking you.

He took the herd and drove them away and left nothing.

O Allah! If I did that for Your sake only, please relieve us from the present suffering.

The rock shifted completely; they got out and walked away.» (Bukhari)

BIBLIOGRAPHY

al-Albâni, Muhammad Nâṣir ad-Deen. *Jilbâb al-Mara'at al-Muslimah*. Dâr as-Sâlam, 2002.

Badawi, Jamal. *The Muslim Woman's Dress*. London: Ta-Ha Publishers, Ltd., 1981.

al-Bayhaqi, Abu Bakr Aḥmad ibn Ḥusayn. *As-Sunan al-Kubrâ*. Beirut: Dar al-Kutub al-'Ilmiya.

Cachon, Gérard and Christian Terwiesch. *Matching Supply and Demand: An Introduction to Operations Management*. New York: McGraw Hill, 2005.

al-Dabbi, Abu Bakr. *Akhbaar al-Qudaah*. Thesis submitted for the degree of Doctor of Philosophy. University of London: Department of Law, School of Oriental and African Studies, 2000.

El-Gamal, Mahmoud Amin. *A Basic Guide to Contemporary Islamic Banking and Finance*. http://www.ruf.rice.edu/~elgamal/files/primer.pdf. Accessed October 23, 2011.

_____. *Islamic Finance – Law, Economics and Practice*. Cambridge: Cambridge University Press, 2008.

al-Hashimi, Muhammad Ali. *The Ideal Muslimah*. Riyadh: International Islamic Publishing House, 2010.

Ibn Bâz. *Majmoo' Fatâwâ*. http://www.binbaz.org.sa/mat/8829. Accessed October 23, 2011.

Ibn Ḥajar al-'Asqalâni, Aḥmad ibn 'Ali. *Al-Qawl al-Musaddad fee Musnad Aḥmad*. Cairo: Maktabat Ibn Taymiyah, 1401 AH/1980.

Ibn Ḥazm, 'Ali ibn Aḥmad. *Al-Iḥkâm fee Uṣool al-Aḥkâm*. Cairo: Maktabat 'Âṭif, 1978.

Ibn Humayd, 'Abd-Allaah. *Fatâwâ Samâhat al-Imâm 'Abdullâh ibn Humayd.*

Ibn Katheer, Ismâ'eel. *Tafseer Ibn Kathir.* Translated by Shaykh Safiur-Rahman al-Mubarakpuri. Riyadh: Darussalam, 2000.

Ibn al-'Uthaymeen, Muhammad ibn Sâlih. *Liqâ' al-Bâb al-Maftooh.*

_____. *Majmoo' Fatâwâ wa Rasâ'il Ibn 'Uthaymeen.* Riyadh: Dar al-Watan an-Nashar, 1413 AH.

Jabnoun, Naceur. *Islam and Management.* Riyadh: International Islamic Publishing House, 2008.

al-Jawziyah, Ibn al-Qayyim. *Zâd al-Ma'âd.* Ar-Risâlah Est. and Maktabat al-Manâr al-Islâmiyah, 1401 AH.

Khan, Dr. Muhammad Muhsin and Dr. Muhammad Taqi-ud-din al-Hilali. *The Noble Qur'an.* Madinah: King Fahd Complex for the Printing of the Qur'an, 1994.

Lazear, Edward P. and Sherwin Rosen. "Rank-Order Tournaments as Optimum Labor Contracts." *The Journal of Political Economy,* 89, no. 5 (October 1981): 841-864.

Mobabaya, Dr. Norlain. *Da'wah According to the Qur'an and Sunnah.* Riyadh: Darussalam, 1999.

al-Mubarakpuri, Shaykh Safiur-Rahman. *The Sealed Nectar (Ar-Raheeq Al-Makhtum).* Riyadh: Darussalam, 2002.

an-Nawawi. *Sharh an-Nawawi 'alâ Saheeh Muslim.* Cairo: Dar us-Salâm.

Saheeh International. *The Qur'an: Arabic Text with Corresponding English Meanings.* Jeddah: Abul Qasim Publishing House, 1997.

Sallabi, Dr. Ali Muhammad. *'Uthmân ibn Affân: His Life and Times.* Riyadh: International Islamic Publishing House, 2013.

Spence, Michael. "Job Market Signaling." *The Quarterly Journal of Economics,* 87, no. 3 (August 1973): 355–374.

at-Tabari, Ibn Jareer. *Tafseer at-Tabari,* Beirut: Dâr al-Fikr.

_____. *Tahdheeb al-Âthâr at-Tabari.* 1406 AH. http://www.almeshkat.net/books/open.php?cat=8&book=2194. Accessed October 23, 2011.

GLOSSARY OF ISLAMIC TERMS*

abu (or *abi*)	أبو، أبي	father (of)
ahl as-Sunnah wal-jamâ'ah	أهل السنّة والجماعة	'people of the Sunnah and the community'
alḥamdulillâh	الحمد لله	all praise is for Allah
âmeen	آمين	O Allah, accept our invocation; amen
'aml	عمل	actions
Anṣâr	نصار	'helpers': the Muslim citizens of Madinah who gave refuge to the Prophet (ﷺ) and the other Muslim emigrants from Makkah
'aqeedah (pl. *'aqâ'id)*	عقيدة	belief system that is based upon a firm conviction in all the fundamentals of faith and of the oneness of Allah; firm creed that one's heart is fixed upon without any wavering or doubt, and that excludes any supposition, doubt, or suspicion

---

* The Arabic words are transliterated according to the conventions of the Transliteration Chart found in this book. If a word has become part of the English language (that is, it is found in a dictionary of Standard English), that spelling is used in this book and appears first in this Glossary, with the transliterated form in brackets after it.

'Âshoorâ'	عاشوراء	the tenth day of the Islamic month of Muḥarram; it is recommended that Muslims fast on this day to commemorate the victory of Prophet Moosâ/ Moses (ﷺ) over the Pharaoh
as-salâmu 'alaykum wa raḥmat-ullâhi wa barakâtuhu	السلام عليكم ورحمة الله وبركاته	a greeting, which means 'peace be upon you, and the mercy and blessings of Allah'.
'awrah	عورة	the part of a person's body that must be screened from public view; for males it is the area between the navel and the knees, and for females it is everything except the hands and the face
bay' al-âjil	بيع العاجل	credit sales
bid'ah	بدعة	innovation, *esp.* undesired innovation in matters of religion
da'wah	دعوة	disseminating the teachings of Islam and calling people to accept and embrace Islam
deen	دين	religion
dhikr Allâh	ذكر الله	remembrance of Allah; specifically, remembering Allah through praising and supplicating to Him
eemân	إيمان	faith; belief in all the six pillars of the creed of Islam

Eid (*'eed*)	عيد	*lit.* festival; one of the two annual Islamic celebrations: one at the end of Ramadan and the other at the culmination of the Hajj
fiqh	فقه	Islamic jurisprudence; understanding or interpreting Islamic law
ghamoos	غموس	*lit.* to immerse; false, referring to swearing a false oath by Allah (which immerses a person in sin), especially one which deprives another Muslim of his or her property
gharar	غرر	'a lack of clarity'; ambiguity, uncertainty
Hadith (*ḥadeeth*)	حديث	the collected statements and actions of Prophet Muhammad (ﷺ) that with the Qur'an form the basis of Islamic law
hadith (*ḥadeeth*)	حديث	a statement or action of Prophet Muhammad (ﷺ) that was remembered and recorded by his Companions and followers
Hajj (*ḥajj*)	حج	the major pilgrimage to the Sacred Mosque, site of the Kaaba at Makkah, to be undertaken by every able Muslim once in his/her lifetime
halal (*ḥalâl*)	حلال	permitted according to Islamic law
haram (*ḥarâm*)	حرام	forbidden according to Islamic law
ḥasanah	حسنة	blessing, reward
hijab (*ḥijâb*)	حجاب	veil ordained by Allah for believing women

iḥrâm	إحرام	the state of consecration for Hajj or 'umrah; the special clothing worn by the pilgrim in such a state
iḥsân	إحسان	goodness, perfection, excellence; to worship Allah as if you see Him, but even if you do not see Him you know that He sees you
ijârah	اجارة	this is a contract that involves hiring or leasing; services of an individual or an organization are rented out or leased against a mutually agreed-upon fee
ijtihâd	إجتهاد	to use one's knowledge of the Qur'an and the Sunnah to derive rulings on matters not specifically mentioned in either source of Islamic law
inshallah *(in shâ'Allah)*	أإن شاءالله	God willing
istikhârah	إستخارة	a prayer by which one seeks guidance from Allah
jinn (sg. *jinni*)	جن	non-human, rational beings created by Allah from fire, often referred to as 'demons' or 'devils'. They have free will like humans: some are Muslims, others disbelievers; some are obedient to Allah, others disobedient. Satan is a jinni. Some people try to 'foretell' the future by contacting a jinni. Some disobedient jinn mislead people into thinking that they can tell them what will happen in the future, near or far,

or that the jinn can provide people with riches or some sort of power.

kufr	الكفر	disbelief in Allah and/or what He has revealed
maḥram	محرم	a degree of consanguinity precluding marriage; a man whom a woman may never marry due to a close blood or marriage relationship: for example, father, brother, son, uncle, and father-in-law
meelâd	ميلاد	a 'ceremonial chanting session' to praise Prophet Muhammad (ﷺ); most of the poetic verses recited in his honour border on *shirk* (associating partners with Allah); professional reciters are called to conduct these sessions.
mudârabah	مداربة	a contract whereby the parties to an investment agree to share the profit and loss of an investment venture; in this venture, one party provides the capital while the other manages the enterprise
murâbaḥah	مرابحة	a sale and purchase transaction for the financing of an asset; here, the cost and profit margin (mark-up) are made public and agreed to by all the parties involved
mushârakah	مشاركة	a partnership or a joint venture whereby all the parties involved agree on profit-loss sharing
ribâ	الربا	usury; charging interest on debt

salam contract	سلام	a contract in which the buyer pays in advance for a specific quantity of goods to be supplied on a specific date in the future. For example, a farmer may need money for living expenses until his crops are ready to harvest; if he sells them in advance at a lower than normal price, the seller and buyer both benefit.
ṣalât or *ṣalâh*	صلاة	formal prayer: a combination of physical postures, recitation, and supplication
shab-e-barât	شب برات	a *bid'ah* celebration in the middle of the month of Sha'bân, common in the Indian subcontinent
shahâdah	الشهادة	testimony, *usu.* the statement *lâ ilâha illâ Allâh, Muḥammadun rasool Ullâh* (There is none worthy of worship other than God [Allah]; Muhammad is the Messenger of God)
Sharia (*shari'ah*)	شرعة	Islamic law derived from the Qur'an and the Sunnah
shaykh	شيخ	teacher, mentor; scholar
shirk	الشرك	associating partners with Allah
shoorâ	الشورىٰ	a consultation body in the Islamic polity
soorah or *soorat*	سورة	chapter of the Qur'an

sukuk *(sukook)*	سكوك	an Islamic financial certificate that is the equivalent of a bond
Sunnah	سنَّة	the practice and collected sayings of Prophet Muhammad (ﷺ) that together with the Qur'an forms the basis of Islamic law
ṭâghoot	طاغوت	idols; everything evil that is worshipped; false judges
taqwâ	التقوىٰ	fearful awareness of Allah; being mindful of Allah; pious dedication; being careful not to transgress the bounds set by Allah
tawakkul	التوكّل	surrender to the divine will; relying on Allah while striving to do one's best
tawarruq	تورق	a transaction whereby a customer buys something on credit and then immediately sells the product to a third party to obtain the cash
tawḥeed	التوحيد	the oneness of Allah: that He alone deserves to be worshipped and that He has no partners
tawḥeed al-asmâ' waṣ-ṣifât	توحيد الأسماء و الصفات	oneness of the divine names and attributes
tawḥeed ar-ruboobiyah	توحيد الربوبية	oneness of the divine Lordship
tawḥeed al-uloohiyah	توحيد الألوهية	oneness of the divine nature

Ummah   أُمَة   community or nation: *usu*. used to refer to the entire global community of Muslims

'umrah   عمرة   minor, non-obligatory pilgrimage to Makkah

zakâh (or *zakât*)   زكاة   obligatory charity: an 'alms tax' on wealth payable by Muslims and to be distributed to other Muslims who qualify as recipients

INDEX

NOTES

NOTES

....

....

....

....

....

....

....

....

....

....

....

....

....

....

....

....

NOTES

....

....

....

....

....

....

....

....

....

....

....

....

....

....

....

....

NOTES

NOTES

NOTES

....

....

....

....

....

....

....

....

....

....

....

....

....

....

....

....

NOTES

....
....
....
....
....
....
....
....
....
....
....
....
....
....
....
....

NOTES

....

....

....

....

....

....

....

....

....

....

....

....

....

....

....

....

....